A Traveller's History of Russia and the USSR

THE AUTHOR   Peter Neville is a Lecturer in Contemporary European History at the University of Luton and is also a tutor for the Open University. He is the author of several books on modern history including *A Traveller's History of Ireland* in this series. He is a frequent visitor to Eastern Europe and Russia and the Commonwealth of Independent States.

SERIES EDITOR   Professor Denis Judd is a Fellow of the Royal Historical Society and Professor of History at the University of North London. He has published over 20 books including biographies of Joseph Chamberlain, Prince Philip, George VI and Alison Uttley, historical and military subjects, stories for children and two novels. He has reviewed extensively in the national press and in journals, and has written several radio programmes.

The front cover shows a detail from a Revolutionary poster of 1920 by an unknown artist.
© *The Society for Cultural Relations with the USSR*

A Traveller's History of Russia

PETER NEVILLE

Series Editor   DENIS JUDD
Line Drawings   DAVID WOODROFFE

Interlink Books
An imprint of Interlink Publishing Group, Inc.
New York • Northampton

To my mother

First American edition published 2001 by

INTERLINK BOOKS
An imprint of Interlink Publishing Group, Inc.
99 Seventh Avenue, Brooklyn, New York 11215 and
46 Crosby Street, Northampton, Massachusetts 01060
www.interlinkbooks.com

Text © Peter Neville 1990, 1994, 1997, 2001
Preface © Denis Judd 1990, 1994, 1997, 2001

The right of Peter Neville to be identified as author of this work has been asserted by him in accordance with the Copyright, Designs, and Patents Act 1988.

Library of Congress Cataloging-in-Publication Data
Neville, Peter
A traveller's history of Russia/Peter Neville; line drawings, David Woodroffe.
—1st American ed.
      p.   cm.
Includes bibliographical references.
ISBN 1-56656-273-2
    1. Soviet Union-History.   I. Soviet Union—Description and travel—
1970—Guidebooks. I. Title.
DK37.N48 1994
914.704'854–dc20   90-34708

Printed and bound in Canada

To request a free copy of our 48-page full-color catalog, please call
1-800-238-LINK, visit our web site at **www.interlinkbooks.com**,
or write to us at: **Interlink Publishing**
46 Crosby Street, Northampton, Massachusetts 01060

Table of Contents

Preface

Peter Neville has performed a miracle of compression in the writing of this lively, comprehensive and sharp-eyed *Traveller's History*. His opening pages vividly remind the reader of the physical immensity of Russia: 'The USSR is the largest country on the globe, covering some 22.4 million square kilometres or one sixth of the earth's land surface. It extends over one third of Asia and more than half of Europe.' While Georgia in the south can enjoy sub-tropical temperatures, the Siberian winter can be as cold as minus 60°C. Russia was, and the Soviet Union is, 'a land of forest, marsh and plain, of immeasurable empty spaces, and of distant horizons.'

The great flat lands of European Russia, the vast plains of central Asia, the huge, navigable rivers, were both Russia's bane and her salvation. Goths, Huns and Mongols from the east could sweep on horseback with comparative ease beyond the western fringes of Russia into Europe. Conversely, invaders from the west – Teutonic Knights, the armies of Napoleon and Hitler – could be pulled into an illimitable hinterland and eventually, exhausted and disorientated, destroyed. Peter Neville quotes a Nazi general's observation that the scale and monotony of the Russian landscape served merely to depress his hitherto victorious troops.

Although Cold War propagandists chose to caricature the Soviet Union as an aggressive, essentially oriental, monolith, the truth is that for much of their history the Slavs of European Russia have done their best to balance between East and West. Often there has been a desperate drive to 'Westernise'. But although Britain, and her various allies, have eagerly accepted Russian military assistance against the forces unleashed by the French Revolution, and against Germany in two world wars, it has, too often, been tempting to portray the Russians as the Scythians of Alexander Blok's last great poem:

> Yes – we are the Scythians! Yes – we are Asiatics
> With slanting and repacious eyes!

Is Russia the enigma that Winston Churchill perceived?

Certainly the contrast between the successes of Soviet space technology and the economy's failure to provide adequate staple foodstuffs in the shops is a puzzling phenomenon. Also Russian history is full of paradox and apparent contradictions. Who is more truly a representative of the Russian past, or of the national psyche, Ivan the Terrible or Pavlova? Peter the Great or Chekhov? Stalin or Tchaikovsky? Catherine the Great or Gorbachev? And, in any case, what is Russia – the vast sprawling whole or the European core? The Ukraine or Azerbaijan? Leningrad or Samarkand?

It takes a week to travel by train from Moscow to Vladivostock. In this fleet-footed and well balanced book the would-be traveller can do much better than that, and on the way there are many wonders to behold, many joys to savour.

Denis Judd

CHAPTER ONE

The Coming of the Slavs

When we think of Russia, we think of her vastness. During World War II a German general noted how his troops 'were depressed by the monotony of the landscape, and the immensity of the stretches of forest, marsh, and plain'.[1] For Russia is, and was, a land of forest, marsh and plain, of immeasurable empty spaces, and of distant horizons. Only the United States of America perhaps compares with her experience of battle against the elements of hardy colonists, and even it (Alaska excepted) lacks the extremes of climate present in what we now know as the USSR.

This is a theme which will be touched on from time to time in this book (which also makes use of the observations of contemporary Western observers). The *physical* similarities of these two great land masses have also been noted in one description of 'a green-yellow ocean, besprinkled with millions of spring flowers' and another which talks of 'the green, ocean-like expanse of prairie, stretching swell beyond swell beyond swell to the horizon'. The first comes from Gogol's *Taras Bulba*, written in 1834, and describes the steppelands of his native Russia, the second is from Francis Parkman's *The Oregon Trail* written a decade later.

Geography

Russia has its own distinctive geographical features. One of them is the relative absence of great physical barriers, because although the Pamirs in Soviet Asia rise to 7,000 metres, even the Ural Mountains are low lying – a reality which opened the Russian heartland to nomadic invasion from the east.

By contrast, Russia is a land of great rivers like the Dvina (flowing into the Baltic), the Dnepr (Dnieper, flowing into the Black Sea), and the Volga which runs into the Caspian Sea. It was along these rivers and their tributaries that the original Slav settlements, such as Kiev, Smolensk, Polotsk and Novgorod, grew up. As far back as the fifth century BC the Greek historian Herodotus had described the Dnieper as 'the most productive river . . . in the whole world, excepting only the Nile'. The Dnieper itself flows through frozen tundra in the north, then great tracts of Russian forest, and finally through the famous 'black earth' (*chernozem*) regions of the south on its way to the Black Sea. These black earth regions stretch from the bread-basket of the Ukraine away eastwards into Siberia, whose bleak plains merge in turn with the arid desert lands to the north and east of the Caspian Sea. For the modern traveller, an indication of Russia's size would be given by a journey on the famous Trans-Siberian Railway: from Moscow in the west to Vladivostok in the east takes a week of non-stop rail travel!

Within this vast landmass there are great climatic variations. Georgia can bask in subtropical temperatures, while Siberia suffers icy blasts at well below -60°C. Such harsh climatic conditions are reflected in the figures for population distribution. In 1987 the Ukraine, covering 603,7000 square kilometres, had a population of 51.2 million whereas remote Kazakhstan, with an area of 2,717,300 square kilometres, had only 16.2 million people. On occasion stark statistics serve us best. The USSR is the largest country on the globe, covering some 22.4 million square kilometres or one sixth of the earth's land surface. It extends over one third of Asia and more than half of Europe.

Prehistoric Russia

Paleolithic and Neolithic remains are common across the USSR today, and as the Neolithic period ebbed away into the Bronze Age, primitive agricultural communities emerged in the black earth zone of European Russia. The best-known civilisation from this period in the USSR was named after the Tripolye area south of Kiev, which flourished between the fourth and third centuries BC.

Particular significance surrounds the evolution of the relationship

A gold coin from the third century BC which was found on the site of
Panticapeum (modern Kerch) in the Crimea

between man and the horse, so that by the end of the second millennium
BC archaeological evidence shows that mounted nomads inhabited the
Russian steppelands. Their very mobility gave them an important
advantage over the primitive farmers who worked the land in the black
earth provinces. In this way a distinctive feature of Russian history was
beginning to emerge, whereby the flat lands of European Russia were at
the mercy of successive waves of nomadic horsemen.

The Scythians

> Yes – we are the Scythians! Yes – we are Asiatics
> With slanting and rapacious eyes!

In his last great poem, 'The Scythians', written only three months after
the October Revolution, Alexander Blok attempted to explore Russian
ambivalence towards Europe and Asia, but he probably did less than
justice to Scythian civilisation in the process.

In the fifth century BC Herodotus had observed Scythian funeral
ceremonies and bore witness to their sophistication. Scythian barrow
(kurgan) burial mounds are found in the Kuban steppeland north of the
Caucasus, and westwards in the Crimea and the lower reaches of the
Dnieper in the Ukraine. Historical records also suggest that the Scythian
kingdom in Southern Russia was capable of defying the Graeco–Maced-
onian army of Alexander the Great (356–323 BC, before it was overrun
by the nomadic Sarmatians.

An example of Scythian art – a griffin's head

The Scythians were goldsmiths of some skill and imagination, who favoured the representation not only of horses and stags but also of fantastic mythical creatures like griffins. The impressive Scythian remnants at Pazyryk, which were preserved by the permafrost in the Altay mountains of western Siberia, date from the period between the fifth and third centuries BC and contain many such objects.

Greek mythology also seems to link the civilisations of the Mediterranean world with the Scythians. One of its earliest legends concerned the story of Jason and the Argonauts and their search for the 'Golden Fleece', and in a recent attempt to restage the journey a replica of a Bronze Age ship sailed from northern Greece to the southern Soviet Republic of Georgia. The results, according to one expert, were convincing enough to 'have indicated a core of possible historical truth in the legend'.[2] It leaves unanswered, of course, the age-old question the Russians have asked themselves about their country. Is she European or Asiatic?

The Slavs

At the time known in Western European history as the Dark Ages, the

Russian lands were peopled by the succession of nomadic tribesmen who followed the Scythians – Sarmatians, Goths, Huns, Avars, Khazars. 'One after another,' the historians Lionel Kochan and Richard Abraham tell us, 'warlike hordes from the east and north had made their way across the exposed steppelands and along the navigable rivers.'³

In the sixth century AD, the distinctive grouping known as the Slavs had appeared, and they began gradually to move eastwards from the Carpathian mountains. This process seems to have been quickened by the death of the Hun chieftain Attila in 453. The Huns had terrorised Western Europe, until their decisive defeat at the hands of the Franks near Châlons in 451. Thereafter three separate branches of the Slav family moved into Central and Eastern Europe. It was the eastern Slavs who followed the routes of the rivers Dnieper and Volga, and were to be the forefathers of the Great Russians (or ordinary Russians in modern terms), Ukrainians (Little Russians) and Belorussians (White Russians). These Slavs were, in their turn, conquered by the Khazars, a race of Turkic origin who seem to have been benevolent taskmasters. They exercised the loosest of political controls and were content (like the Ottoman Turks in the Balkans in later centuries) merely to exact annual tributes from their Slav vassals. This experience underlined a major feature of the early history of Russia: she had never been part of the Roman Empire with its sophisticated mechanisms of centralised control; she was also 'the only country of geographical Europe that owed virtually nothing to the common cultural and spiritual heritage of the west'.⁴ Did this vacuum explain the ambiguity many Russians later felt about their relationship with the West? Some historians like Tibor Szamuely have thought so.

The Khazar Khanagate was triangular in shape, running from the Caspian Sea to the Sea of Azov, with its sides resting on the Volga and the lower Don. Its people were but one of the series of restless nomads who occupied the Russian heartland and relied on farming and trading for a living. The Khanagate was well placed to do the latter, because it lay across the trade routes linking the rich Arab caliphate to the east and the urban centres of Europe to the north-west. The Slav contribution to their Khazar masters took the form of honey, wax and slaves, and the area around the river Dnieper became part of the so-called 'great way' which ran from the Gulf of Finland in the north to the gates of Constantinople in the south.

What were those early Slavs like? We have this description from the writings of Ibn Fadlan, the ambassador from the Baghdad caliphate to Kiev around AD 920.

> Never have I seen people of more perfect physique; they are as tall as date palms, and reddish in colour . . . Each man has tattooed upon him trees, figures and the like from the fingernails to the neck. Each woman carries on her bosom a container made of iron, copper, silver or gold depending upon her man's wealth. Round her neck she wears gold or silver rings.

Certain facts are evident from Ibn Fadlan's description. The so-called 'Rus' were in fact descendants of the Varangians from Scandinavia and the Baltic (or Vikings to give them their more common name) who had been invited by the eastern Slavs to come and 'rule as princes over us' late in the ninth century. This was because the Slav lands, known to the Varangians as 'the kingdom of towns' (there may have been as many as 600), had dissolved into chaos under the increasingly loose control of the Khazar empire.

Kiev Rus

In 862 the city of Novgorod on the River Volkhov fell to the Varangian chief, Rurik. After his death in 879 his successor Oleg led a raid towards Byzantium; on the way he captured Smolensk and Lyubech, and in 882 he took Kiev which he made his capital. Historians have stressed that this Varangian conquest, like the Khazar one before it, was essentially superficial. The Varangians did not 'come to build a state; rather did they become the ruling stratum of princes over the mass of Slav society'.[5] They seem to have been assimilated by the Slavs very quickly – more quickly, for example, than the Normans were in England after their conquest in 1066. For instance, Oleg's successor Igor gave his son a Slav name, Svyatoslav.

Igor had succeeded Oleg in 913 and when he was killed in 945 his wife Olga ruled as regent during Svyatoslav's minority. She was an early convert to Christianity, and the conversion of Kiev Rus (the Varangian name for the Slav lands) was a historical watershed which was a direct result of the trading links established between Kiev and Byzantium. The relationship was, in its early stages, an ambivalent one. In 907 a fleet from Kiev under Oleg had sailed down the Bosphorus and menaced Constantinople, but lacking the siege engines to breech its massive walls settled for a peace treaty instead. This treaty established regular trading relations between Byzantium and Kiev, and allowed the empire to recruit Russians as mercenaries (Byzantine emperors had a famous Varangian guard). Russian contingents took part in Byzantine expeditions against Syria and Cyprus in 910, and against Crete in the following year. From the Byzantine point of view Kiev provided a useful counterweight to the powerful Bulgarian kingdom on their northern flank. But the Russians also proved to be unreliable allies. In 941 a Russian fleet devastated the coast of Asia Minor and, although the Byzantines caught up with the booty-laden sailors, the threat remained. In 943 Igor made a pact with the nomadic Pechenegs, and a joint Russo–Pecheneg force then appeared under the walls of Constantinople. Once again the stout walls of the imperial city saved it.

Svyatoslav seems to have behaved like the archetypal Viking, more interested in making war than governing. He overthrew the Khazar Khanagate to the south and conquered the area around Kuban, before penetrating to the Sea of Azov. He then took advantage of Bulgarian weakness to destroy the Bulgar kingdom and establish his rule on both sides of the River Danube. Only in 971 was the Byzantine soldier emperor John Tzimiskes able to advance into Bulgaria and drive Svyatoslav back to the Danube and into the fortress of Silistria where he surrendered. Nevertheless, Svyatoslav's incursions had ensured the permanent disappearance of the once powerful Bulgar kingdom although his own career proved to be short-lived. In 972, on his way back to Kiev, he was attacked by Pecheneg tribesmen near the cataracts of the River Dnieper and his army was utterly destroyed. According to legend, Svyatoslav's skull was made into a drinking vessel for a Pecheneg prince. Never again was Kiev Rus to dominate such large tracts of territory.

KIEV AND BYZANTIUM

Svyatoslav's successor was his eldest son, Yaropolk, whose reign ended violently at the hands of his younger brother Vladimir. Although Olga's Christianity had failed to moderate the violence of Svyatoslav's and Yaropolk's reigns, her influence remained and Vladimir was baptised in 989. His reward was the hand of the sister of the Byzantine emperor Basil II, which cemented the alliance between his city and Constantinople. If his subjects were initially unenthusiastic about Christianity, this conversion had two priceless advantages from Vladimir's point of view: firstly it provided divine sanction for his rule over a squabbling and troublesome set of relatives and neighbours; secondly, it allowed Vladimir to bask in the glory of his link with the Byzantine purple, the oldest and most sacred monarchy of the day.

Otherwise the Russian Orthodox Church was distinctive from its Byzantine mother. The Slavonic liturgy gave the Russians a language close to their own. Most of the first priests, and many of their books, came from Bulgaria, although Constantinople insisted on appointing the head of its sister church. Byzantine help was in any case essential in the construction of the new Russian ecclesiastical system, and the foreign appointment had its advantages. The Byzantine origins of the Russian Church would also mean that it would side with Constantinople rather than Rome, when the Christian world was divided by the schism of 1054. Whether the very close links between Church and State, which were pioneered in Kiev Rus and became a characteristic of tsarism, were altogether healthy is a matter for debate. This phenomen of 'caesaropapism' helped to strengthen the nascent Kiev state, but also encouraged the anti-intellectualism which was its other characteristic.

In this context, it is significant that the Slavonic word for the Orthodox religion is 'pravoslavie' which means 'true worship' or 'right glory'. This indicates the way in which liturgy (i.e. the forms of worship) has been more important than dogmatic substance in the history of Russian Christianity. This pragmatism is actually reflected in the famous story of how Vladimir came to be converted to Christianity in the first instance. According to the version given in the Russian Chronicle, Vladimir sent envoys to investigate Judaism, Islam, Roman and Byzantine Christianity. He was won over to the last because the envoys were so impressed by the mass in the great cathedral of St Sophia that they could not tell whether they were in heaven or on earth. Vladimir

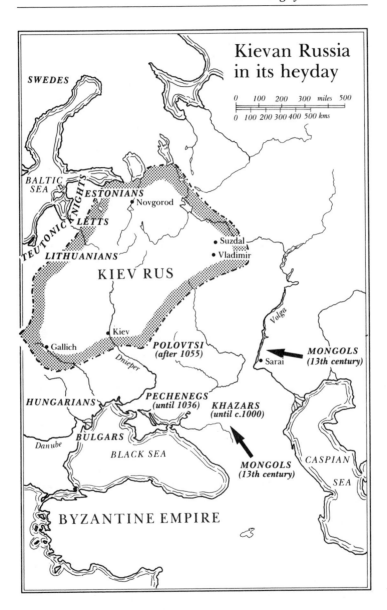

Kievan Russia in its heyday

SWEDES

0   100   200   300   *miles*   500
0   100 200 300 400 500 *kms*

BALTIC SEA

ESTONIANS

● Novgorod

TEUTONIC KNIGHTS

LETTS

LITHUANIANS

● Suzdal
● Vladimir

KIEV RUS

Volga

● Kiev

● Gallich

POLOVTSI (after 1055)

Dnieper

MONGOLS (13th century)

● Sarai

HUNGARIANS

PECHENEGS (until 1036)

KHAZARS (until c.1000)

Danube

BULGARS

BLACK SEA

MONGOLS (13th century)

CASPIAN SEA

BYZANTINE EMPIRE

was equally impressed, and ordered the mass baptism of his people according to the Byzantine rite. This story is probably a legend, but it underlines the point about the primacy of the Byzantine link. Yaroslav the Wise (1019–54), Vladimir's son, acknowledged this by accepting the leadership of Constantinople, and naming the cathedral in Kiev after the great mother church in the Byzantine capital.

THE HEYDAY OF KIEV RUS

At the height of its power and glory in the mid-eleventh century, Kiev was an impressive sight for foreign observers. It was, according to the German chronicler Adam of Bremen, 'the fairest jewel' in the Greek world with its 400 churches and eight cosmopolitan markets. Kiev had primarily an agricultural economy, but it was well sited and a centre for the sale of furs like sable, beaver and fox. Distinctive, too, was its system of government, administered by the prince, who was assisted in this task by the growing class of landed aristocrats known as the boyars. In the towns, authority was further devolved to the *vyeche*, or popular assemblies, made up of the free adult males of the municipality. Under them, a new class of artisans or skilled workers was emerging with expertise in leather-processing, linen manufacture and coarse textiles, while in the countryside most Kievans were *smerdi* or free farmers. These were men who owned their own homes, animals and implements; unlike the serfs of the western feudal system, they could leave their land and move about freely, although Kiev was still a slave-holding society. There were also landless labourers, known as *zakupi*, who hired out their labour to the *smerdi*, but they were free men unlike the *kholopi* at the bottom of the Kievan social structure, who were virtually slaves. The rights of all were safeguarded by the *Russkaya Pravda*, the eleventh-century legal code which determined the obligations and duties owed by one class to another.

THE DECLINE OF KIEV

After the death of Yaroslav in 1054, Kiev fell into a steady decline. This was partly Yaroslav's own doing because in his will he divided his kingdom between all five of his sons, rather than following the Roman principle of primogeniture (the first born inherits all). The will led to internecine strife in Kiev, and the situation was worsened by the raiding of the nomadic Cumans (Polovtsians). Although Yaroslav had been able to defeat the marauding Pechenegs in 1036, the Cumans were a far more dangerous foe. In 1096 their army reached the very walls of Kiev itself. Only Vladimir Monomakh (1113–25) was able to unite the various factions against the invader, routing the Cumans and establishing a peace which lasted until the death of his son Mstislav in 1132. But by the middle of the twelfth century resistance had become impossible (in 1160, 10,000 slaves were carried off by the Cumans from Smolensk alone). The population of Kiev began gradually to flee northwards, while their barbarian enemies occupied the mouth of the Dnieper.

Political instability was accompanied by economic collapse after the Third Crusade in 1204 sacked Constantinople instead of marching to the Holy Land. This was, in fact, a logical consequence of centuries of enmity between Byzantium and the Latin West, but it ruined Kiev's trade. Byzantine trade fell into the hands of the rapacious Venetians and Genoese, and the Kievans were cut off from their formerly profitable trade with Constantinople. In its weakened economic condition, the Kiev state was also beset by a new wave of northern enemies like the Lithuanians, Swedes and Teutonic Knights (an order of medieval German knights). In the south-west the growing power of the Magyars (Hungarians) pressed in on Kiev's borders also.

The noted Belgian historian, Henri Pirenne, wrote that this 'migration from south to north determined the future of the Russian people'[6] and it is hard to disagree. In the frozen north they were forced to become farmers and hunters rather than merchants, and only during the reign of Peter the Great did Russia become a commercial power once again. Although Novgorod became something of a commercial centre from the early thirteenth century onwards, this was the result of the efforts of the German Hanseatic League rather than a consequence of Russian enterprise. Kiev itself was reduced to the status of a middling-sized fortress town, which even lost its position as a capital city in 1169 when it was sacked by Prince Andrey Bogolyubsky who moved the capital to Vladimir in his native principality of Rostov–Suzdal. Southern Russia was therefore hopelessly divided by the 1230s. And then came the Mongols.

CHAPTER TWO

The Bloody Swamp of Mongol Slavery

During the centuries of Viking attack on the British Isles, Anglo-Saxon monks are said to have prayed for deliverance from 'the fury of the Norsemen'. Arguably their Russian counterparts had even greater need to pray for divine intercession in the two centuries that followed the year 1237. For never was Russia's vulnerability to the nomadic invader from the east more savagely demonstrated than during the period of the Mongol Conquest, when she lay at the mercy of an enemy more ruthless, more organised and more astute than any of the other barbaric hordes that had devastated her lands.

To geographical vulnerability, alas, was added chronic political division, which could only assist the Mongols in their task. In the end, northern Russia was only saved from a similar fate by the existence of even more tempting targets for Mongol ambition. But before the tide of Mongol conquest ebbed in Russia, it had transformed her society even more fundamentally than the Viking depradations had changed Western Europe.

The origins of the Mongol invasion of Russia lay in the dynastic settlement which followed the death of Genghis Khan in 1227. It was this settlement which brought the Mongols directly into conflict with the states of the Near and Middle East. Thus Jalal-ad-Din Mengubirdi, ruler of Khwarizm, was defeated and eliminated between 1230 and 1232 by the Mongol *noyan* (ruler) Tchermogan, who went on to conquer western Iran, Azerbaijan (1233), Georgia (1236) and Greater Armenia (1239). At this stage the Mongols were massing at the frontiers of the Seljuk sultanates of Asia Minor, which they then invaded and overthrew at the battle of Kose Dagh in 1243. This victory allowed Bayju Noyan to set up a Mongol protectorate over eastern Mongolia. The invasion of southern Russia in 1237 therefore has to be seen in the wider context of a massive westward sweep by the Mongol hordes.

From the Mongol perspective, their invasion of southern Russia could not have been better timed, for they were the benefactors of the political collapse which had left the former state of Kiev Rus weak and divided. Clearly, too, the small principalities into which Kiev had divided did not take the initial Mongol threat seriously enough. But in the Mongol war machine they faced a more formidable and ruthless foe than any European army had ever encountered before. Our word 'horde' comes from the Mongol word 'ordu' but its English usage is misleading: ordu in Mongolian meant 'camp', but Mongol ordus were organised and disciplined in a way unseen in Europe since the zenith of the Roman Empire. There was nothing horde-like about their battle tactics or strategy, and their command structure, organisation and tactics deserve detailed analysis here.

THE MONGOL WAR MACHINE

The Mongol command structure was deceptively simple. Each clan was led by a khan, under whom were noyans (barons in Western European terms); the underclass of knights were known as bahadurs. Each Mongol tribe was divided into patriarchal clans, and each clan had its own independent ordu or camp.

The life of a Mongol tribesman was hard. The rival clans constantly raided one another, which was partly because, though polygamous, Mongols were not allowed to marry inside their own clan, but also because of their warlike and wayward nature. It was Genghis Khan's greatest achievement that he disciplined these doughty horsemen for his own purposes. Amongst other regulations he made horse-stealing a capital offence, prevented anyone holding a Mongol slave, and broke down old clan loyalties by dispersing his warriors throughout the Mongol host.

Such discipline was imposed on a hardy race of warriors who had limitless stamina, great expertise in archery and horsemanship, and a callous indifference to the suffering of other human beings, be they enemy or innocent. It was the qualities of 'cohesion and persistence'[1] in particular which made the Mongols such terrifying opponents and got for them the nickname 'The Devil's Horsemen'. And devilish they were too with their fur-lined blue or brown tunics and tough little Mongolian or Przewalski mounts (although at an average of 13–14 hands Mongol horses were larger than legend suggests) which they could ride for days on end. Each horseman would be followed by at least three remounts so that he was constantly on the move, eating as he did so. For preference he rode a mare whose milk he could use, but in an extreme he would slit a horse's leg and drink its blood for sustenance. Weaker, ridden-out horses could also be killed for food, but the Mongol was not cruel to his horse by the standards of the day. It was his most valuable possession and, as James Chambers points out in his excellent study, 'Mongol horses were better cared for than the horses of any other army'.[2] They were better used in battle too, as a mobile base for the arsenal of Mongol arrows which saturated an invariably more static enemy. These were fired by the light cavalry while the heavy cavalry, wearing chain-mail, carried a combination of battle-axe, mace and twelve-foot lance.

Crucially, the Mongol bow, though smaller and shorter in range than the English longbow, was technically superior. The Mongol 'thumb lock' involved the drawing back of the bowstring by a stone worn on the right thumb, which released the arrow more rapidly than the fingers could. The Mongol bowman also had a more formidable array of specialised arrows to loose upon his unfortunate foe: they included special armour-piercing arrows, incendiaries, arrows tipped with small grenades, and red-hot whistling arrows for signalling. All these could be shot at full gallop, and the bowman could also bend and string his bow on horseback. The description of such a force as 'mounted artillery' would not be an inaccurate one. Another alarming dimension was added by the average Mongol's habit of slashing his cheeks to stop a beard from growing, which produced intimidating scars. The additional use of the lasso might suggest to a western reader that he or she was confronting a particularly unpleasant citizen of Dodge City. Confirmed perhaps by the fact that Mongols never washed, and kept on their silk undershirts until they began to rot (although this did have a valuable function in preventing infection in arrow wounds). Little was left to chance, however. Each warrior's saddlebag contained a change of clothing, a cooking-pot, portions of yoghurt, millet and dried meat, a leather water-bottle, a fishing line and needle and thread. The saddlebag had a dual purpose since it was waterproof and could be used for fording rivers.

There is also evidence that the Mongols had a crude but effective system of espionage. Merchants were used to spy out the land before campaigns were launched, maps were secretly copied for use during the campaign, and misleading information spread about the timing of the next Mongol onslaught (what would be known today as 'black propaganda').

All this preparation, nevertheless, would have been useless without the legendary courage of the Mongol warrior. The clansmen had an opportunity to display this, and to perfect their cavalry tactics, in what was known as the 'great hunt'. This was a massive hunting expedition which could last as long as three months and during which the Mongol army became 'a huge human amphitheatre with thousands of terrified animals crowded into its arena'.[3] It was apparently a point of honour during the great hunt that no animal should escape this terrifying sweep, after which the Khan took his pick of the best. The warriors also seized this opportunity to show off their courage, in barehanded combat with tigers. Not surprisingly some perished in the process, but the great hunt demonstrated the ambivalence of Mongol tradition, in which callousness was mixed in equal measure with respect for the gallant foe. Tradition decreed that when the hunt was over the Khan would grant the lives of any surviving animals on the request of his warriors.

This link with nomadic hunting custom went hand in hand with a Roman-style penchant for military organisation. Each Mongol army was divided into multiples of ten, the largest of which was a division of 10,000 men known as a *tumen*. Each *tumen* was divided into ten regiments of a thousand men, called *minghans*, which were subdivided in turn into ten troops of ten, called *arbans*. A primitive element of democracy allowed the men in each *arban* to elect their commander, and the ten *arban* commanders then elected the commander of the *jagun*. Above that level the commanders were appointed by the Khan himself.

Every Mongol army was accompanied by several minghans of artillery and engineers, although the Mongols were not particularly skilled at siegecraft. Initially they copied the techniques of the Chinese, using catapults to lob missiles over distances of up to 150 yards. The latter could also be used to hurl incendiary missiles into besieged towns, and to support the barrage of arrows fired by archers on the battlefield. By the time of the Mongol invasion of Russia they were also using incendiary grenades and arrows tipped with naphtha and quick-lime.

The speed of Mongol advance made good communications essential. A flag system (not unlike the more recent semaphore system) was used during the day and torches at night to link the army with other Mongol formations and its domestic base. Throughout the Mongol Empire, a highly efficient system of staging-posts or 'yams' was also established, which could be loosely compared with the pony express system in nineteenth-century USA. Messengers wore leather belts with bells on them, which warned the staging-post of their coming, and the yam would then provide food, shelter and remounts. This enabled Mongol messengers to travel as much as 120 miles in a day.

There were other parallels with ancient history, although there is no evidence that the Mongols studied Roman campaigns. But the classic Mongol battle-plan bore an uncanny resemblance to that used by the great Carthaginian Hannibal in his rout of the Romans at Cannae in 216 BC. Where Hannibal had used a retreating infantry screen to lure the Romans to destruction, the Mongols used a 'suicide corps', or *mangudai*, of light cavalry for the same purpose.

As the enemy force spread out over the field it would be bombarded on the flanks by Mongol archers, and finally attacked by the heavy cavalry at the sound of a huge kettle-drum (the *naccara*). This charge was invariably decisive in the Russian campaign, and was always the final act in a Mongol battle-plan. The overall effect of such tactics has been likened to a sort of thirteenth-century blitzkrieg, and it was no accident that World War II generals like Patton and Rommel were admirers of the great Mongol general Subedei. Mongol battle tactics are still the focus of study in modern military schools and academies.

The Mongol Invasion

This then was the formidable foe which was massing on the frontiers of southern Russia in the winter of 1237. That summer the Mongols had destroyed the Bulgar kingdom on the Middle Volga, in characteristic fashion putting 50,000 inhabitants of its capital city to the sword. This should have been a warning to the divided Russian princelings, but they persisted in understimating the Mongol threat. Such complacency played into the hands of Subedei who sent a vast army of 120,000 warriors across the frozen Volga, after which they advanced unobserved through the thick forest on its western bank.

The Mongol plan was simple. Subedei recognised that the strongest Russian leader was Grand Duke (or Grand Prince) Yuri of Suzdal, and he aimed to divide his principality and that of Novgorod from the states of Chernigov and Kiev by laying waste to a corridor of territory through southern Russia. Having terrorised and confused the rival Russian states, his forces would then isolate and destroy Suzdal itself. The small state of Ryazan on the fringes of Russia was selected for attack in the initial stage, because it was judged to be the weakest, with its rulers hopelessly divided, and as a vassal state of Suzdal it would be bound to be supported by the Grand Duke (this part of Subedei's assessment proved to be incorrect).

Two brothers, Yuri and Roman, were in contention with their cousins Oleg and Yaroslav, and each princeling had his own urban base. When the Mongol host appeared, Prince Roman rode for Suzdal and asked the Grand Duke Yuri for help, but he said (not unreasonably but failing to discern the nature of the threat facing his vassal kingdom) that the four princes should stop squabbling and unite against the Mongols. Although the other three Ryazan princes won a small initial success against the invaders, they were soon enveloped in the capital (also named Ryazan) themselves. The Mongols built a wooden palisade around Ryazan, to cut it off from outside aid, and stormed the city after just five days. It was then that the Russians began to understand what the 'Mongol terror' meant. The rulers and their families were slaughtered, citizens were flayed alive in the streets, and all the young women (including nuns) were systematically raped.

Even then the Grand Duke Yuri remained strangely lethargic, and watched the fall of his own capital Suzdal without intervening. This time the Mongols, confident of ultimate victory, spared the nuns and priests

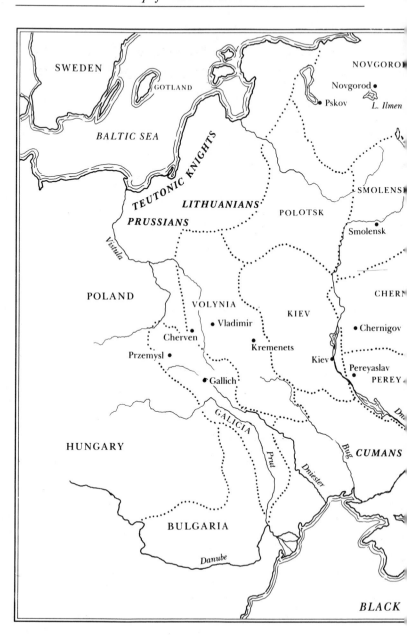

SWEDEN

GOTLAND

NOVGOROD

Novgorod •

• Pskov   *L. Ilmen*

BALTIC SEA

TEUTONIC KNIGHTS

LITHUANIANS

POLOTSK

SMOLENSK

PRUSSIANS

Smolensk

Vistula

POLAND

VOLYNIA

• Vladimir

KIEV

CHERN

Cherven

Kremenets

• Chernigov

Przemysl •

Kiev •

• Gallich

Pereyaslav

PEREY

GALICIA

HUNGARY

Prut

Bug

CUMANS

Dniester

Dm

BULGARIA

Danube

BLACK

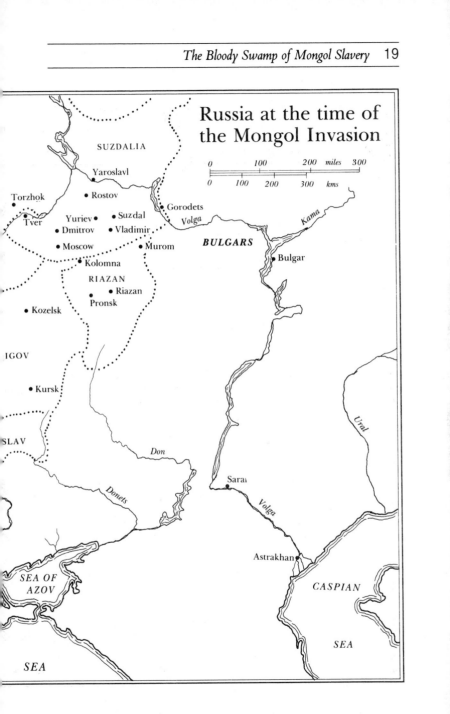

of Suzdal, and immediately laid siege to the city of Vladimir where the Grand Duke had left his wife and children for safekeeping. It availed him little for it too was stormed in February 1238. When his wife refused to come down from the cathedral choir-loft where she was hiding, the Mongols burnt her and her children to death.

The day of reckoning for the Grand Duke himself came soon afterwards. One Mongol army under Khan Batu laid siege to Novgorod, while Subedei sought out the reluctant Yuri to force him to battle. Vainly did the Grand Duke wait for a relieving force from Novgorod, and his scouts could only report 'My Lord, the Tartars [the Russian name for the Mongols] have surrounded us'. In the first week of March 1238 the Suzdalian army was destroyed in battle on the River Sit, together with its Grand Prince.

Novgorod would surely have suffered the same fate had it not been for the courageous resistance of the fortress of Torzhok. This held up Batu's force for two weeks and then an early spring thaw flooded the southern part of the state and made it impossible to advance further. Batu was forced to give up the investment of Novgorod and, crucially for Russia, it never did capitulate. Thereafter the Mongols laid waste to the state of Chernigov, taking care to avoid the walled towns. In one instance, however, the garrison of Kozelsk, afraid perhaps of the fate of Ryazan and Vladimir, sallied out and took the Mongols by surprise. The Mongol vanguard was defeated but retribution soon followed. Kozelsk was sacked with such ferocity that even the Mongols referred to it afterwards as the 'City of Sorrow'.

Satiated perhaps with blood and plunder, the Mongols then rested through the summer of 1239 in the lush steppeland of the Western Ukraine. Fresh horses were brought from Mongolia and the warriors contented themselves for the next twelve months with raiding old enemies like the Cumans, Alans, and Circassian nomadic tribesmen in surrounding territories. There also appear to have been divisions between the leaders about which strategy to follow, so that only in the summer of 1240 was the offensive against Russia resumed. Cities like Chernigov and Pereyaslav were captured, and in mid-November the Mongol vanguard under Mangku reached Kiev, by now but a pale shadow of its former glory. Even so the Mongols were much impressed by the city, high on the banks overlooking the Dnieper, and they called it 'the court of the golden heads' (a reference to the golden domes of its thirty churches). Such respect did not, of course, save Kiev from its fate, although its fall was precipitated by the killing of Mongol ambassadors by its governor, Dimitri. This apparent folly derived from Dimitri's decision to fight the Mongols regardless of the fears of Kiev's citizens, who he suspected would settle for Mongol rule and the payment of an annual tribute. When Batu arrived with reinforcements from the north on 6 December 1240, Kiev was stormed amidst an orgy of slaughter during which Byzantine treasures were looted and the bones of Christian saints scattered in the streets. Yet with their traditional respect for a courageous foe, the Mongols spared the life of Dimitri whose ill-advised decision had brought about the slaughter of his fellow citizens. However, they left the Cathedral of Saint Sophia standing (it was the *only* building left standing in Kiev) which contained the bones of Yaroslav the Wise.

A Mongol mounted archer

After the fall of Kiev three weeks then sufficed to take the Mongol horsemen to the western fringes of Russia; unsurprisingly they encountered little resistance. So began what Karl Marx was to describe as 'the bloody swamp of Mongol slavery', which Novgorod was fortunate to escape for the Mongols, lured by the prospect of more booty in neighbouring Poland, left a mere 30,000 men to maintain their control of southern Russia. Their terrible reputation ensured that it would be enough.

In 1242 the Mongols set up their headquarters in Saray (not far from modern Volgograd) but the control they exercised (like the Khazars before them) was loose. Their primary concern was an annual tribute – it is significant that the words for 'money', 'goods' and 'exchequer' in modern Russian are of Tartar origin. Russian princes did have to travel to Saray to obtain their authorisation to rule from their Mongol masters, but thereafter the khans left their Russian vassals alone, providing Mongol financial requirements were met.

Historians are agreed that the Mongol impact on Russia was essentially negative. Their 'yoke' cut Russia off from Byzantium, and also severed her links with the Latin West. These, it should be remembered, were not inconsiderable. Yaroslav the Wise had married a daughter of the king of Sweden, and his three daughters were married to the kings of France, Norway and Hungary respectively. Anna, the wife of Henri I of France (1031–60), was apparently able to sign her name while her husband could not! In cultural terms, therefore, the Mongol invasion was a disaster for Russia, as her celebrated poet Pushkin recognised in the nineteenth century. 'The Tartars', he wrote, 'were unlike the Moors: having conquered Russia, they gave her neither algebra nor Aristotle.'

What the invasion did give the Russians, however, was the political cohesion which flowed from the rise of Muscovy, which was in itself a consequence of the Mongol conquest. Karamzin, 'the father of modern Russian historiography',[4] wrote of the Mongol despotism:

> Batu's invasion overthrew Russia ... but upon further examination we discover that the calamity was a blessing in disguise, that the destruction contained the boon of unity ... Another hundred years or more might have

passed in princely feuds. What would have been their result? Probably the doom of our country . . . Moscow, in fact, owes its greatness to the Khans.[5]

Even if this point is conceded it still has to be recognised that throughout the Mongol period standards of craftsmanship and monastic scholarship declined in Russia, and she ceased to be, to use the Varangian term, the 'kingdom of towns'. It was an historical freak that the small town of Moscow, stormed by the Mongols in 1238 on their way to Vladimir and then part of Suzdalia, should provide the territorial heartland for the rise of the modern Russian state.

CHAPTER THREE

The Rise of Muscovy
1265–1462

The Defeat of the Teutonic Knights

As we have seen, Novgorod was fortunate to have survived the Mongol onslaught between 1237 and 1240, after which the nomadic warriors turned their attentions towards Hungary and Poland. In the long run, however, it was succession problems within the Mongol empire which diverted Batu's attentions eastwards, and saved north-western Russia from his armies. Batu, although he was the first 'Khan of the Golden Horde', a name derived from the Mongol treasures at Saray, never became Supreme Khan, and his energies were absorbed by internal feuding within the Mongol leadership.

But Novgorod had other enemies, who sought to take advantage of the Mongol diversion into Eastern Europe. Chief amongst them were the formidable order of Teutonic Knights, whose avowed intention was the overthrow of the schismatic Russians who had defied the papacy in 1054. This religious aspect gave the Knights a papal sanction for what they claimed was a crusade, but which was in reality a plundering expedition.

The military order of Teutonic Knights had been founded in 1198, but unlike its sister orders, the Templars and Hospitallers, it was not based in the Holy Land. Instead it sought the apparently softer target of the Baltic coastline and East Prussia, where conquest was followed by a German settlement. Only members of the German nobility were allowed to become members and its *hochmeister* (high master) was accorded the status of a prince of the Holy Roman Empire. By 1240 the Teutonic Knights were a major military presence in the Baltic provinces, and in that year they seized the town of Pskov in preparation for a wholesale offensive against Novgorod in the (alleged) cause of the 'True Cross'.

In their way these heavily-armoured knights, with their flowing white cloaks and black crosses, were as frightening a phenomenon as the Mongols, and they certainly remained so in Russian folk memory. Unlike the Mongols, however, they did not do their homework, and in 1242 were lured by Alexander Nevsky onto the frozen ice of Lake Peipus. The weight of their armour cracked the ice and many thousands drowned; those who did not were finished off by Nevsky's lightly-armed horsemen (brilliantly portrayed in Sergei Eisenstein's film *Alexander Nevsky*). Nevsky himself was a prince of Novgorod and took his name from the river Neva in commemoration of his victory over the Swedes in 1240. He realised that heroics would not save Russia from the Mongol yoke. While the power of the Teutonic Knights was broken for ever on Lake Peipus, the Mongols were another matter.

THE EXPERIENCE OF MONGOL RULE

In fact, the first of the Russian princes to offer his allegiance to Batu was Nevsky's father Yaroslav of Novgorod, who went to Saray in 1242. The death of his brother Yuri during the Mongol invasion had made him Grand Prince of Vladimir and Suzdal, but this was meaningless without the sanction of the Golden Horde. Having been subjected to the required Mongol rituals (like walking between two fires, which was supposed to remove all evil intentions), Yaroslav returned home with his *yarlyk*, or authorisation to rule.

Others were not so lucky, and it was customary for Russian princes to draw up their wills before leaving for Saray. This may have been a result of the treatment received by the princes of Chernigov at Batu's hands: Andrei was executed by the Mongols for no more serious an offence than exporting horses, while his brother Michael was executed for refusing to kneel before a statue of Genghis Khan. In 1246 Yaroslav's luck also ran out when he attended the election of the Supreme Khan at Karakorum, the capital of the entire Mongol empire. He was sent in place of Batu as his representative and fell victim to the internal machinations of the empire. For the dowager empress, Torogone, infuriated by Batu's infringement of tradition in failing to attend the election, had Yaroslav poisoned so that he died within the week. She then invited Alexander Nevsky to Karakorum to be confirmed as his father's heir! (This particular subplot was unusual, since the Russian princes dealt normally only with the Khan of the Golden Horde.)

The Origins of Muscovy

It is to Alexander Nevsky's youngest son Daniel (Daniil) that the rise of Muscovy, or Moscow, can first be attributed. Under his rule (1261–1303) Moscow (Moskva) rose from being merely the capital of a minor principality to a status of some significance among the Russian princedoms, though not yet to a position of dominance. It doubled its size and became a centre of refuge for Russians fleeing from more exposed principalities. It also had obvious geographical advantages: it linked up with all the important river systems of northern and western Russia, but it also lay across the two most important trade routes from the Baltic to the Caspian, along the Western Dvina and the Volga.

Early Muscovite history was dominated by the struggle with the neighbouring city of Tver, and it was during this period that a distinctively Muscovite version of statecraft appeared. In 1326 the Tverites rose up against the Mongol yoke and appealed to fellow Russians to join them. This fell on deaf ears in Moscow, and indeed the ruler, Ivan I Kalita ('Moneybags') (1325–41), was asked by the Golden Horde to crush the uprising, and did so with the greatest severity. As a reward the Mongols made Ivan Grand Duke of Vladimir, and with their approval he subsequently added the title 'all of Russia'. He also won the right to collect taxes on behalf of the Golden Horde and to exercise judicial authority over all the other Rusian princes.

Thus, under Ivan I the three major characteristics of the grand princes of Muscovy were already present. Firstly, there was what has been justly called 'sycophantic grovelling before the Mongols'[1] (the Grand Duke Vasily II, Ivan the Great's father, was so nauseatingly obsequious that the Mongols put his eyes out). Secondly, there was an obsessional hoarding of money which was the origin of Ivan's own nickname. Lastly, there was a policy of territorial acquisition by whatever means, fair or foul. This last element sometimes involved backing the winner in internecine

Mongol wars (as in 1392 when Moscow got Nizhny-Novgorod for supporting the Golden Horde against Timur (Tamerlane). In Ivan Kalita's case these principles were adhered to with considerable success. During his reign much treasure was hoarded away and Moscow absorbed some Trans-Volgan territories, although Ivan opted for tribute rather than direct rule. It also obtained another important advantage when after 1327 the Orthodox Metropolitan opted to reside in Moscow, as did his successors. This allowed the grand princes to acquire the sanctity associated with divine approval, whereas the Tverites made the fatal error of seeking help from Catholic Lithuania. Hatred of the Latin Catholic West was an early, and increasingly dominant, feature of Muscovy.

The pattern of Muscovite history after the death of Ivan Kalita was characterised by struggle. Mongol raids continued between 1368 and 1408, 'cutting down all Christians all the time like grass', and in Lithuania and Novgorod Muscovy had 'tough rivals'.[2] Lithuania, whose rulers were still pagan in the fourteenth century, was involved in a religious power struggle with Moscow over the Orthodox patriarchate because it had more Orthodox believers. The struggle effectively ended in 1385 when Lithuania adopted Catholicism as the state religion, but as late as 1458 it installed a rival Orthodox Metropolitan in Kiev.   .

The importance of the Orthodox patriarch was demonstrated during the minority of the Grand Duke Dimitri Donskoy (1359–89), when the Metropolitan Alexei acted as regent, thus setting a precedent for clerical involvement in Muscovite government.

Dimitri Donskoy

The reign of Dimitri Donskoy was then a crucial period in the rolling back of Mongol domination, although it did not end it. In 1378 a Mongol raid failed for the first time, and in 1380 Donskoy, having provoked a punitive attack by the Mongols, decisively defeated them at Kulikovo on the River Don (the full Russian name for the battlefield is Kulikovo Pole – the Field of Snipe). The Grand Duke Dimitri then became, like Alexander Nevsky, a heroic legendary figure, but like many subjects of myth his exploits were granted the rosy hue of legend rather than fact.

Dimitri Donskoy Grand Prince of Moscow. He, like Alexander Nevsky was
later canonised

In the first instance, his victory at Kulikovo owed much to the absence
of a Lithuanian contingent promised to the Mongol commander Mamai.
In the second, Kulikovo did not prevent a subsequent Mongol raid in
1382 which succeeded in capturing Moscow despite its new stone
fortress known as the Kremlin (from the Russian 'kreml' as fortress).
Mamai's successor Tokhtamysh then reimposed the tribute to the
Mongols, which the Muscovites were forced to pay for another hundred
years – this reality did not suit Muscovite historians who continued to
claim that Donskoy (named after the headwaters of the River Don)
threw off the Mongol yoke after a famous, though historically doubtful
blessing, by St Sergius of Zagorsk (c. 1321–91). It was Tamerlane (Timur
the Lame) who really destroyed the power of the Golden Horde in 1395.

Dimitri Donskoy's successor, the Grand Duke Vasily I (1389–1425),
was able to offer a further example of growing Muscovite confidence by
complaining that 'we have a Church but no Emperor'. This was a
reference to the chronic political weakness of the Byzantine empire,
which by the 1390s had been reduced to a few islands and the city of
Constantinople. The Grand Duke seems to have accepted the rebuke,

although, as we have seen, the Muscovites had already won the argument about the home of the Russian Metropolitan. Muscovy continued to press its case to be 'The Third Rome' supplanting Rome and Constantinople.

Several points about Moscow's early history also need to be noted. In an age when succession rights were vital and frequently led to catastrophic civil wars, Moscow alone of the Russian states adopted the system of primogeniture. This gave her more social cohesion than her rivals. Another characteristic of Muscovy which helped to bring about its eventual triumph was a direct consequence of its subjection to the Mongol yoke. Even the use of the title 'White Tsar' to describe the grand princes of Moscow derived directly from the former title of the Khan of the Golden Horde. Finally the historians Milner-Gulland and Dejevsky have pointed out that Muscovy also possessed other inestimable advantages. After 1359 six successive rulers (Dimitri, Vasily I, Vasily II, Ivan III, Vasily III and Ivan IV) reigned for a period of 225 years during which the shortest reign was twenty-eight years and the longest fifty-one. It was a 'rather astonishing record in a turbulent and disease-ridden time'[3].

The Mongol Legacy

Most important in its influence on the evolution of the modern Russian state was the Mongol capacity for centralisation, which even allowed them to hold a census of their subjects, an achievement far beyond the Western European states of the medieval period (with the sole exception of the Domesday Book in England). Moscow copied the Mongol system of conscription, which produced a sophisticated military machine, and also their fiscal system which gave the grand princes a capacity to raise revenue by taxation. So while the Mongols destroyed cultural links with the rest of Europe, they certainly left their stamp on the administrative structure of the Muscovite state, and later of the tsarist one.

Less desirably, perhaps, the Muscovites also aped the Mongol capacity for ruthless *realpolitik*. When the situation demanded, the grand dukes were subservient to a degree before their Mongol masters, but copied them in dealing with their so-called 'apanage' (or vassal) states.

Paradoxically, in western eyes, Russian historians have often approved of the ruthless servility of Ivan Moneybags and his successors. Karamzin, for example, wrote approvingly of those princes who 'crawled on their knees at the Orda [Horde], but returning thence with a gracious yarlyk of the Khan they commanded with greater boldness than they used to do in the days of our political independence'.[4] Vernadsky too, while noting that the 'Mongolian state was built upon the principle of unquestioning submission of the individual to the group',[5] refrains from criticising this development. The context in fact is one of approval for the concept of individual service to the state, which was to become such an essential component of the Russian political tradition. While Karl Marx wrote scathingly about Kalita's system as 'the machiavellism of the usurping slave', his own adherents in the USSR have begun to question whether they too have not fallen victim to 'the terrible and abject school of Mongolian slavery'[6] which the prophet of socialism described. What is beyond dispute is the crucial and devastating impact of the Mongol Conquest on modern Russian history.

CHAPTER FOUR

The Consolidation of the Muscovite State
1462–1584

The establishment of the Muscovite state in the fourteenth and fifteenth centuries was followed by a period of consolidation which lasted until the closing quarter of the sixteenth century. This covered the reigns of Ivan the Great or Ivan III (1462–1505), Vasily III (1505–33) and Ivan IV (1533–84) who is more commonly known as Ivan the Terrible (a more correct translation of the Russian word 'Grozny' would be 'Dread').

The Reigns of Ivan the Great and Vasily III

Ivan III's reign gave Muscovy the secure territorial heartland which his predecessors had craved. Tver (known today as Kalinin) was brought under Muscovite control, and Ivan also had military successes over the Lithuanians and the Kazan Tartars. More significantly, in 1480 he formally ended Moscow's subjection to the Golden Horde, thus ending two centuries of Mongol domination.

He also secured the capitulation of Novgorod in 1477, and the terms he granted to the rival city were characterised by the usual Muscovite ruthlessness. 'Our grand-princely dominion,' Ivan told the Novgorodites, 'is of this wise: there is to be no assembly and no bell in our land Novgorod, and no lieutenant; our rule is to be exercised by ourselves.' When subsequently Novgorod conspired against him, Ivan replied in kind, dispossessing four-fifths of the landowning class, and 'removing' many of them to central Muscovy, so establishing a tradition which was kept up by Ivan the Terrible and his successors.

Ivan III's reign was also notable for various changes in the social structure and customs of Muscovy. The process of so-called 'selection' from the aristocracy became common for state service, although to begin with it was on a purely voluntary basis. Conversely the 'right of departure' of the Grand Duke's vassals or apanage princes gradually disappeared. This was because by the end of Ivan the Great's reign the only realistic alternative to service with Muscovy was with Lithuania, and in Orthodox eyes this was treason. So this feature of the looser Russian feudal system died out.

The characteristics of Ivan's reign were continued under his successor Vasily III. In 1510 the concept of Moscow as the 'Third Rome' was put forward by the monk Filofey (Philotheos) of Pskov:

> Know then, O pious Tsar, that all the Orthodox Christian realms have converged in thy single empire. Thou art the only Tsar of the Christians in all the universe ... Observe and hearken O pious Tsar, that all Christian Empires have converged in thy single one, that two Romes have fallen, but the third stands, and no fourth can ever be. Thy Christian Empire shall fall to no one.

Vasily III

Given this central acceptance of the concept of Holy Russia as the rightful representative of true Christianity (particularly since the fall of Constantinople in 1453), it is not surprising that in pre-revolutionary Russia the normal mode of address for a group of fellow citizens was 'Christians' or 'Orthodox'.

Ivan the Terrible

The childhood of Ivan IV was as disturbed as the last decades of his reign. Nominally Grand Duke at the age of three, Ivan's fate rested in the hands of his mother, a Lithuanian princess who acted as Regent after the death of his father. But she was poisoned when Ivan was eight, whereupon the boy became the pawn of the leading nobles, although at the tender age of thirteen he showed his mettle by prompting the murder of one of them.

Ivan's period of personal rule really started in 1547, when at the behest of the Metropolitan Makary he was crowned Tsar (or Caesar). Significantly this was the first occasion that a grand prince of Muscovy had laid claim to this title. (The ornate ritual surrounding the occasion was superbly conveyed in Eisenstein's film *Ivan the Terrible*, made in 1944. So too was the shadowy paranoia of Ivan's court, rife with intrigue and faction – at least until Ivan established his personal despotism.)

Ivan was marked by his childhood experiences. The unhealthy mixture of dependence on the one hand and fawning minions on the other was almost bound to distort any young man's personality. It is known that he tortured animals in his youth, and the execution later of one of his mother's ex-lovers points to a lingering resentment against the woman who, he claimed, gave him no affection. It is, of course, tempting for the historian also to play the role of psychoanalyst and deduce that Ivan was deranged, but the conclusion of Kochan and Abraham seems a reasonable one nonetheless: 'It would have been surprising had the Russian tsar not been a seriously disturbed person; he may well also have suffered severe mental illness.'[1] But Ivan was a creature of his time, and it is right that we place any speculations about lunacy in the context of the aura of sycophancy and duplicity which surrounded him.

Ivan demonstrated his capacity for personal initiative by abandoning tradition and marrying the daughter of a boyar family, Anastasia Zakharina, who bore him six children. She is often credited with being a moderating influence on Ivan until her death in 1560, and it is certainly true that the tsar never achieved marital happiness again although he married a further five times (and took lovers of both sexes). Anastasia's alleged influence over her husband offers one explanation for Ivan's relatively mild reaction to the events surrounding the 'succession crisis' of 1553, when he fell seriously ill. When it seemed that the young tsar might die, the boyars (high-ranking noblemen) saw an opportunity to install his cousin Vladimir Staritsky on the throne rather than risk the accession of one of his wife's hated relatives, the Zakharins. Ivan's unexpected recovery sabotaged this plan, but he knew of it and did not forgive the participants.

Otherwise the period 1547–60 was dominated by the so-called 'Chosen Council', an advisory council whose leading figures were Adashev and the priest Sylvester. Like the tsaritsa, they too were of humble origin, and the young Ivan resented their influence. There is no evidence, however, for his subsequent claim that Adashev and Sylvester were central figures in a boyar plot against him. In fact the rule of the 'Chosen Council' coincided with some signal successes for the Muscovite state.

The Kazan Tartars were conquered in 1552, and Astrakhan was annexed in 1556. In conjunction with this expansion of Muscovy's territorial base, there was also a re-establishment of commercial ties with the West, when the Englishman Richard Chancellor made his pioneering voyage to the White Sea in 1553 (see p. 00).

At home the Chosen council was responsible for the introduction of the *Domostroy*, a code of domestic behaviour borrowed from the rich merchants of Novgorod. At the time it was regarded as a model for the treatment of upper-class Russian women, but they later came to regard it as an instrument of oppression.

IVAN'S REIGN OF TERROR

These successes, however, did not save the Chosen Council from Ivan's disfavour, and by 1560 Adashev and Sylvester were in disgrace. Ivan's capacity for paranoia was then unfortunately enhanced by the death of his wife Anastasia, and by reverses in an ill-advised campaign against the German barons of Livonia. His fury at the latter in 1562 caused him to leave Moscow altogether and live in Alexandrov. He only agreed to return if the boyars placed no obstacles in the path of his absolute rule.

So began the dark chapter in Muscovite history known as the *oprichnina*. It took its name from the special court set up by Ivan, with powers of life and death over about a half of his realm. Under its auspices the *oprichniki* (the men apart), a private army of 6000 black-cowled fanatics, were allowed to strike down all the tsar's alleged enemies regardless of their age and sex. What followed was an orgy of torture and butchery (in which Ivan frequently participated personally) by this sinister quasi-monastic organisation, with its emblem of the dog. (The analogy with the Stalinist secret police drawn by Eisenstein, in the second part of his film *Ivan the Terrible*, is obvious.) No one was safe from the excesses of the *oprichniki*. In 1567 the blood purge included among its victims Ivan's own relatives, the Staritskys, and still the reign of terror went on.

In 1569–70 the classic pattern of such purges was reaffirmed when both Pskov and Novgorod were sacked by Ivan's forces spearheaded by the *oprichniki*. An external threat was used to justify internal persecution. The fall of Novgorod was a particularly ghastly example of the tsar's blood lust, although it can be understood in the context of the Muscovite grand dukes' traditional suspicion of their neighbouring city. Novgorod was, after all, a rich, cultured centre for foreign trade, a role unique in Russia at that time, which made it the natural target for Muscovite jealousy. But whatever demon afflicted Ivan IV was given its head at Novgorod, as Tibor Szamuely has noted:

> Thousands, perhaps even tens of thousands of peaceful inhabitants were put to death by various fiendish methods born in the fertile imagination of their lawful sovereign: impaling, flaying alive, boiling, roasting on spits, frying in gigantic skillets, evisceration and most mercifully drowning.[2]

What was the explanation for this wilful destruction of Russia's only remaining centre for international trade? There is apparently none, other than the fact that, in his mania for authoritarianism, Ivan IV saw

Novgorod, with its distinct culture and history, as a threat to Muscovite absolutism. This may offer apparently irrevocable proof of Ivan's lunacy, but he was sane enough to follow the precedent of confiscations from the Novgorodites set up by Ivan III. Other contemporary rulers were also capable of such savagery. After the crushing of the Catholic revolt known as the 'Pilgrimage of Grace' in 1537, Henry VIII of England demanded that Catholic monks 'be tied up' and tortured, and his wrath extended even to those women who removed their executed husbands' corpses at night.

Ivan justified the activities of the *oprichnina* on the grounds that his position was endangered by boyar opposition and conspiracy. There is virtually no evidence that such a conspiracy existed after his return to Moscow in 1562, and it is much more likely that his reign of terror was a direct consequence of Ivan's own experience in the succession crisis of 1553. The terror of the 1560s can then be seen as belated revenge by a man deeply imbued with the belief that his cause was both righteous and sacred. In his mind the very suggestion of opposition was tantamount to treason, and given his uncertain temper, likely to be followed by savage reprisals. Nevertheless, in his celebrated correspondence with his former favourite Prince Kurbsky, who had fled to Lithuania, Ivan continued to defend his actions as a justified response to boyar sedition. When Kurbsky reproved him for destroying Russia's ancient liberties, the Dread Tsar replied angrily:

> And as for the godless [i.e. foreign] peoples – why mention them? For none of these rule their own kingdoms. As their servants order them, so too do they rule. But as for the Russian autocracy they themselves [i.e. the autocrats] from the beginning have ruled all their dominions, and not the boyars and not the grandees.[3]

Ivan's thesis was, of course, false. The early history of Russia did not justify his assertion that the power of the grand dukes had always been absolute. Instead Ivan himself was creating the evil precedent for Russia of rewriting history to suit the needs of the present.

THE CHURCH UNDER IVAN THE TERRIBLE

Even a bloody tyrant like Ivan IV needed the sanction of holy Church.

Indeed, he showed a curious rectitude in ensuring that even his victims obtained a suitably religious burial. When one of Russia's many 'holy fools' denounced his slaughter of the innocents at Pskov, he also went unpunished. This was because Ivan, though superstitious to a degree (like most contemporaries he believed in witchcraft – but even England's highly educated Elizabeth I took John Dee's predictions about the fatal year 1588 at their face value)[4] was as afraid of eternal damnation as anyone else. But he fully shared Filofey's belief that Moscow was the true centre of Christianity. Thus when fleeing Polish Protestants wished to enter Russia, Ivan thundered, 'Rome is enticement, and you are darkness,' and rejected their request. In a similar fashion he was fond of reminding Polish kings that his title came from God, whereas they were elected by the nobility. Despite this certainty Ivan did not always get his own way with the Orthodox Church. In 1550, for example, it refused to agree to his plan for the secularisation of its lands, and Ivan was fobbed off with a promise that Orthodox clergy would lead more saintly lives and avoid the sins of the flesh.

The relationship, in fact, was one of mutual dependence. Ivan needed the Church as an agency of social control over a peasantry which suffered badly in the difficult conditions between 1550 and 1600. Clerics told their flocks that their sufferings were not the fault of the Dread

Ivan IV (Ivan the Terrible)

Tsar, and that they would in any case be rewarded in heaven. They were also comforted by the assurance that they, the Russians, were the only true Christians.

Historians have, with some justice, criticised the Church for encouraging Russian nationalism at the expense of the wider Orthodox community (those living in the Ottoman Empire). Particular criticism has been levelled at the *Stoglav* (or Hundred Chapters) of 1552, a series of decrees which legitimised rituals and customs which were peculiar to the Russian Church, and which other Orthodox regarded as heretical. In the context of Ivan IV's reign, however, such measures are not surprising. For both Tsar and Church alike were terrified by the advent of the free-thinking German Reformation, with its apparent emphasis on the individual conscience in religious belief and practice. Ivan IV could hardly be expected to detect the subtleties of historical development in Germany, which would in fact lead to an obsessive Lutheran loyalty to the state. So he closed his frontiers to western influence, and burnt or imprisoned any clerics who were deemed to have propagated the falsehoods of the Reformation.

This fear of the Reformation also had a decisive influence on the development of the Russian Orthodox Church itself. For the sixteenth century was characterised by the struggle between the 'Possessors' and the 'Non-Possessors' for the soul of the Church, which naturally concerned the tsars whose fate was so intimately bound up with it. It was an age-old argument which had also arisen in the medieval Catholic Church, when St Francis of Assisi had preached the virtues of poverty and asceticism to an increasingly worldly and complacent clergy. In Russia this teaching was put forward by the Bulgarian-born Metropolitan of Moscow, Cyprian of Tirnovo, who demanded both the separation of church and state and a clergy free from material possessions. His supporters, of whom there were many in the Orthodox monasteries, were known as the Non-Possessors. Their opponents were called the Possessors or Josephans (after their leader Joseph, abbot of Volokolamsk) and they saw no objection to the church accumulating wealth. But an important qualification needs to be added here, which is that the Possessors wished to acquire such wealth in order to *dominate* the state. This, of course, was something that Ivan IV was not prepared to tolerate, and when in 1569 the Metropolitan Philip (a Possessor) attacked the tsar for his cruelty and immorality, he was tortured to death. Steven Runciman, therefore, accurately observes that the Possessors 'buttressed up the Tsar's autocracy more than they had intended'.[5]

The struggle between the Possessors and the Non-Possessors was a crucial one, because the latter were forced into the role of non-conformity in Russian history. Although they were driven out of the monasteries by Ivan the Terrible and his successors, their influence was not destroyed; from it, a century later, flowed the movement known as the Old Believers and the tradition in Russia of *startsy* (holy men), of whom Grigory Rasputin was the most celebrated and notorious example. Conversely, the triumph of their rivals meant that ultimately the Orthodox Church became the pliant instrument of the autocracy.

THE ECONOMY

On the face of it, Ivan the Terrible's theory of boyar conspiracy stands up because an increasingly impoverished and desperate nobility had to seek state service as a means of obtaining revenue. In 1550 Ivan's government took advantage of this dependence by making state service compulsory for the *votchinniki* (those landowners who held their estates by hereditary right). The Domostroy Code had already made such service compulsory for the *pomeshchiki*, those landowners (largely the younger children of boyars who did not inherit) who held land in fief as vassals of the tsar. Such weakness should, according to Ivan's theory, have bred resentment against the autocracy, but it does not appear to have done so. Instead the boyars' relationship with Ivan seems to have been a servile and supine one.

The weakness of the aristocracy under Ivan was accompanied by an equivalent deterioration in the status of the peasantry. In part, this was a result of a shortage of labour in the second half of the sixteenth century, which had given rise to the *Sudebnik* (Law Code) of 1550 during the period of the Chosen Council. Among other things, this tried to regulate the movement of peasants between estates by preventing them from leaving before the harvest was reaped, and then only on payment of a dwelling tax. Further legislation was initiated in 1581 by Ivan himself which introduced the practice of 'forbidden years' when peasants could not be transferred from estate to estate. A census was also held in rural areas.

The overall effect of the socio-economic changes in Ivan's reign was that Russia moved *backwards* in relation to what had taken place in Western Europe. Restrictions on social mobility and labour service were combined with a decline of the *posadi* or commercial centres in the relatively few urban centres (exclusive of the deliberate destruction of Novgorod in 1570). In most respects, therefore, Ivan's rule was damaging to the Muscovite economy.

The major exception was the eastward expansion of Muscovy into Siberia, a process which naturally reminds western readers of the opening of the American West. The key figures here were the Stroganovs, a family of merchants who obtained a vaguely worded charter from Ivan IV to seek their fortune in the wilds of Siberia. Their agent was Yermak, the leader of a band of wild Cossack horsemen who defeated the khan of the Siberian Tartars but proved increasingly difficult to control. Ultimately the tsar had to send his own troops to secure Yermak's seizure of the Siberian capital (modern Tobolsk) but it proved to be a worthwhile gesture. Meantime the Stroganovs evolved into that rare creature in early Russian history, a mercantile dynasty with moneybags of its own.

FOREIGN RELATIONS

The important success in Siberia was linked to another breakthrough in Muscovy's relationship with the West, which has been briefly referred to earlier. This was the arrival of Richard Chancellor at the mouth of the Northern Dvina in 1553, which was actually part of his contribution to the age-old English obsession with the North-West Passage. Ivan was pleased to see these visitors because trading links with England, then as diplomatically isolated as Muscovy, would lessen his dependence on the German Hanseatic League (which included such ports as Rostock, Lübeck and Hamburg). Chancellor's expedition was speedily followed by the setting up of the Russia Company in London in 1556. Ivan granted it the privilege of tax-free trade with his realm and the operation of English trading counters in Kholmogory, Vologda and Moscow itself.

The English response to these favours was condescending in the extreme, and they regarded the Muscovites as little better than savages.

Their agent Tuberville, with some claim to be a minor poet, leaves us this damning description of his new trading partners:

> Wilde Irish are as civil as the Russians in their kind,
> Hard Choice which is best of both, bloody, rude and blind.

In fairness to the Russians one should point out that the English were notorious for their chauvinism throughout Europe. The unfortunate Spanish entourage of Philip II, whose marriage to Mary Tudor in 1554 was deeply unpopular in England, went in fear of their lives in the streets of London. Ivan's own interest in marriage to an Englishwoman stayed strictly in the realm of daydreams, although it is known that he corresponded with that confirmed spinster Elizabeth I. Perhaps all the Englishwomen of the day should have counted their blessings. When some foreign women were thought (probably wrongly) to have been laughing at Ivan IV at court, he had them stripped and forced to pick up seed corn which was sprinkled all over the palace floor!

Elsewhere Ivan's plans went increasingly astray. Reference has already been made to the failure in Livonia, which even Ivan had reluctantly to accept by 1582, but a more significant one took place in Poland–Lithuania. This dual kingdom, which had been united by the Union of Lublin in 1569 under the House of Jagellon, was at this time by far Muscovy's most important neighbour. About half of Muscovite trade went through there, and in the 1570s there was talk of Ivan himself acceding to its throne. This opportunity was created by the idiosyncratic Polish system of elective monarchy, which left the realm without a monarch between 1574 and 1587. But the dream never became a reality. Ivan IV was far too autocratic to tolerate the independent pretensions of the Polish nobility, and his people were unlikely to accept the fusion of Catholic Poland and Lithuania with 'God's land'. The scheme therefore collapsed, and in its totality Ivan's foreign policy has to be regarded as a failure.

THE LAST PHASE

Ivan's erratic moods were not tempered by age. In a fit of jealous rage he killed his eldest son, Ivan, and his daughter-in-law, and his excesses went uncurbed because there was no mechanism for doing so in such an

The Great Seal of Ivan IV

absolute autocracy. Then nemesis finally overtook him in a gruesome form, vividly described by the agent of the Russia Company, Sir John Horsey. In 1584 Sir John noted:

> The Emperor began grievously to swell in his cods, with which he had most horribly offended above fifty years altogether, boasting of a thousand virgins he had deflowered and thousands of children of his begetting destroyed.

For some time he lingered on with a pathetic and unchristianlike belief in witchcraft and spells. Precious stones like emeralds and rubies, we are told, were carried daily into the royal chambers so that the dying despot could invoke their magic powers. But the exercise availed him little and Ivan the Terrible died, somewhat bizarrely, as he was about to start a game of chess. The succession at least was secure, although it passed to Ivan's half-witted second son, Fyodor.

THE LEGACY OF IVAN THE TERRIBLE

Controversy has raged between Soviet and western historians about Ivan's reign. On one point there is none, which is that Ivan vastly increased the autocratic powers of the tsar, and destroyed even those limited representative institutions which Muscovy had. The *Zemsky Sobor* (Assembly of the Land), which Ivan had tolerated, just became a rubber stamp for the tsar's decisions, and its powerlessness was witheringly summed up by Queen Elizabeth's ambassador Giles Fletcher:

> for to propound bils which every man thinketh good for the publike benefite (as the manner is in England) the Russe Parliament knoweth no such custome nor libertie to subjects.

When Ivan's belief in his role as the agent of divine will is recalled, Fletcher's observations about the Zemsky Sobor at work will occasion little surprise.

The real debate has been about whether Ivan's ruthless suppression of all individual rights and liberties was justified by domestic circumstances. Many Soviet historians have argued that it was because Russia's geographical and military vulnerability (which was real enough) made such methods inevitable. Western historians have presented the view that Ivan's methods were peculiarly harsh even by the standards of the day, so that he cannot be compared to Western European monarchs like Louis XI and Henry VIII.[6] The flaw in this argument would seem to be that, although Ivan's excesses *were* worse than those of his western counterparts, so was his inheritance. The grand dukes of Muscovy had learnt about kingship while they were tethered to the Mongol yoke, and as late as 1571 the Crimean Tartars had raided Moscow itself.

Remarkably, the Russian people did not share historians' reservations about Ivan the Terrible, even those of the generation who suffered so cruelly at his hands. In the folk memory of the people he was 'Ivan the Conqueror', harsh but fair, and the father of the modern Russian state. More remarkable perhaps is that this memory of the reign was largely wrong. The conquests were those of others, and the people of Novgorod might have disputed Ivan's reputation for fairness.

CHAPTER FIVE

The Time of Troubles

The period known to Russian history as 'the Time of Troubles' lasted from 1598 to 1613, but this chapter will also deal with the reign of Ivan the Terrible's ill-fated son Fyodor (1584–98). The seeds of Russia's troubles were laid in his reign, and indeed during that of his father.

Fyodor was a retarded youth whose simple pleasures included bell-ringing, watching fights between men and bears, and laughing at the antics of court jesters and dwarfs. It soon became evident that he was incapable of ruling his realm, and he had to be superseded by a series of regents.

Boris Godunov

The first regent was Nikita Romanov, the young tsar's maternal uncle, but he died in 1586 and was replaced by the aristocratic Boris Godunov, whose reputation has been somewhat distorted by the works of Pushkin and Mussorgsky. Boris came from a family of Mongol origin which had gone into service with the grand dukes of Muscovy in the fourteenth century. He himself rose rapidly during the period of the *oprichnina*, although its influence had been destroyed by the time he took over the regency. He then consolidated his position by marrying off his sister Irina to the tsar, a move which did not, of course, enhance his popularity with older aristocratic families in Muscovy who were deeply jealous.

The pattern of conspiracy and revolt which characterised the next two decades in Muscovy was now rapidly established and there were several plots against Boris Godunov's life in the early years of his regency. Boris replied in kind, and when the Mstislavsky and Shuisky families were implicated they were tortured, and then executed or exiled. Merchants of lower social rank who were found to be involved were publicly beheaded.

CHURCH/STATE RELATIONS

Having silenced the political opposition, Boris went on to take control of the Church. He had his own nominee Iov (Job) appointed as Metropolitan of Moscow, and in 1588 persuaded the visiting Patriarch of Constantinople (the head of the Orthodox Church) to establish Moscow itself as a separate Patriarchate. Iov became Patriarch of Moscow and 'All Russia', and was effectively removed from the control of his supposedly senior colleague in Constantinople. As Gudunov well knew, the latter was little more than an Ottoman puppet and in no position to argue. Between 1595 and 1695 there were no less than sixty-one changes on the patriarchal throne in Constantinople although they affected only thirty-one individuals. This was a result of the fact that after the death of the great Ottoman Sultan Suleiman the Magnificent in 1566, the synod in Constantinople 'would be ordered to depose a patriarch on some flimsy excuse, though he might later be allowed to buy his way back to the throne'.[1] One patriarch only lasted seventeen days in 1603, and this detracted from the prestige of Constantinople vis à vis Moscow. The claims of Moscow to be the 'Third Rome' were accordingly enhanced by the chaos and corruption in its sister patriarchate. It also meant of course that the Russian Orthodox Church was more firmly under state control than ever, and that there was no real countervailing influence (as there would have been, for example, in contemporary Catholic states with the influence of the Papacy).

GODUNOV'S FOREIGN POLICY

By 1587 Boris Godunov's position at home was secure enough to allow him brazenly to tear up Ivan the Terrible's will, and Kochan and Abraham describe the regent as a 'consummate bureaucratic politician'.[2] He recognised the significance of the land question and passed decrees to force the peasantry to remain on the land, while abroad he was a much more adept diplomat than Ivan IV had been. Like Ivan he tried to unite the dual kingdom of Poland-Lithuania under the Russian tsars, in this instance by trying to influence the Polish election of 1587. Unfortunately he failed and independent Poland was soon to test severely the resilience and resolve of the Russian people.

Internal expansion, a feature of the previous reign, also continued under Boris resulting in the foundation of the towns of Ivangorod, Yam and Karelia. But this success did not make Boris Godunov's rule any more palatable for his opponents, and his reliance on the half-witted Fyodor made him vulnerable to a new device in Russian history, but one which was to become increasingly common in the coming centuries. This was the royal pretender, usually someone who had 'died' in mysterious circumstances and whose imperial title (as claimed) mesmerised a credulous peasantry.

THE FIRST 'FALSE DIMITRY'

The first of these was the first 'false Dimitry' who claimed to be the authentic younger son of Ivan IV by his marriage to Maria Nagaya. Dimitry who has been described as 'a pampered epileptic'[3] was found bleeding to death by his doting mother in 1591. In her grief, Maria blamed the ambitious Boris Godunov for her son's death, and his enemies were only too willing to accept her story. (It is, in fact, much more likely that the unfortunate Dimitry stabbed himself to death in an epileptic fit.)

Seven years then passed until the death of the simple-minded Fyodor allowed Godunov to obtain the throne when he had set aside the claims of Fyodor's wife Irene, his sister, who was forced to become a nun. Muscovy was apparently not ready for a tsaritsa. Godunov then ascended the throne after (at his insistence) election by both the Zemsky Sobor and the Boyars Council, the first time that such and election had taken place.

Five years later Tsar Boris was challenged by the first 'false Dimitry' who was in fact one Grigory Otrepyev, a former supporter of the Romanovs who had fallen on hard times. Otrepyev turned up at the castle of a Polish aristocrat called Adam Wisniewicki, who had an eye for the main chance and introduced him to other important Polish nobles, and in particular to George Mniszek, governor of Sandomir who saw, as did the false Dimitry, a chance to restore his family's fortunes. Mniszek agreed that his daughter, Marina should marry the Pretender. As Grigory then converted to Catholicism, he also received the backing of the Papal Nuncio in Poland who saw a means of counterbalancing the losses of the Reformation with the acquisition of Orthodox Russia. In this he was wildly optimistic, as no Russian would tolerate a union with the Latin heretics.

The Polish king Sigismund III was apparently not deceived by the claims of the false Dimitry, but he also saw the opportunity to extend Polish power at the expense of Muscovy. In 1604 he met Grigory at Cracow, recognised him as tsar and gave him a pension. The Pretender was joined by an army of some 4,000 Poles which moved off in the direction of Moscow, on the way it was joined by dispossessed Cossacks and peasants, most of whom had run away from their feudal masters.

EDUCATION

At this point Boris Godunov (1598–1605) died suddenly from a stroke (although there were stories about poison) leaving a somewhat undeserved reputation for being a despotic tsar. In fact Boris was in many respects quite enlightened. He was the first Russian ruler to be really interested in education, and apparently considered founding a university. Russian students were even sent abroad to complete their education, and four are known to have come to England (1603). They must have liked what they found, for they all refused to return and one

Tsar Boris Gudunov

actually became an Anglican clergyman! Persistent Russian efforts to get them back over the next twenty years failed completely.

Ultimately Boris Godunov was undone by a severe economic crisis even before the appearance of the false Dimitry. Poor harvests between 1601 and 1603 devastated the villages, not only depopulating them, but also causing speculation on the grain market. The result was catastrophic with cases of cannibalism reported, and peasants reduced to eating the bark of birch trees. In this context it is not hard to understand the effect the apparently miraculous appearance of the false Dimitry had on a superstitious and illiterate peasantry.

The death of Tsar Boris seemed to resolve the situation in the Pretender's favour, for although Godunov's son succeeded him as Fyodor II he was brutally murdered. Grigory seems to have been a curious creature. A French mercenary captain describes him as having spiky red hair, a wart on his nose, and a most unRussian tendency to be garrulous in council.

Grigory also displayed a most unRussian capacity for liberal reforms. He freed a quarter of all bonded slaves, banned the recovery of serfs who had fled from their estates, and doubled the pay of government officials. Suspicions about his lineage had apparently been satisfied by the personal identification of Maria Nagoya, who had been released from the convent where she had been mewed up, and doubtless had little desire to continue her incarceration. It couldn't last, of course. The Muscovite mob became mutinous about the airs and graces of Marina Mniszek, now married to Grigory, and her Polish entourage, and the Russian nobility could never accept this renegade Catholic with his humanitarian ways, as one of their own. The red-haired imposter lasted a year until Vasilly Shuisky led an uprising against him in May 1606. Less fortunate than his English counterpart Lambert Simnel (whom Henry VII allowed to work in his kitchens) Grigory was killed, and his ashes were fired from a cannon in the direction of Poland.

FOREIGN INTERVENTION

The next phase of the 'Time of Troubles' was if anything even more chaotic. It was characterised firstly by a cohesive peasant movement against feudalism, and secondly by large-scale foreign intervention in

Muscovite affairs. Together these phenomena effectively prevented Shuisky, who was proclaimed tsar by the Boyar Council and the Muscovite mob, from ever controlling more than half of the realm.

The key figure on the domestic front was Ivan Bolotnikov, the son of a poor boyar whose family had been forced into slavery as a result of the economic crisis of the 1570s. Bolotnikov then survived various privations which included a spell as an Ottoman galley slave, before returning to Muscovy, via Hungary and Poland, at the head of some ten thousand Cossacks.

The important point about Bolotnikov was that he had a cohesive programme, based on his so-called 'excellent charters', which was a challenge to the feudal system. He called on bonded slaves and peasants alike, to revolt and seize the estates of the tsar's fief holders (*pomeshchiki*). Such was the programme's popular appeal that it carried Bolotnikov and his followers to the gates of Moscow (1607). But its very radicalism alienated the boyars and merchants, and Bolotnikov's populism did not prove a strong enough force to take Moscow, and he began to lose

The Trinity Monastery of St Sergius at Zagorsk

support. A retreat to Tula was followed by a siege by Shuisky's forces and a surrender in the autumn of 1607.

At this point a second 'false Dimitry' appeared. Like his predecessor, he married Marina Mniszek (who bore him a child) and won the support of the Metropolitan Filaret Romanov. Unlike the first false Dimitry though, this 'Thief' or 'Scoundrel', as he was nicknamed, never got within more than six miles of Moscow. His forces were never strong enough to lay siege to the capital, although a Polish contingent did besiege the historic monastery of the Trinity of Saint Sergius close to it. The heroic resistance of the monks boosted the prestige of the Orthodox Church, and its perceived role as national unifier.

Events now took on a new foreign dimension, and were in themselves an admission of the weakness of the rival forces inside Muscovy. First of all, Shuisky appealed to Charles IX of Sweden who provided him with a mixed force of six thousand English, Scots and French mercenaries. This in turn provoked the intervention of the Polish king Sigismund III who laid siege to the strategically placed town of Smolensk in 1609. It fell after a siege of twenty-one months, while the Poles conquered large tracts of Muscovy.

Some boyars sided with the Poles, and it was with their assistance in 1610 that Sigismund's son Vladislav was proclaimed tsar and Shuisky was deposed. Meantime the Swedes had captured Novgorod and reduced Russia to a state of anarchy, experienced again only in the twentieth century. It was in this desperate state of affairs that the innate resilience and fortitude of the Russian people was displayed at its best. In 1611 there was a wave of national feeling against the 'Latin heretics' which resulted in an attempt to oust the Poles from Moscow. This failed, but Muscovy had now found two leaders in Minin and Pozharsky from the Volga and northern districts. In 1612 the Poles were driven out of Moscow. At this point a crucial decision was taken whereby the Zemsky Sobor nominated the sixteen-year-old Michael Romanov for the *hereditary* title of tsar, so rejecting the Polish system of elective monarchy because, as the Russians told the Poles,

> Your way is freedom for you but for us it is unfreedom. You do not have freedom but licence . . . if the Tsar himself acts unjustly, it is his will: it is

easier to suffer injury from the Tsar than from one's brother; for he is the common ruler.

Michael Romanov was of good pedigree, being a relative of Ivan the Terrible's first wife Anastasia, and the son of the Metropolitan Filaret. But if the 'Time of Troubles' is judged by historians to end with his elevation to the throne, it far from ended the troubles of the realm. Nevertheless the beginning of the Romanov dynasty in 1613, followed a period of Polish ascendancy which as B.H. Sumner says 'left the bitterest memories'[4] in Muscovy. This was why Minin and Pozharsky became heroes in Russian folklore for saving the motherland from 'our enemies and outragers of Christian faith the Polish and Lithuanian men'.

CHAPTER SIX

Years of Recovery
1613–1682

Michael Romanov

The situation in Muscovy at the accession of Michael Romanov (1613–45) was distinctly unpromising. Large areas of the state were still occupied by the Poles and Swedes; law and order had broken down, and gangs of marauding ex-peasants roamed the countryside; the treasury was empty and the economy disrupted. All these problems were abruptly thrust upon a sixteen-year-old boy.

So bad indeed were the circumstances facing the young Michael Romanov that he was soon forced to approach the wealthy Stroganov family for a loan both in cash and kind (fish, salt and grain). Few Muscovites would have predicted that this bankrupt dynasty would rule Russia for the next 300 years. That is was able to do so was in large part due to the remarkable resilience of the Russian peasants and their ability to eke out a living in the most catastropic economic and political conditions. Remarkable too was the ability of Russian merchants to maintain their contacts with the outside world at the height of the Time of Troubles, so that Anglo-Dutch trade with Russia continued via the Arctic Circle port of Archangel. Kochan and Abraham note how the canny Russian merchants ensured that foreign traders were made to pay for their purchases in bullion, which then stayed in Russia and contributed to the growth of a money economy.

It was clear, too, that emergent Rusian power was making itself felt on the European stage for the first time. The great French statesman Cardinal Richelieu encouraged the Romanovs to apply pressure on neighbouring Poland so that she made peace with Sweden. This in turn brought about the decisive intervention of the great Swedish king Gustavus Adolphus in the Thirty Years War (1618–48) in Germany. A grateful Sweden then supplied her ally with advisers to train the Muscovite army, while more foreign merchants flocked to the foreign quarter of the capital. No longer was Russia to be a barbaric and mysterious backwater unknown to the West, even if her laws and customs struck Western observers as being quaint in the extreme. Muscovite administration now included a professional Foreign Office (Posolsky Prikaz) which both read and translated extracts from foreign newspapers, and provided the tsars with accurate information about places as far away as Hamburg.

Much of this growing sophistication can be attributed to the influence of the tsar's father Filaret Romanov, who returned from years in captivity in Poland in 1619. Filaret encouraged his son's influence in European science and technology, but his knowledge of the western world did not prevent him from being a doughty defender of the Russian principle of absolutism. Throughout Michael Romanov's reign a battle raged between the Romanovs (father and son) and the National Assembly or Zemsky Sobor.

THE DECLINE OF THE ASSEMBLY

To begin with the crafty Filaret realised that he would have to work with the Assembly if the damage done during the Time of Troubles was to be repaired. Thus in 1619 municipal reforms enabled the tax burden to be equalised, and allowed for the return of citizens who had become serfs to avoid paying urban taxation. Thereafter, although Filaret Romanov discouraged the ambitious clamourings of the Assembly by ensuring that it didn't meet between 1621 and 1631, he 'was no more able to abolish the Assembly than Charles I was able to dispense with Parliament'.[1] Charles I (1625–49), it should be remembered, tried to rule England without Parliament during the period known as the 'Eleven Years Tyranny' from 1629 to 1640.

As matters turned out the tide of history favoured absolutism not only in Russia but throughout Europe. Although the Assembly of 1648–9 refused to support Russia's war with Poland, its influence declined in the 1650s and it ceased to be of major account. Instead the Romanovs began to rely increasingly on the more sectional Boyar Duma or parliament.

THE CHURCH

The relationship between Church and State was never closer in Russia than during the reign of the first Romanov. For while the son looked after the temporal realm, his father looked after the spiritual although, as we have seen, the latter's influence overflowed into the secular world as well.

Filaret was a progressive in spiritual matters, and he interested himself in the attempts by the metropolitan of Kiev, Peter Mogila, to fight off the attempts of the Catholic Poles to impose their religion on the Ukraine. Mogila's theological seminary in Kiev was also reputedly the most modern in the Orthodox world. The rare tandem of father and son continued until the death of Filaret Romanov in 1633.

The Reign of Alexis

The second Romanov tsar also interested himself in matters spiritual.

Tsar Alexis receiving foreign ambassadors (c. 1660)

Indeed his reputation for piety was so great that by the age of sixteen he had already acquired the nickname of 'The Young Monk'. His English court physician, Doctor Collins, noted in some wonder how his royal master would prostrate himself as many as 1500 times at midnight prayers on special feast days!

'His Imperial Majesty', reported Collins, 'is a goodly person about two months older than King Charles II,' who was both 'severe in his chastisements but very careful of his subjects' love'. This last-named virtue was apparently demonstrated at feasts in the Kremlin, where as many as seventy dishes were commonly served to the greedy participants. But Tsar Alexis, his doctor noted, ate sparingly and sent many of his dishes to selected boyars as gifts.

Though pious, Alexis (1645–76) maintained himself with the full panoply of imperial majesty, and was outraged when he learnt of the execution of Charles I of England in 1649. Russian funds helped keep young Charles II afloat during the Cromwellian Commonwealth, and an embassy sent by the English king to thank Alexis in 1664 has left this striking description of tsarist pomp and majesty:

> The Tsar like a sparkling sun darted forth most sumptuous rays, being most magnificently placed upon his throne, with his sceptre in his hand and having his crown on his head. His throne was of massy silver gilt, wrought curiously on top with several works and pyramids; and being seven or eight steps higher than the floor, it rendered the person of the Prince transcendently majestic.

If the cult of tsarism could have this effect on foreign observers, it takes but little imagination to understand the ruler's absolute sway over the masses. A favourite peasant saying was, 'It is very high up to God; it is a very long way to the tsar.'

RUSSIA IN THE MID-SEVENTEENTH CENTURY

What was this newly emergent Russian state like? It had a population of some eight million, the same as neighbouring Poland but less than half that of the France of Louis XIV (England had just over five million). It was still overwhelmingly rural in character, with only a fraction of the people living in urban centres like Moscow, Novgorod, Nizhny-

Russia in the reign of Tsar Alexis

FINLAND

L. Onega

★ **Olonets 16**

Helsingfors

Gulf of Finland

L. Ladoga

BALTIC SEA

★ **Novgorod 1650**

• Riga

★ **Pskov 1650**

Tver

LITHUANIA   *Western Dvina*   • Nevel   Rzhev •   •

• Kovno   Polotsk •   **Moscow**

PRUSSIA   • Vilna   • Vitebsk   **1648, 166**

Kaluga

                                    • Smolensk

            Borisov   Orsha •   • Andrusovo   Kazelsk • Tul

      • Grodno   •

      Minsk •   Kazelsk •

      POLAND   • Or

  • Brest-Litovsk   Gomel •   • Starodub

      • Pinsk   • Mozyr   **Kursk 1648** ★

      VOLHYNIA   • Kiev

  • Lvov   • Zbarazh   Poltava •   **Chuguyev** ★

         Vinnitsa •   **1648**

  Kamenets •   UKRAINE

                Dniester   *Bug*

                                  Zaporozhian Cossacks

                                       KHANATE O

OTTOMAN   Perekop •   *SEA O*

                                        AZOV

  Danube

EMPIRE   *BLACK SEA*

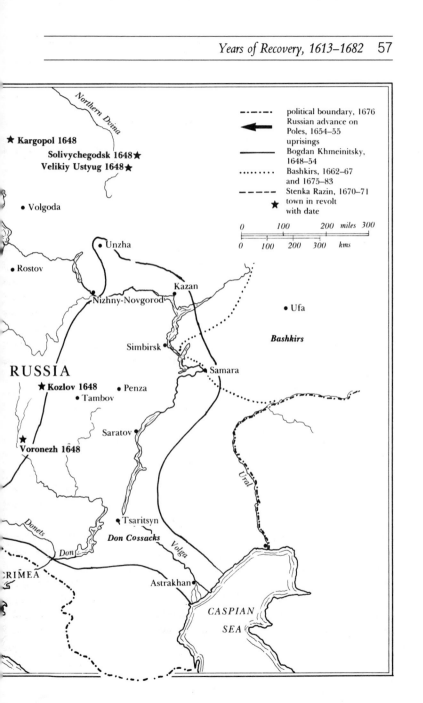

★ **Kargopol 1648**
     Solivychegodsk 1648★
  Velikiy Ustyug 1648★

• Volgoda

Northern Dvina

- - · - - · — political boundary, 1676
◀━━━ Russian advance on
              Poles, 1654–55
              uprisings
━━━━━ Bogdan Khmeinitsky,
              1648–54
· · · · · · · · Bashkirs, 1662–67
              and 1675–83
– – – – – Stenka Razin, 1670–71
★ town in revolt
              with date

```
0        100        200   miles  300
0     100    200    300   kms
```

• Rostov

● Unzha

● Kazan

Nizhny-Novgorod ●

• Ufa

Simbirsk ●

Bashkirs

RUSSIA

★ **Kozlov 1648**   • Penza
       • Tambov

● Samara

Saratov •

★
Voronezh 1648

Ural

● Tsaritsyn

Donets

Don Cossacks

Don

Volga

:RIMEA

Astrakhan ●

CASPIAN

SEA

Novgorod, Pskov, Archangel and Rostov. There was still too a reminder of the bad old days of Mongol tyranny with the spasmodic raiding of the Crimean Tartars into Muscovite territory. 'These massive raids,' writes one historian, 'bringing thousands of Russian slaves annually into the Ottoman slave markets, were a source of embarrassment and anguish to the tsars in the Kremlin'[2].

Life was wretchedly hard for the ordinary peasant, living in a log cabin and helplessly dependent on the whims of his master and the climate. Hundreds of days of frozen, arctic winter dominated the peasants' lives and made the coming of a spring unusually important. In old Russia, Mayday was doubly significant, not only as a symbol of rebirth and renaissance, but as a marker for a summer spent in backbreaking work in the fields. If Tolstoy was later to write in lyrical terms about the virtues of toil in the fields, the seventeenth-century peasant never found his lot less than hard, as the rising level of agrarian discontent indicated. Every man wore a cross around his neck from birth to death, to remind him (if he needed reminding) that his was a fallen and transitory state. For the peasant labouring in the vast steppelands the tsar was indeed a 'long way' off.

THE ULOZHENIE

Trapped as he was by nature and tradition, the Russian peasant found his fate institutionalised by the *Ulozhenie* or Russian Code of Laws of 1649, the single most important reform of Tsar Alexis' reign. It was the first time the shambolic Rusian legal system had been codified, and it provided for a regimentation of society which was almost totalitarian in its soulless neatness.

The population was to be divided into three main classes, and then further divided into smaller categories which accurately described their occupations. So 'serving men' were divided into fourteen sections 'from royal councillor to lowliest musketeer'.[3] Tax bound men; those paying the *tyaglo* or family tax were further divided into seven separate categories of townspeople and four of peasants. Last of all came those who did not pay the family tax, the slowly disappearing class of 'freemen' and the four varieties of bonded slaves.

The Russian Code of Laws was crucial in two major ways. First of all, it destroyed the old class of *votchinniki, hereditary* landowners: after 1649 all landowners effectively became *pomeshchiki*, that is their right to hold land was tied to *state service*, although the Code did allow land then to be passed down within families. Secondly, the *Ulozhenie* invented an entirely new social grouping, that of 'townspeople', although Russia's towns and cities never had the entrepreneurial drive of their counterparts in England and Holland. This was largely because the traders and artisans who serviced the court in Moscow had still been effectively categorised as peasants and lacked all opportunity to improve their social status. The English observer, Giles Fletcher, had noted the effect of this debilitating system on the inhabitants of Russia's great towns and cities. The townspeople, he wrote,

> give themselves much to idleness and drinking: as passing for no more than from hand to mouth . . . because the people, being oppressed and spoiled of their gettings, are discouraged from their laboures.

The *Ulozhenie* changed this by making all townspeople chattels of the state. The towns became crown property, all townspeople were permanently tied to their calling and its particular tax liability, and attempts to escape from it (through marriage, for example) incurred the death penalty. In the long run, therefore, the *Ulozhenie* was a recipe for social and economic inertia and no improvement on the previous stystem.

THE CHURCH

Tsar Alexis shared his grandfather's concern over ecclesiastical affairs. He invited clerics from Kiev to Muscovy, and also fell under the influence of the Greek patriarch of Jerusalem, Paisios. Paisios was responsible for drawing the tsar's attention to the abbot Nikon, whose abilities were so impressive that in 1649 Alexis appointed him metropolitan of Novgorod, the second greatest see in the realm. Nikon's influence over the tsar became so great that in 1652 he forced Alexis to do penance for the murder of his predecessor Archbishop Philip, and in that same year he was elected patriarch of the Russian Church. Nikon was also a reformer, who tried to improve the standards of the parish clergy, partly by importing books which he forced them to read. He insisted on better discipline within the monastic houses, and recovered some of the lands seized by the boyars during the Time of Troubles. The Russian liturgy was also revised to bring it into line with the Byzantine liturgy of St John Chrysostom.

Such thoroughgoing reform was bound to be unpopular in a traditional institution like the Russian Orthodox Church. Churchgoers resented using the unfamiliar rite of Constantinople, and their pastors disliked reading books which were printed in the heretic West (there were no printing presses in the Orthodox world). The Old Believers, the spiritual descendants of the Non-Possessors, under the influence of leaders like the Archpriest Avvakum refused to implement the new changes and were brutally repressed. Nikon was perceived by the Old Believers as an agent of foreign heretics who was in league with the devil and his works. These included instrumental music, representational art and tobacco, which the Old Believers called 'bewitched grass'. Stories were spread about Nikon being the Antichrist, and there was a strong strain of old Byzantine iconoclasm about the movement. Daily Avvakum thundered against the blasphemy of icons which showed the Holy Family in representational form, and accused the reformers of painting

> the image of Immanuel the Saviour with plump face, red lips, dimpled fingers and large fat legs, and altogether make him look like a German, fat-bellied, corpulent, omitting only to paint the sword at his side. And all this was invented by the dirty cur Nikon.

Such dogmatism was bound to lead to disaster. To escape persecution the Old Believers fled to the territories of the Volga, the Don, the White Sea and even beyond the Ural Mountain. They were followed to their sanctuaries by tsarist soldiers who burnt many as heretics. 'Some communities', Robert K. Massie tells us, 'tired of waiting, crowded together – men, women, and children – into their wooden hut churches, barricaded the doors and, singing the old liturgies, burned the buildings down over their own heads.'[4]

In all this the patriarch had the support of the tsar, but Nikon had occasioned a schism within the Russian Church which was as traumatic in its own way as the German Reformation in Western Europe. Unlike

England and the German princedoms, however, the unity of church and state in Russia ensured victory for the former. The Nikonites in any case represented change in Russia just as the Protestants did elsewhere.

Then Nikon overplayed his hand, so confident was he of the young tsar's support. Foreign observers noted that the boyars went more in fear of the patriarch than they did of Alexis, and the young man began to grow resentful. Matters came to a head when Nikon wrote a book declaring the superiority of church over state, and in 1658 there was an open row over church ceremonial in which the angry tsar described the patriarch as a 'stupid clown'. Like many a man used to the exercise of absolute power, Nikon had come to regard himself (fatally) as indispensable. In an ostentatious show of piety the patriarch then retired to the seclusion of the New Jerusalem Monastery for two years. But Alexis called his bluff and did not reinstate him; in 1660 he called together a synod of churchmen who accused Nikon of having 'of his own free will abandoned the most exalted patriarchal throne of Great Russia and so having abandoned his flock and thus caused confusion and interminable contention'. In 1666 a formal trial condemned him to exile and rejected his claim that the church was superior to the state. His last years (he died in 1681) were spent as a spiritual healer, living in a tiny cell while loaded down with chains to mortify his flesh. This repentance eventually won even Alexis' sympathy, and his son Tsar Fyodor eventually secured the posthumous restoration of Nikon's title of patriarch. His reforms also remained intact but, as Massie points out, 'never again would a patriarch wield such power'.[5]

SUCCESSION PROBLEMS

In an autocracy like seventeenth-century Russia, the succession to the imperial throne was a vital issue, and after the hereditary principle was restored in 1613 it became even more crucial. Alexis' first wife, Maria Miloslavskaya, had borne him no less than thirteen children, of whom five were sons. But when in 1669 she died, followed shortly afterwards by two of her four surviving sons, including the sixteen-year-old Tsarevich Alexis, the heir to the throne, there was something of a succession crisis. Although Alexis still had two surviving male heirs, Fyodor was a sickly ten-year-old, while three-year-old Ivan was half-blind, lame, and grew up with a serious speech impediment. In these circumstances it was imperative that Alexis should marry again.

The normal practice for Russian tsars was to marry into a native aristocratic family, because a marriage alliance with Western heretics was ruled out on religious grounds. Yet this was a process fraught with conflict and subterfuge as the rival families fought over the prize. (In 1616, for example, Michael Romanov's choice, Maria Khlopfa, was drugged by the rival Saltykov family, who convinced the tsar that she was incurably ill and then had her and her family packed off to exile in Siberia. Alexis himself had fallen victim to this marital skulduggery when he had chosen Euphemia Vsevolozhskaya as his first wife, only for a group of court ladies to convince him that she was an epileptic after twisting her hair so tightly that the poor girl had fainted clean away!) There were therefore no rules in such a contest and the late tsaritsa's family, the Miloslavskys, had no intention of seeing their influence supplanted by that of some upstart. In the event, Alexis met his second wife, Natalya, the mother of Peter the Great, in the house of his chief minister, Artemon Matveev. The latter himself was regarded with suspicion in boyar circles, because he had a Scottish wife, Mary Hamilton, who had supported King Charles I and fled after his defeat and execution. Mary didn't help combat Russian prejudice by openly flouting the native custom which decreed that married women should remain out of sight on the second floor of their husbands' houses.

The Miloslavskys were outraged when Alexis selected the high-spirited Natalya Naryshkina (a mere nineteen) to be his bride, and adopted the usual battery of ploys to have her removed from the tsar's sight and affections. These included a story that Matveev has secretly poisoned Alexis so that he would fall victim to Natalya's charms. But though subsequent investigation delayed their marriage for nine months, the tsar did marry Natalya in February 1671. Nevertheless the young tsaritsa was only safe from the spite of the Miloslavskys while her husband lived. They could not forgive her common origins as the daughter of an obscure landowner in the faraway province of Tarus.

Fyodor III

Alexis died unexpectedly in 1676 at the age of forty-seven, and was succeeded by Fyodor (1676–82) who suffered from a scurvy-like disease which made his legs swell and forced him to be carried to his coronation. The Miloslavskys naturally saw an opportunity for revenge on the Tsaritsa Natalya and her two children, Peter and Natalya. Fortunately for them, Tsar Fyodor inherited his father's affable and kind-hearted character. He apparently bore no ill will towards his half-brother or his young stepmother and protected them from the malice of his family. Nonetheless the Miloslavskys demanded their pound of flesh and Matveev was selected as their victim. The former chief minister was first exiled and then imprisoned, but the kind-hearted Fyodor prevented the Miloslavskys' vengeance from being carried any further.

Although forced to rule most of the time from a supine position because of his illness, Fyodor III (a well-educated youth) did contrive to enact one major reform in his brief reign. This was the abolition of the system of aristocratic preference known as the *mestnichestvo*. This system had made all state appointments dependent on the candidate's social

An iconic portrait of Tsar Fyodor III

rank, which naturally led to gross inefficiency in government. The direst effects were felt in the army where officers would refuse to take orders from their social inferiors. Fyodor acted decisively against this antediluvian practice and all documents relating to the system of precedence were called in and unceremoniously burnt. Although the tsar did not live to see his new system fully implemented, it was ruthlessly enforced by the modernising Peter the Great.

In 1682 the sickly Fyodor made the mistake, despite warnings from his advisers, of marrying a fourteen-year-old girl. Within three months he was dead. Worse still, he died without a male heir and Muscovy faced yet another succession crisis.

Foreign Relations 1613–82

The immediate priority of Muscovite foreign policy after the Time of Troubles was to end foreign intervention in the state's affairs. This was speedily achieved as far as the Swedes were concerned, and their occupation of Novgorod was ended by the Peace of Stolbovo in 1617. In return for an indemnity of 20,000 silver roubles, the Swedes renounced their claim to the throne of Muscovy but kept the whole coastline along the gulf of Finland – which meant that the Muscovites were still cut off from the Baltic Sea.

The Poles, in the words of Lionel Kochan and Richard Abraham, 'proved a harder nut to crack'.[6] They refused to recognise the new tsar and in 1618 launched a new offensive which took them to the gates of Moscow. But they failed to take the capital and they were never to advance so far again. An armistice gave the Poles the provinces of Smolensk and Seversk, and among the prisoners released was Metropolitan Filaret, the new tsar's father.

The outbreak of the Thirty Years War in Germany then allowed Muscovy to flex its muscles as a European power, under the guidance of the wily Filaret. Elected Patriarch, he effectively controlled government until his death. He had the considerable advantage, with all his countrymen, of regarding both the Latin and Protestant heretics with equal contempt, but in this instance he encouraged the Swedish king, Gustavus Adolphus, 'the Lion of the North', to attack the Catholic

Habsburgs. For their part the Muscovites were supposed to attack Smolensk but fate decreed otherwise. Gustavus Adolphus, though victorious, was killed in the battle of Lützen in 1632, and Filaret died in 1633. The Turks also proved to be unreliable allies, and the result was the so-called 'eternal peace' between Poland and Muscovy in 1634 (the Thirty Years War between the Habsburgs, Sweden and France dragged on until 1648). Nevertheless the Muscovites had shown their mettle, and the Poles were forced by Filaret's diplomacy to surrender their claim to the throne which had survived from the time of Sigismund III.

In 1642 Azov had been seized from the Don Cossacks, although the truce that followed it did not last long. At this time the Cossacks were the mercenaries of Europe, playing – with greater panache – the role filled by the dour Swiss in the fourteenth and fifteenth centuries. They had the misfortune, however, to be sandwiched between the southward drive of Muscovy and the northward expansion of Poland–Lithuania. A further complication was religion, for under Jesuit inspiration a Uniate Church appeared in the Ukraine which, though Orthodox in rite, accepted papal authority. So when in 1648 the Cossack *hetman* (leader) Bogdan Khmelnitsky appealed to Alexis for help against the Catholic Poles, it was swiftly forthcoming.

There was desultory warfare between Sweden and Muscovy between 1656 and 1658, but Poland was always perceived to be the main enemy. As Alexis himself noted, 'It is not meet for a dog to eat even one morsel of Orthodox bread.' He therefore rejected the advice of his minister Ordyn-Nashchokin, a western-orientated inhabitant of Pskov, who argued that a war against the Swedes and the capture of Riga was more important than the reduction of the Ukraine. Also, as Bernard Sumner points out, Alexis unlike Ivan IV 'avoided challenging Sweden and Poland at the same time'.[7] Events proved in any case that Alexis' caution was wise. When Charles X of Sweden invaded Poland and proclaimed himself its king in 1655 the Muscovites responded by laying siege to Riga as Nashchokin had wished. But they were defeated, and Sweden was subsequently able to ensure that she retained Estonia and Livonia.

By contrast the Muscovites were more successful against the declining power of Poland (whose last great feat in European affairs was Jan Sobieski's defeat of the Ottomans outside Vienna in 1683). They won the war of 1658–67 and the treaty of Andrusov gave Alexis the provinces of Smolensk and Seversk, and the greater prize (in historic significance) of the Ukraine and Kiev, the cradle of Old Russian civilisation.

Everywhere but in the Baltic the early Romanov years saw the heartland of Muscovy expand into what would be the modern Russian state. What Ivan the Terrible began in the Far East his successors also continued.

CHAPTER SEVEN

The Reign of Peter the Great
1689–1725

The succession crisis was headed off by the decisive action of the Patriarch Joachim, who was convinced that Fyodor's retarded brother Ivan could not be allowed to rule alone. His half-brother Peter, by contrast, was a robust ten-year-old and far more likely to survive in the long run (everyone had been surprised that Fyodor had lived to inherit the throne). Normal procedures were therefore circumvented by Joachim, who realised that the period of weeks required to convene the Zemsky Sobor would create a dangerous interregnum. Peter was acknowledged as ruler by the acclamation of the Muscovite crowd, which demanded that he accept the throne. His confused silence was deemed to indicate acceptance, but his reticence is understandable. Although his mother Natalya was made regent their position was still very insecure.

Indeed, his elevation to the throne and his mother's regency lasted just two weeks. This was because the Miloslavskys had found a formidable champion in Peter's half-sister Sophia. She it was who spread rumours that Natalya was plotting the murder of her brother Ivan whom Peter had just supplanted. These rumours were subtly placed among the *Streltsy* (or musketeers), Russia's first professional soldiers and a sort of Slav version of the Praetorian Guard.

The *Streltsy*, who had already fallen out with the Naryshkin clan, were easily prevailed upon to march on the Kremlin. Then, although the former tsaritsa half convinced them of her innocence by displaying the live Ivan, they sighted the equally hated Matveev. He was hurled down the Kremlin's Red Staircase, and hacked to death in full view of the regent and her son. Now there was no holding the *Streltsy* as they hunted through the Kremlin for Natalya's relatives. One brother, Afanasy, was found hiding behind the altar of the Church of Resurrection and soon cut to pieces, but the other Naryshkins had gone to ground in the Kremlin's labyrinthine corridors.

For two days the *Streltsy* hunted their quarry, until eventually their most hated enemy, Ivan Naryshkin, gave himself up to protect his sister and her son. Ivan was horribly racked, dragged to Red Square and suspended upside down at the mercy of the mob. The remains of Matveev, Naryshkin and other supporters were then trodden into the mud of the square. Three other Naryshkin brothers were able to steal out of the Kremlin disguised as peasants.

The Regency of Sophia

The immediate effect of this gruesome massacre was to put Sophia in Natalya's place as regent, and elevate her epileptic brother, Ivan, to the position of co-tsar with Peter. This poor youth, whose disabilities were well known among the Moscow populace, owed his sudden promotion entirely to the wiles of his elder sister and the pikes of the *Streltsy*.

His half-brother Peter was traumatised by the experience of the *Streltsy* uprising. For the rest of his life Peter the Great was to hate Moscow, with its canting clerics and fearful memories. He never forgot the dark days of 1682, and if not the sole cause of the building of St Petersburg (and consequent demotion of Moscow as capital city), those events were a crucial component in the decision to build it. Peter was also to take a fearful vengeance on the *Streltsy* which reflected the severity of the trauma he had been through in 1682.

To a degree, Sophia's treatment of her half-brother paralleled that of the dead Fyodor. Peter was allowed, indeed encouraged, to indulge his interest in matters martial and a special fortress was built for him on the River Yauza near Moscow. Here Peter fought out mock battles with the soldiers of his own Preobrazhensky and Semenovsky regiments, destined to be the most famous guards regiments in Russian history. In this sense Peter's training camp was 'the first Russian military academy'.[2] It was characteristic of the young Peter that he took the lowest rank, that of drummer boy, and only accepted promotion when he had acquired the necessary expertise. This was to become an established trait of his character which was demonstrated most strongly in the area of his greatest enthusiasm, the sea. As a youth he experimented on ponds and lakes, and sought the help of foreigners like Franz Timmermann for his scientific studies. Lifelong friendships began in this way, because only foreigners could provide Peter with up-to-date knowledge.

Peter's progress was watched warily by Sophia. Nine years his senior, and as regent the effective ruler of Russia from 1682 to 1689, she was herself a remarkable woman, high spirited and well educated, who rejected the enclosed world of the imperial terem where the royal princesses were little better than prisoners. So prudish were the customs surrounding the upbringing of a tsarevna that medical examinations had to be conducted through a mesh of gauze lest the doctor come into contact with naked female flesh.

Sophia was the first woman to rule Russia and little information is available about her although a French agent left this grotesque picture in 1689:

> Her mind and her great ability bear no relation to the deformity of her person, as she is immensely fat, with a head as large as a bushel, hairs on her face, and tumours on her legs, and at least forty years old. But in the same degree that her stature is broad, short and coarse, her mind is shrewd, subtle, unprejudiced and full of policy.

This was an example of the Anne of Cleves syndrome in reverse (Henry VIII had been duped into marrying his fourth wife by an overflattering portrait). No other contemporary account refers to her in such unflattering terms, and this seems to have been an early example of black propaganda. More to the point, perhaps, was the fact that the very shrewdness referred to in the passage had caused Sophia to align Russia with Habsburg Austria *against* France. She was also only thirty-two.

If Sophia was shrewd and subtle, she was also strong-willed and insisted on ruling with her lover, Vasily Golitsyn. There were also suspicions that the ambitious princess was planning to set aside her two brothers and assume the imperial purple herself. Whether this was the case or not, Sophia was before her time and Russia was not ready for an empress.

This became evident in 1689 when Peter, now seventeen, won over the important support of General Patrick Gordon, and deposed his half-sister and Golitsyn. Sophia was not forced to take the veil, but Peter was sufficiently fearful of her abilities to ensure that she was safely mewed up in a convent for the rest of her days. He himself described Sophia as 'a princess endowed with all the accomplishments of body and mind to perfection had it not been for her boundless ambition and insatiable desire for governing'. Due allowance needs to be made here for sibling rivalry. Peter's own 'insatiable desire for governing' was to be even more striking than his sister's.

Peter the Great

This desire had to be restrained until 1696 when sickly Ivan died, and Peter became tsar in his own right. In the meantime he busied himself by acquiring those practical skills and that knowledge which he deemed it right that a seventeenth-century tsar should have. Under his influence, for example, a terrified and unwilling aristocracy was forced to put to sea on the Sea of Azov so that Russia could have her first real navy.

The physical presence of Peter the Great dominates modern Russian history. He 'was Russia'[3], as Tibor Szamuely rightly says, and was also in Pushkin's immortal phrase a 'mighty lord of fate'. Impressive he certainly was at six foot seven inches tall, with a physique to match. Yet with this strength went a serious disability which afflicted him from his early twenties onwards. This epileptic type of malady, which is variously attributed to the memory of 1682 and an episode of high fever, varied in intensity. At its mildest the disease showed only as a facial tic, but in its severest form the young tsar's face and neck were seized by contortions which could render him unconscious. Such situations demanded the soothing presence of a woman, usually his second wife Catherine. She, Robert Massie tells us, would then comfort the stricken giant by stroking 'his forehead and temples, speaking to him softly and reassuringly'.[4] It was as if Peter's giant frame encapsulated both the strength and the vulnerability of his huge realm.

In his second marriage Peter found happiness and contentment, whereas his loyal but very traditional first wife, Eudoxia, had evoked increasing feelings of boredom and irritation. Eventually she was divorced and packed off to a convent.

The corollary to Peter's physical ailment was his immense energy and curiosity. In 1697, with an entourage of 200, he embarked on a lengthy tour of Western Europe. Contrary to what some contemporaries thought it was essentially a 'fact-finding tour', but Peter was still taking a considerable risk. There were malcontents at home who favoured Sophia and the Miloslavskys and it would take many weeks to alert the tsar in the event of trouble. But the scale of the expedition demonstrated the degree to which Peter recognised the need for the modernisation of his country.

The first stop was the Baltic and Peter stayed at the ports of Riga and Libau (Liepaja), before moving on to Holland. The Dutch Republic was an acknowledged centre of maritime expertise, and for a while Peter and some of his companions worked as apprentice shipwrights in Amsterdam to enable them to study Dutch shipbuilding techniques. The same motive took Peter to England for four months, where he met William III, was given a loan of the royal yacht, and visited the ports of Portsmouth and Chatham and the Woolwich Arsenal in his quest for knowledge on naval and military affairs. Generally the behaviour of Peter's party was restrained but there were exceptions. The main sufferer was the noted diarist John Evelyn, in whose London house the Russian visitors were staying. Unused to the refinements of a fine garden, which Evelyn had laid out with infinite pains, Peter wrecked it by hurtling around in wheelbarrows with his companions! The bill for the damage to Evelyn's house and garden came to the massive sum, for those days, of £350.

The Russians then moved on via Holland to Vienna, where significant news awaited Peter. A letter from Prince Romodanovsky, who carried the macabre title of Minister in Charge of Flogging and the Torture, told him that the *Streltsy* were once again on the march. Their complaints were common enough ones for professional soldiers. Their pay was in arrears, and they had been exiled (quite deliberately) to far-off Azov under unpopular foreign commanders. But there was also a dangerous religious dimension because many of them were Old Believers.

What followed in the winter of 1698–9 was like something out of the darkest pages of the *oprichnina*, and Peter's behaviour was strongly reminiscent of that of the Dread Tsar: despite all his links with the West, the same propensity for dark, savage and almost demonic cruelty surfaced in this 26-year-old tsar. This cruelty may, as Robert Massie suggests, have been occasioned by *realpolitik* (political pragmatism), but it was none the less fearful for all that. 'Day after day in September and October of that year, and again in January 1699 men were flogged with the knout, broken on the wheel, roasted over a slow fire.'[5] In all some 1200 *Streltsy* died, and for months afterwards their corpses were on show throughout Moscow.

Although she denied having anything to do with it, another victim of the *Streltsy* uprising was Sophia. Peter believed, but could not prove, that she was implicated, and this time he forced her to shave her head and take the veil, under the name Susanna. She died in 1710 at the age of forty-seven, in the first decade of a century which was to be notable in Russia for its tsaritsas.

In 1698 Peter the Great banned the wearing of beards to the gentry and merchant class

A bizarre feature of the campaign against the *Streltsy* was that it went hand in hand with Peter's 'westernising' policy. The day after he returned from Western Europe, he started a campaign against beards. Boyars were alarmed to find the tsar, together with his court jester, personally taking part in the ceremonial of shaving. Resistance meant a fine but most of the aristocracy preferred to pay rather than lose their beards (priests and peasants were exempt from the new law).

Church/State Relations

Peter the Great 'had little feeling for religion',[6] and with his closest intimates, the so-called 'Jolly Company', he enjoyed mocking the ornate ceremonial of the Orthodox Church. He had none of his father's natural piety, although he would have been acutely aware of Tsar Alexis' difficulties with the Patriarch Nikon. He loathed his own Patriarch Joachim, even though the latter's desertion of Sophia had played a crucial part in her downfall. But he moved carefully where the Church was concerned and when Joachim died he allowed the election of the new Patriarch Adrian. Only when Adrian died in 1700 did Peter seize his opportunity.

Initially Peter cocked a snook at the Church by bringing in his own nominee, Stephen Yavorsky, who was a product of the Kiev school of theology, and therefore likely to be hostile to the Orthodox establishment. Even Stephen, however, felt obliged to protest when in 1721 Peter introduced an ecclesiastical code which effectively destroyed the independence of the Church. This created the Holy Governing Synod (a ministry of religion), on which sat twelve clerics, three of whom were bishops and all of whom were imperial appointees. Above them was the secular official known as the Procurator of the Holy Synod, who was responsible for enforcing Synod decisions through an inspectorate, and who had a general overview of the whole Church. The code also provided for 'secularisation' (i.e. confiscation) of all church land and for the payment of clerical salaries by the state. Ecclesiastical courts also found their jurisdiction was limited strictly to areas of clerical law and practice. At a stroke Tsar Peter had broken the theocracy which had dominated Muscovy since the time of Ivan Moneybags.

Peter's code was a devastating blow for the Orthodox Church, from which it never really recovered. No attempt was made to educate the lower clergy, and even the higher clergy were forced to learn Latin and German philosophy which they didn't understand. The religious art, which had been such a feature of Russian Orthodoxy, also fell into decline in the eighteenth century, and Steven Runciman detects a general spiritual malaise thereafter. This is hardly surprising because the procurators of the Holy Synod regarded themselves primarily as agents of the tsar, and were often openly hostily to Orthodoxy. The decline in the Church's status is underlined by the fact that in the nineteenth century Nicholas I was happy to let the office of procurator fall to an ex-cavalry officer called Protasov.

The Modernisation of Russia

Tsar Peter's hostility to the Church, as much as his antipathy to the beards of the boyars, reflected his opposition to all the ways of old Russia, with its dark superstitions and backwardness. In every sphere of Russian life the giant tsar bustled about, issuing decrees at a frantic pace and generally discomforting the privileged establishment. There were local government reforms, and new taxes based on the Dutch model. There was a professional army, drawn from a levy on monasteries and landowners; but Peter was careful to exempt the peasants who tilled the soil – his drafts were filled by domestic serfs and slaves. Lastly there was Peter's personal delight, the new Russian navy, the product of laborious hours on the Yauza and Azov, and in Amsterdam. He set up an Admiralty, and a shipbuilding yard at Voronezh staffed with foreign advisers. And from it in due course emerged the first all Russian-built 60-gun warship, designed by the tsar himself.

Peter's enthusiasm for the maritime also made him anxious to expand Russia's export trade but most of his landbound countrymen were lukewarm in their support. Only the merchants of far-off Pskov and Novgorod, with their interest in the Baltic, and their counterparts in Moscow, who had a trading outpost in Archangel, shared his desire to expand commercial links with the West. In this, as in so many other areas, Peter the Great was an innovator.

The Great Northern War

The single most dominant feature of Peter the Great's reign was the Great Northern War with Sweden (1700–21). Defeat would mean exclusion from the Baltic, which had been controlled by the dominant power in the area throughout the seventeenth century. Victory would mean that Russia would become a major European power with a significant influence on the continent's affairs.

The national struggle was interwoven with a fascinating subsidiary duel between two remarkable men, Tsar Peter himself and Charles XII, the warrior king of Sweden. Charles was the antithesis of Peter in almost every way: a mere five foot nine, a misogynist who had given up drinking, and a military leader of genius and daring. What the two men did have in common was a belief in their divine mission and a tenacity of purpose, which meant that their personal feud continued until the death of the Swedish monarch in 1718. While Charles lived Peter could never be at ease.

In 1700 the Swedes had the best army in Europe, and it showed its mettle by defeating Russia's Protestant ally, Denmark, in a lightning campaign which forced the Danes to make peace in the Treaty of Travendal. Peter's other ally, Augustus II of Poland, a womaniser and a drinker like the tsar, proved to be a tardy friend who had already incurred the wrath of the strait-laced Charles XII by deserting the Swedish alliance. Peter was effectively left to fight the Swedes alone, and having occupied Ingria, he laid siege to the port of Narva with a force of 40,000 men.

NARVA

While the Russians were attempting to reduce the Swedish-held fortress Peter heard that Charles XII had landed on the Baltic coast 150 miles away. He was not unduly alarmed because the Swedes were outnumbered four to one and weather conditions were appalling. Peter didn't know his man. If ever a leader had charisma (that much overused word of our times) it was Charles XII. He force-marched his tiny army to Narva while Peter handed over the command of his force to the Duc de Croy, one of the many foreign officers in his army. In doing so Peter was not, as has been suggested, motivated by cowardice but by the need to see his recalcitrant Polish ally at Novgorod. Nothing in Peter's career suggests that he was a physical coward.

Peter's mistake was to imagine that the Swedish army would act like other armies and avoid combat in fearsome winter conditions. Nor did he allow for the speed of the Swedish advance, or the audacity of the eighteen-year-old Swedish king, who proceeded to launch a frontal attack on 9-foot earthworks with a 6-foot ditch around them. Charles himself had horses shot from under him, lost one of his boots, and found a spent musket ball in his necktie after the fighting was over. Small wonder that the Swedish troops worshipped the young warrior king, who calmly told them not to fear death because it would only come in the Lord's time and that there was nothing that they could do about it. Meantime he shared all their privations and was able to ask of them the impossible.

The result was the rout of the Russian army, most of which fled before the Swedish bayonets with the cry that 'the Germans have betrayed us'. This was partly true because the Russian officers showed themselves to be more combative than the foreigners, but the Swedes were the finest infantry in Europe and Peter's troops were no match for them. Even so Peter's own creations, the Preobrazhensky and Semenovsky regiments, fought well, and the battle of Narva was still a close-run thing. The Swedes were exhausted after their forced march, and many of them got hopelessly drunk on brandy they found in the Russian lines. One wing of Peter's army was undefeated, and it alone was bigger than the entire Swedish force, but its commander General Wreide opted to surrender when he heard of the rout of the Russians on the southern front. The commander-in-chief, De Croy, and nine other generals were taken prisoner after the battle which had cost the Russians 8000 men.

Peter was devastated by this defeat and humiliated by the accusation that he had 'fled' from the battlefield (Charles XII rubbed salt into the wound by striking a medal which showed the tsar's flight from Narva). Yet in the long run it was Peter rather than Charles XII who benefited from the experience of Narva. The Swedish king was openly contemptuous of his Russian opponent and fatally overconfident about his own prowess. After Narva, because of his obsession with dealing out punishment to the treacherous Augustus of Poland, the heroic obstinacy he showed in 1700 became a vice rather than a virtue.

By the time Charles turned his forces against Peter again, his enemy was a far more formidable proposition and Charles' tactical brilliance on the battlefield was neutralised by strategic myopia. Like the Germans in the Second World War, he couldn't decide what his primary objective should be: Smolensk offered the key to Moscow, but the new capital of St Petersburg offered another tempting prize. Ultimately Charles was duped into a useless alliance with the Cossack *hetman* Mazepa, who lacked real popular support. This southern imbroglio presented Peter with valuable time for defensive measures and it wasn't wasted. By the time Charles XII was in a position to launch a major offensive against the Russians, Peter had initiated a 'scorched earth' policy which destroyed all the crops and forced and the Swedes to rely on a cumbersome supply system for food. The flirtation with the Ukrainian Cossacks meant that the Swedish forces were divided in two and the main army was separated from the baggage train commanded by General Löwenhaupt. In October 1708 Löwenhaupt's force was attacked and destroyed at Lesnaya.

POLTAVA

The winter of 1708–9 was one of the severest in memory, and a more resolute (and possibly less obstinate) commander than Charles XII would have cut his losses and retreated to his Swedish heartland. Nothing in his character, however, indicates that he would even entertain the concept of failure. Natural obstinacy and courage were fatally combined with a contempt for the Russians who had fled from the field of Narva.

In the spring of 1709, for reasons best known to himself, Charles XII laid siege to the town of Poltava some 200 miles from Kiev in the Ukraine. Peter rushed southwards to relieve the town which had no great strategic importance. Fate then dealt the Swedes a cruel blow when Charles, who had led a charmed life on the battlefield up to that point, was hit by a musket ball while out inspecting his troops. Typically, the king didn't tell anyone about his wound for three hours, and then exhorted an anxious doctor to 'slash away, slash away' at the royal footwear. Although he avoided amputation Charles was too disabled to manage a field command, and had to be carried around on a litter. The command of the Swedish army, therefore, fell upon the veteran Marshal

Rehnskjold, who was barely on speaking terms with the infantry commander Löwenhaupt. This personal feud, while probably not affecting the ultimate result of the Battle of Poltava, caused some confusion in the Swedish ranks.

For Peter the incapacity of his Swedish rival was decisive because he then decided to take on the Swedes on the battlefield. In fact the odds were heavily in the Russians' favour, because the Swedes had only 19,000 men to face Peter's 42,000. But Peter remembered Narva and began to build a new system of earthworks to blunt the effectiveness of the famous Swedish infantry.

Charles XII agreed with Rehnskjold that attack was the best form of defence and, as at Narva, the Swedes launched a frontal attack on the Russian positions. This time the veteran Swedes found an enemy more worthy of their mettle, with powerful artillery and an effective cavalry force under Prince Menshikov. Despite a valiant effort by the Swedish infantry the disparity in numbers proved to be too great; Rehnskjold was taken prisoner and the Swedes were routed, although Charles managed to escape. Meanwhile the old canard about Tsar Peter's alleged 'cowardice' at Narva was well and truly laid to rest. A horse was shot from under him, and one musket ball was deflected from his chest by an old icon while another knocked off his hat. As long as the battle raged the tsar's giant frame was conspicuous and an obvious target for Swedish musketry. Once it was over Peter was generous, and a little diffident in the treatment of his famous foes. 'Where is my brother Charles?' he asked the captured Swedish officers, but the two men were destined never to meet.

Swedish military power was shattered at Poltava, where 6000 of their finest infantry fell, and it never recovered.[7] Russia was saved from invasion and, although the Great Northern War dragged on to 1721, she was never under real threat again. That it did so was due to the obduracy of Charles XII who fled to Turkey after Poltava and spent the next nine years raising up coalitions against his greatest enemy. Peace feelers from Peter were consistently rejected. In the end Charles died as he had lived, with a reckless disregard for his personal safety; in 1718, while laying siege to a town in Norway (then ruled by Russia's ally Denmark), he was shot by a sniper as he looked out of a siege trench.

Charles XII was brought back to Stockholm, which he had not seen for eighteen years, and buried in the Riddarhom Church with the other kings of the House of Vasa. When Peter heard the news of his arch-enemy's death he wept for 'my poor Charles'. Such is the strange chivalry of the battlefield. Thereafter, the Swedes lost all stomach for more fighting, but three years were spent in haggling over peace terms before the Great Northern War was ended by the Treaty of Nystadt of 1721, which confirmed Russian dominance in the Baltic. Livonia, Estonia, Ingria, part of Karelia, the city of Vyborg, and the islands of Ösel and Dago were ceded by Sweden to Russia. Had their warrior king been able to concede defeat earlier, the Swedes would have got off more lightly.

The Black Sea Front

The victory over Sweden had given Peter the Great one of 'the windows on the West' which he craved, but his attempt to open up a passage to the Black Sea had been far less successful. The Russo–Turkish war of 1710–11 was a disaster for Peter, whose Turkish enemy was egged on by the vengeful Charles XII, who had found temporary sanctuary in the Ottoman Empire. In 1711 Peter and the Tsaritsa Catherine were surrounded with their forces on the banks of the River Pruth. Fortunately for the Tsar he was able to buy off the Turkish grand vizier (effectively the Ottoman prime minister), and Russia only had to cede Azov which Peter had captured in 1696.

Although the route to the Black Sea was blocked by the Ottomans, Peter was able to continue the eastward expansion which had started in the reign of Ivan the Terrible. He cultivated good relations with the Shah of Persia, and in 1723 annexed Baku (later to be a centre of the Soviet oil industry) on the shores of the Caspian Sea. The strains of the Great Northern War prevented a more wholehearted forward policy in the East.

The Building of St Petersburg

The Tsar's childhood memories of the *Streltsy* uprising had given him a lifelong hatred of Moscow, but the construction of the new capital of St Petersburg owed something to accident. After Narva Peter wanted to control the mouth of the Neva, and the original conception allowed only for the construction of a fortress. It has also been suggested that, had Peter managed to capture Riga, which was ice-free six months of the year, he would never have built St Petersburg at all. As it was Peter began his life's work with the building of the Fortress of SS Peter and Paul which, with its thirty-foot walls and six bastions, was to become a sort of Russian Bastille. Once this had been done and the approach to the Neva secured, Peter turned to the task of building a new capital city to supplant the hated Moscow.

It was a Herculean task. In Finnish 'neva' is the word for swamp, and the terrain on which the new capital was built was bleak in the extreme. A series of marshy islands marked the Neva's flow into the sea, and it was impossible to grow enough food in the surrounding area to feed the vast army of workmen who were forced to leave their homes and build the new capital. Conditions were atrocious, and diseases like scurvy and malaria decimated the workforce. Flooding was common, as were fires in a largely wooden city, and the aristocracy resented giving up their comfortable Moscow houses to obey the imperial edict requiring them to live in St Petersburg.

The tsar's hand could be seen everywhere. He personally assisted in firefighting, and dictated every aspect of life in the new capital down to the smallest detail. Houses had to conform to his specification, both in terms of height and in the building materials used. When the stonemasons in St Petersburg began to run short of building material Peter banned the use of stone for housebuilding in the rest of the empire. It is clear, though, that when Peter spoke of 'this paradise' he was in a minority of one. The cost in human lives was enormous; contemporary estimates gave a figure of 100,000 dead which is an exaggeration, but a figure of 30,000 is quite probable. The sufferings of the early inhabitants were made even worse by marauding packs of wolves, which were known to eat people in broad daylight.

All this, and the endless whingeing of spoilt aristocrats, made no impact on Peter who single-mindedly went on to finish the project. Ultimately he was to be vindicated by the appearance of 'the Venice of the North', a queen amongst the cities of Europe. Constantly under the threat of Swedish attack before Poltava, St Petersburg was the most long-lasting testimony to the iron will of Tsar Peter – as was the casualty list of those who built it.

The Petrine Reforms

While Peter laboured mightily to make Russia a European power (and the abandonment of Moscow was a symbolic rejection of old Muscovy too), he also worked unceasingly to change Russian society. This involved the implementation of a reform programme which was far more thoroughgoing than the banning of boyars' beards.

At its fountainhead was the great Tsar himself, with an attitude towards the common people which justified taking the most ruthless and autocratic measures. In 1723, two years before his death, Peter wrote: 'Our people are children who would never of their own accord decide to learn.'

To understand this statement is to understand modern Russian history.

Peter the Great by Sir Godfrey Kneller

The former shipwright in the Amsterdam dockyard may have been an admirer of western technology, but he was never prepared to abandon the tradition of Russian absolutism in the interests of modernisation. Neither were his successors.

For most of Peter's reign Russia was at war and this highlighted her financial weakness. By 1724 war expenditure had reached four million roubles, and Peter had been forced into various expedients to increase government revenue. In 1710 an imperial census was followed by the imposition of a household tax, which was followed in 1719 by the levying of a poll-tax on every adult male peasant. This tax, though manifestly unfair, did increase government revenue and also forced the wretched peasantry to put more land under cultivation so that they were able to pay the poll-tax.

At attempt was also made to reform the hopelessly inefficient land tenure system through the Entail Law of 1714. Partly based on the primogeniture system in force in England, it allowed a landowner to nominate one son to inherit the family estate (though not necessarily the eldest one as in England). The object of the Entail Law was to force other sons off the land into government service, but it had not been in place long enough to have any real effect when it was abandoned in 1730.

Peter's most significant reform was the institution in 1722 of the Table of Ranks, which introduced the concept of a *dvoryanstvo* or service gentry. Instead of aristocratic blood lines, merit and seniority would ensure promotion in the government service and also provide the state with more efficient soldiers and bureaucrats. Fourteen parallel grades were created for all ranks in the army, navy and civil service, and promotion to a nominated grade brought ennoblement. This in turn allowed the new nobleman to own serfs and exempted him from the dreaded poll-tax. The Table of Ranks was to survive until 1917 but it only made the plight of the peasantry worse. More of the poll-tax burden fell on them, and they could also be forced to work in mines and factories, or find themselves conscripted into the army to fight Peter's endless wars.

Like several of his successors Peter the Great was perceptive enough to see the evil in serfdom, and he criticised the way in which serfs were sold 'like cattle', but nothing was done about it. The creation of the *dvoryanstvo* meant that the Russian state had traded privilege for loyalty and efficiency, and reform of the social system would have endangered this delicate balance. It would be almost 150 years before a Romanov plucked up the courage to tamper with what Peter had created, and then only in a half-hearted manner. In the meantime, Tsar Peter hedged the privately owned landowners' serfs around with another restrictive law, which forced them to have internal passports. Individual serfs could not leave an estate without the landowner's permission.

Elsewhere structures were evolved to strengthen the absolutist state, and deprive Russia of the last vestiges of any representative institutions. Thus in 1711 Peter introduced the Senate to replace the virtually redundant Boyars' Duma and act for him when he was away fighting his campaigns. The Senate was to be the supreme court of appeal in the realm and was also responsible for tax collection. Although it survived until 1917, it was never more than a rubber stamp for the tsars.

Primitive government ministries or colleges also evolved in the Petrine period, with responsibility for key areas like foreign affairs and the armed forces, but they lacked any really independent powers and the fact that each collegial vice-president was a foreigner underlined Peter's lack of faith in the capacities of his 'childlike' people. The subjection of the Orthodox Church has been referred to earlier in this chapter.

THE NON-RUSSIAN LANDS

As the Russian empire began to expand in the seventeenth and eighteenth centuries, it was forced to evolve a policy for its non-Russian minorities. This was usually a mixture of expediency and chauvinism. Under Peter, the expediency was shown in the treatment of the Baltic German nobility, which was allowed to retain its Lutheran Protestant beliefs because the tsar wished to remain on good terms with Protestant Prussia and its fellow German states.

The Ukrainians, who lacked powerful foreign patrons, fared less well, and their land was sold off to Russian boyars. A Russian governor also strutted around Kiev and two regiments of soldiers were garrisoned in that city. Bottom of the list came the Tartars and the Bashkirs, who were forbidden to own serfs and had Orthodoxy imposed on them at the point of a bayonet.

EDUCATION

It was part of the paradox that made up the man that Peter the Great could have his son tortured to death (see below) and propagate educational reforms. In these he was largely unsuccessful. Although Russia was given an Academy of Sciences she could not sustain a national school system. This was partly because the Church founded an effective system of parochial schools after 1721, and partly perhaps because Peter's mathematical schools smacked of Latin heresy. The state did not therefore become really involved in education.

Peter did better in more functional spheres. In 1700 he introduced the Julian calendar, which Russia continued to use until 1917, and reduced the number of letters in the Cyrillic alphabet. Women were freed from their traditional seclusion in the home, and theatres played in the big cities. Russian-language newspapers were also printed, although they were closely vetted by the authorities.

INDUSTRY

The epic war against the Swedes ensured that the tsar would give priority to arms production, and state-funded munitions factories appeared on a large scale during his reign. But Peter also wished to provide his country with an industrial base which would accelerate the modernisation process. His problem was that Russia lacked that class of entrepreneurs whose drive and enterprise brought wealth and prosperity to countries like Britain and Holland. In their absence the state was forced to provide the capital which private enterprise could not, and Peter sponsored the setting up of paper, wool, linen, silk and cotton industries. The iron-mining industry of the Urals was a particular success story, and by the end of Peter's reign Russia had become the world's largest iron producer. These nascent industries were protected by high tariffs on foreign imports, and encouraged by their exemption from taxation. Russia, like Colbert's France, was modernised from above, although she was still very dependent on foreign technology and advice.

This minor industrial revolution also had its unsavoury side. Coercion was used to supply the new factories with labour, and the victims were generally runaway peasants, prostitutes and vagabonds, the 'have nots' of Russian society. Those peasants who had fled the rigours of Russian rural life now found themselves imprisoned in a new industrial hell where life was accounted equally cheap.

The Succession

The greatest blot on Peter the Great's reputation was the treatment of his own son, the Tsarevich Alexis, the child of his first marriage to Eudoxia Lopukhina. Indeed the whole story of the tsar's relationship with his son would merit an entry in the history of psychoanalysis as a classic example of an Oedipal complex. Peter was fascinated by war and the technology of war. Alexis was not, and his attempts to acquire such knowledge were a conspicuous failure. The more Peter lectured his son on the demands of the imperial throne, 'the more incompetent he became and the more he grew to loathe and fear his father, his father's friends and his father's ways'.[8]

The crisis in the relationship came in 1716 when the demoralised Alexis fled to Vienna and threw himself on the mercy of the Habsburg emperor, Charles VI. For nine months Peter was forced to stomach the fact that a foreign power was hiding the heir to the Russian throne. Finally his patience gave way, and orders were given to kidnap the tsarevich and bring him back to Russia. Once this was done, Alexis was accused of treason, put on trial, and sentenced to death by a court in which his father was both judge and chief prosecutor.

Initially Alexis had only been required to renounce his rights of succession in favour of Peter Petrovich, the tsar's young son by his second wife Catherine. For a while it even seemed that the rift between father and son had been healed. But the increasingly paranoid Peter couldn't rest content with this verdict, and racked and knouted his way through the tsarevich's closest acquaintances. The Tsaritsa Eudoxia was sent to a convent and Peter's half-sister Maria was imprisoned in the Fortress of SS Peter and Paul. Finally Alexis' lover Afrosina, who had gone into exile with him, betrayed the tsarevich by saying that he had conspired against his father and rejoiced at the prospect of his death when Peter had suffered a serious convulsive attack. This was enough for a court packed with Peter's supporters who found the tsarevich guilty of a 'horrid double patricide, first against the Father of his country and next against his Father by nature'. The death sentence had to be approved by Peter himself, but before he could do so he received the news that his son had died in the Peter and Paul fortress.

The death of the Tsarevich Alexis in 1718 is still shrouded in mystery. There were many at the time who believed lurid accounts of it in which Peter beheaded his own son. More plausible is the thesis that Alexis, whose health was never robust, died as a result of the forty lashes from the knout which he received in the week before his death.

Peter's own behaviour did little to counteract such rumour-mongering. He gave no public display of grief and the celebration of the victory at Poltava (the day after the death of the tsarevich) went ahead as usual. Yet Alexis seemed to haunt his father from the grave. The young Tsarevich Peter died and Peter the Great still had no surviving male heir. In 1722 a bizarre succession law was enacted which allowed the tsar to leave the throne to whoever he wished. In 1724 he had his second wife Catherine, who was in fact to succeed him, crowned tsaritsa, but the succession still remained uncertain. On his deathbed in 1725, Peter was to scrawl on a piece of paper, 'Leave all to . . .', but the name was illegible. His failure to resolve the issue of the imperial succession left Russia in dynastic chaos for the next forty years.

The Legacy of Peter the Great

Peter the Great's achievements were immense but his record remains controversial. He broke Swedish power in the Baltic and made Russia into a European power of substance, but the human cost was high. This fact is best demonstrated by demography. At the end of the seventeenth century the Russian population had largely recovered from the horrors of the Time of Troubles, and in 1678 it stood at some sixteen million. But in 1724, the penultimate year of Peter's reign, it had fallen to thirteen million, a percentage drop which, as Szamuely points out, was a demographic catastrophe even greater than 'the Great Patriotic War' of 1941–5.

Critics of Peter the Great have focused their attention on his draconian domestic policies and the legacy of autocracy which he left to

Russia. Vernadsky's verdict is the harshest of all because he accuses Peter of intending 'to establish what is now termed a totalitarian state'.[9] This is hyperbole, because no seventeenth-century regime could possess the repressive instruments of the Hitlerite or Stalinist state. According to Klyuchevsky, Tsar Peter 'spent human resources and lives profligately, unsparingly . . . The Petrine Reform was a struggle between despotism and the people's torpor.'[10] But was not the whole history of modern Russia a struggle between tsarist autocracy and 'the dark mass' of illiterate peasantry? There was barely one tsar (or tsaritsa) who was not profligate with the lives of their subjects when the occasion demanded it.

Curiously, the nineteenth-century revolutionary Chernyshevsky regarded Peter the Great as the ideal Russian patriot, while Stalin invoked his memory when the German invaders were at the gates of Moscow in 1941. There is no doubt that Peter *was* a patriot and an innovator, but his westernising obsession did not lay the deep foundations he would have hoped for. Instead he laid down a veneer of western civilisation and culture which heightened the divisions and tensions in Russian society. A small privileged aristocracy was established which both aped the West and was not of it, and was separated both by its wealth and education from the mass of the people. Alexander Herzen, the nineteenth-century radical writer, said that this French-speaking aristocracy was 'spoiled for Russia by their Western prejudices, and spoiled for the West by their Russian habits'.[11]

The creation of this privileged élite was the work of Peter the Great, and our criticism of him must be tempered by the knowledge that he had little real alternative. The vulnerable position of the Muscovite state which he inherited in 1689 did not allow him to dismantle its social structure completely, even if he had wished to do so. The national emergency was too great, and Peter's more favoured successors still lacked the resolve to grasp this particular nettle.

CHAPTER EIGHT

The Era of Empresses
1725–1762

Until 1725 Russia had never been ruled by a woman in her own right, but in the remaining years of the eighteenth century she had no fewer than four empresses. By contrast, the male rulers during this period were either weak or sickly (in the case of Peter III both). Then in 1796 the succession reverted to the male line once more and never again was Russia ruled by a tsaritsa.

It is also true that, until 1741, Peter the Great's unusual indecisiveness about the succession cost his country dearly. The door was left open for foreign adventurers and it was quite fortuitous that Russia ultimately obtained, in Catherine II, an able and patriotic ruler despite her German background.

Catherine I

The dynastic vacuum left by Peter's death provided an immediate opportunity for overambitious guards officers, just as the death of Tsar Alexis in 1682 had allowed the *Streltsy* to play the role of kingmakers. Their choice fell upon the Tsaritsa Catherine (1725–7), the popular second wife of Peter the Great, and in her interest the claims of Peter's grandson Peter Alexeyevich were set aside. The boy was nine years old in 1725.

Catherine I has been described as 'illiterate and sottish'[1] but, unlike her husband, she did attempt to resolve the succession issue, decreeing that if the Grand Duke Peter Alexeyevich (the future Peter II) should die without heir, the rights of succession should pass to Peter the Great's daughters Anne and Elizabeth and their heirs, with any male heirs taking precedence over females. Any claim to the Russian throne was subject to the provision that the candidate must be a member of the Orthodox Church.

Catherine I had an open and generous personality, and few illusions about her capacity to rule. Real power during her reign rested with the Supreme Privy Council, a small body of leading aristocrats dominated by Peter the Great's old cavalry commander, Prince Menshikov. Under his guidance, Catherine brought about some progressive changes: the poll-tax was cut by a third and the size of the army reduced by a similar amount. Menshikov was fiercely ambitious, but he had rivals, notably Catherine's own favourite, Charles Frederick, Duke of Holstein, who had married Catherine's elder daughter Anne in 1725. In the following year Holstein became a member of the Supreme Privy Council.

Menshikov realised that he was in a vulnerable position because the young Grand Duke Peter, son to the murdered Tsarevich Alexis, was aware of his role in the forcible return of Alexis to Russia in the previous reign. In a wily but self-seeking manoeuvre Menshikov therefore persuaded the empress to make Peter her heir, and also secured her permission for the marriage of the Tsarevich to his own daughter Maria. At a stroke Menshikov had secured his position with the heir to the throne while Catherine still lived. He seems to have had almost prophetic powers because in 1717, after hours spent reviewing troops in the winter cold, the Tsarista Catherine died of a fever.

The Reign of Peter II

The position of Peter II (1727–30) on his accession to the throne was remarkably similar to that of the English King Edward VI (1547–53) when he became king. He was a minor, with two older sisters who had their own claims to the throne, and an overmighty subject (in his case the Duke of Northumberland) who dominated the ruling council and was trying to marry his offspring into the royal family. In the Russian case the situation was simplified somewhat by the death of the Tsarevna Anne in 1728, but she had already given birth to the future Tsar Peter III and so consolidated that German influence in Russia which was such an important feature in the eighteenth century.

Once the Tsaritsa Catherine was dead Menshikov moved swiftly. The 14-year-old Tsar Peter II was moved from the Winter Palace in St Petersburg to Menshikov's own palace on Vasilevsky Island, and the Grand Privy Council was packed with Menshikov's allies, the Golitsyns and the Dolgorukys. Within a month of his accession his engagement to Menshikov's daughter Maria was also publicly announced. Menshikov's position appeared to be unchallengeable, and foreign observers were impressed by his apparent domination. 'Not even Peter the Great', said the Saxon ambassador, 'was so feared, or so obeyed.'

But pride came before a fall, as the young tsar began to resent the arrogant behaviour of his overmighty subject. In the summer of 1727 Menshikov fell ill, and the reins of government fell into the hands of the youthful Peter and his aunt Elizabeth, the last surviving daughter of Peter the Great. People at court noticed that Menshikov was not indispensable, and that Tsar Peter enjoyed being free from his adviser's tutelage. When Menshikov reappeared at court in September 1727 Peter II turned his back on him, and it became clear that the dead empress's favourite was doomed.

Within a matter of weeks. Menshikov was disgraced and exiled to the Ukraine with his family. He wasn't the first court favourite to overplay his hand and forget that he owed his position to the whims and fancies of an autocrat. Doubly galling for him, however, was the knowledge that his dominant role was now taken by the Dolgorukys, who soon persuaded the young tsar to have their former ally sent off to the remote northern Siberian village of Berezov.

Within a year Menshikov was dead, to be followed two years later by the young tsar himself who had contracted smallpox. A marriage alliance with the Dolgorukys (Peter was to marry Catherine Dolgoruky) perished with him, and the onset of smallpox was so rapid that he had been unable to nominate his successor. This task therefore fell upon the Supreme Privy Council, who offered the throne to Anna, Duchess of Kurland, a daughter of Ivan V and niece of Peter the Great. In doing so, they were ignoring the superior claim of the Tsarevna Elizabeth, who was thought to be too irresponsible for the job. The evidence suggests that the lustful Elizabeth, then twenty-one, didn't relish such responsibilities anyway.

The Reign of Anna

In reality the council had other motives than their alleged concern about the flighty behaviour of Elizabeth. Anna was a childless, middle-aged widow who would undoubtedly be easier to control than the boisterous and strong-willed Elizabeth, and her elevation to the throne of All the Russias was subject to several conditions. She was not to marry again, or to nominate her successor, and the right to make war and raise revenue rested with the Supreme Privy Council.

Anna (1730–40) was canny enough to accept the conditions, but she soon freed herself of these constitutional bonds. Once again the Guards regiments were a key factor in her counter coup, which abolished the Supreme Privy Council and restored the powers of the autocracy. She had fortunately not inherited the mental and physical infirmity of her father (Ivan the Fool in Russian history), and had something of the determination of her uncle, Peter the Great. Like Peter too, Anne disliked Moscow, which Peter II had favoured, and moved the capital back to St Petersburg.

It was at this point that German influence really began to make itself felt, for the Tsaritsa Anne had spent eighteen years in Kurland. She brought her first minister in Kurland, Ernst Buren Biron, with her to Russia; another German, Ostermann, ran foreign policy, and Münnich became commander-in-chief of the army.

The other striking feature of Anna's reign was the eccentric nature of the court life. There was a tradition of macabre interest in physical freaks in the tsarist court, and a royal dwarf had betrayed one of the unfortunate Naryshkin brothers in the *Streltsy* uprising of 1682. But under Anna this tendency reached bizarre proportions so that 'midgets, giants, hunchbacks, cripples, the deformed in body and mind were a grotesque and pathetic feature of Anna's entourage'.[2] Otherwise the tsaritsa seemed to share the interest of other Petrine descendants in the bedchamber and the hunting field.

The Reign of Ivan VI

In 1730 the Supreme Privy Council had also passed over the claims of Ivan V's eldest daughter, Catherine. This was because she was believed to be too much under the influence of her German husband, the Duke of Mecklenburg. The Tsaritsa Anna, however, relished the German connections of her family and nominated Catherine's grandson, the infant Ivan VI to succeed her.

It was at this point that the inherent instability of the Petrine succession showed itself. Ivan VI (1740–1) was an infant, who was bound to be dependent on adult relatives for years to come, and sadly for him they proved to be lacking in both compassion and scruples. Before she died in October 1740, the Tsaritsa Anna used the mechanism of the Petrine succession law to leave the throne to the two-month-old son of Ivan V's granddaughter Anna Leopoldovna, the Princess of Brunswick. Anna had already arranged for the infant Ivan and his parents to be brought to Russia. Biron was made regent but he only survived for three weeks. Early in November 1740 Field Marshal Münnich (Minikh) staged a coup d'état with the support of the Guards regiment and proclaimed the Duchess Anna as regent for her son Ivan VI.

This second regency lasted for just a year and then the Grand Duchess Elizabeth, who had been passed over in 1730 and was the darling of the Guards regiments, seized power herself. She claimed to be acting in the interest of her nephew, Duke Charles Peter Ulrich of Holstein, who was Peter the Great's grandson, but remained on the imperial throne herself for the next twenty years. Ivan VI, then fifteen months old, was imprisoned with the rest of his family and was never to know freedom

The Schlüsselburg Fortress where the unfortunate Ivan VI was imprisoned and murdered

again in his short and wretched life. The Tsaritsa Elizabeth left strict instructions that he was to be killed in the event of any rescue attempt, and his jailers were not allowed to converse with him.

These instructions were endorsed by Catherine II, and Ivan was, in fact, killed during an abortive rescue attempt in 1764, as his guards carried out their instructions to the letter.[3] The British ambassador noted that the deposed tsar 'made so stout a resistance, as to break one of their swords, and received eight wounds before he expired'. The memory of this unfortunate youth, who spent twenty-two years in the Schlüsselburg fortress, was to haunt Catherine and her successors in the form of legends about Ivanushka, the innocent tsar who was alleged to be still alive and the rightful claimant to the throne. Ivan's death was the melancholy sequel to a disastrous period during Russia's history when, in just sixteen years, she had two emperors, two empresses, and two regents.

The Reign of Elizabeth

A measure of stability returned to Russia with the accession to the throne of Peter the Great's last surviving child, Elizabeth (1741–62). The new empress was a hedonist, who enjoyed dancing and love-making, often to the exclusion of affairs of state. Like her cousin, the Tsaritsa Anna, her pleasures often took on a peculiar aspect, notably in her inclination to appear in male clothing. The tsaritsa, as her successor Catherine noted, had a shapely leg which contrasted sharply with the blunderings of her male courtiers in the female costumes which Elizabeth required them to wear at court balls!

Garish tales about Elizabeth's sexual escapades tended, however, to ignore the central tragedy of her life. In 1727 her dashing fiancé, Charles Augustus of Holstein-Gottorp, had died of smallpox and the young princess was shattered by this loss. In 1730, as has been noted, she took no interest in the imperial succession, and was only persuaded to depose Ivan VI in 1741 because of the very real threat that his mother would force her into a convent. Elizabeth got her blow in first and 'never doubted for a moment the quasi-divine legitimacy of her power over the Russian people'.[4]

As empress, Elizabeth was a strange mixture of compassion and authoritarianism. She abolished capital punishment, yet ordered two court ladies to have their tongues cut out when they were involved in a court plot in 1743. She drank to excess, and a French diplomat noted how the imperial 'dress and corsets have to be cut open' when Elizabeth was in her cups. She beat maidservants, and her ministers were plainly terrified of her imperious temper which could exile them to Siberia in a moment.

Nevertheless, the tsaritsa, unmarried and childless as she was, had to secure the imperial succession and turned for a solution to the family of her lost fiancé. Charles Peter Ulrich of Holstein, the son of her dead sister Anne, was nominated as Elizabeth's heir, and the courts of Germany were scoured for a suitable bride. Frederick the Great of Prussia offered his help (he was anxious to preserve the Russian alliance in his struggle with Elizabeth's sister empress, the Austrian Maria Theresa), and in 1744 his influence secured the hand of Sophie of Anhalt-Zerbst for that ugly duckling, the future Tsar Peter III.

The choice of Peter was in itself an odd one. Elizabeth had been able to seize the throne because she, rather than the German Mecklenburgs, represented the true Russian blood royal. Now, as Henri Troyat has pointed out, she had made another German her heir, although she was by inclination a Francophile (the French ambassador de la Chétardie was one of her lovers). She had her doubts about Peter, who obstinately stuck to his German ways, but the choice of his fiancée proved to be an inspired one. Charles Peter was rechristened Peter Fedorovich, while his bride-to-be became Catherine Alexeyevna after the tsaritsa's mother.

With the succession secured, Elizabeth continued on her path of energetic hedonism (she was reputed to have 15,000 dresses) and left the governance of her empire to her chancellor, Bestuzhev-Ryumin, who had opposed the marriage alliance with Prussia's protégé. She was pleased by Catherine's sensible adherence to Russian ways, but perturbed by her nephew's failure to provide an heir when he married her in 1745. The sickly youth, whose early years had been ruined by a bullying German tutor, was intimidated by his formidable aunt, who was not above boxing his ears on occasion. But Peter was still more interested in his collection of toy soldiers than in performing his marital duties. It is one of the major mysteries of Elizabeth's reign that she insisted on bequeathing her throne to such an unpromising candidate, who was almost certainly not the father of Catherine's son, the future Tsar Paul.

The Empress Elizabeth was a dangerous woman to cross, as Chancellor Bestuzhev-Ryumin found out to his cost when his plot to make Catherine regent for the six-year-old Paul was discovered. Her ministers were undoubtedly fortunate that Elizabeth gave most of her time to sex and drink, and the longer her reign lasted the more the tsaritsa craved her sensual pleasures. Ultimately they were her undoing and on 5 January 1762 the last of Peter the Great's children died in St Petersburg. She was just fifty years old.

The Reign of Peter III

Peter III (January–June 1762) 'had nothing but contempt for the nation he had been put at the head of'.[5] This was demonstrated at his aunt's funeral, when he pulled faces and laughed out loud during the service. He ignored his wife and openly favoured his mistress, Mademoiselle Vorontsova, despite the fact that she was ugly and squint-eyed. The dominant feature of his personality was his Prussophilia and admiration for Frederick the Great. The new tsar forced his troops to wear Prussian uniforms and to adopt Prussian-style discipline, while his beloved Holstein regiment was singled out for special favour. The then British ambassador, Keith, noted how his passion 'for the King of Prussia is beyond all expression'. Accession to the imperial throne merely allowed Peter to indulge his military mania to extremes, as the unfortunate inhabitants of St Petersburg were made painfully aware during the continuous artillery salvos which sounded off night and day in the capital.

PETER III'S REFORMS

Curiously, although Peter III gave every appearance of being mentally disturbed, he did introduce some important reforms during his short reign. This action may in part have been motivated by the desire to ape his hero Frederick of Prussia, who was a supporter of the eighteenth-century Enlightenment as well as being a military genius, but it was unfortunate for Peter that any credit due to him for these reforms was neutralised by his outrageous and provocative behaviour at court.

Peter's most important reform was the ukase (edict) which abolished compulsory state service for the aristocracy. Instead, Peter decreed that, while the obligation to serve the state would continue in wartime, state service would be voluntary in peacetime. The aristocracy would be free to travel abroad and to take service with foreign rulers, although few of them took advantage of this concession. They also knew that retirement from state service would prevent them from appearing at court ever again, and catching the tsar's eye. Many would have felt doubtless that they were better off well away from Peter III and his eccentric whims, but the reform marked a major turning point nonetheless. Russia now had a large, western-orientated leisured class for the first time in her history. Peter completed his reform package by abolishing the secret police, and preventing the sale of serfs to Russia's new factory-owning class.

Peter also aroused the dangerous enmity of the Orthodox Church by confiscating its property and openly attending Lutheran services in the Winter Palace. Although both he and Catherine had to convert to Orthodoxy to establish their dynastic credentials, Peter (unlike his wife) made no attempt to placate the Orthodox establishment, and outraged it by ordering priests to cut off their beards. This process of

The Great Palace at Tsarskoye Selo (renamed Pushkin) built in the 1750s

secularisation was continued when he made clerics dependent on the state for their salaries. He also demanded that the Old Believers should be allowed to worship freely, so that the Orthodox clergy began to pray that God should free them from this 'Anti-Christ'.

Catherine's Coup d'état

PETER III's ASSASSINATION

Under the influence of his mistress Vorontsova, Peter III's attitude towards his wife Catherine became more and more insulting. By the summer of 1762 he was threatening to send her to a convent, and the French chargé d'affaires, Beranger, took this threat at its face value. The tsar's 'insane and barbaric ferociousness', he reported to his master Louis XV, 'made his threats to crush his wife quite believable'. Matters came to a head at a public banquet, when Peter called Catherine a fool when she failed to rise for a toast to Frederick the Great, which was normal practice for members of the imperial family. Catherine was no fool, and she was already quite adept at the political infighting which was a characteristic of the imperial court in the eighteenth century. While Peter relentlessly drilled his beloved Holsteiners, Catherine attracted support both by her devotion to the Orthodox Church and her sober behaviour, which contrasted sharply with the bizarre antics of her husband's entourage. Public sobriety, it should be added, did not carry over to the tsaritsa's private life, which was dominated by a passionate love affair with the guards officer, Grigory Orlov. Showing characteristic skill in blending romance and statecraft, Catherine was to use Grigory and his brother Alexey to win the vital support of the Preobrazhensky and Izmailovsky guards regiments for her cause.

On 28 June 1762 Catherine and her supporters struck, arresting the terrified tsar and claiming that he had planned 'to destroy Us and to deprive Us of life'. Peter was forced to abdicate and was held at his house at Rapsha before being imprisoned in the Schlüsselburg fortress. A week later he was dead in mysterious circumstances which almost certainly involved the Orlovs. (By one of history's stranger ironies, Mikhail Gorbachev was presented with a portrait of the ill-starred Peter III in

Britain in 1989. His response went unrecorded!) The official version said that Peter had died of 'haemorrhoidal colic' but few people believed this version of events. For years rumours spread about strangulation and poison, and at Peter's lying-in-state it was noticed that a large hat covered the dead tsar's darkened face, while his neck was covered by a silk scarf (possibly to disguise marks of strangulation).[6]

It is unlikely that Catherine gave direct orders for the tsar's murder, but equally unlikely that she warned the Orlovs off. She wished to rule as Tsaritsa of All the Russias and not merely as regent for her son Paul, and Peter III was in her way. She had also borne Grigory Orlov's child and was unlikely to take action against its father or his brother. Catherine feigned regret at Peter's death, but few observers were deceived. Her husband's murder was to haunt her throughout her reign because, as John T. Alexander stresses, nothing 'could camouflage the fact that Catherine had usurped the throne from a legitimate monarch by force and deceit'.[7]

Foreign Relations 1725–62

A remarkable aspect of eighteenth-century Russian history is the degree to which that country's power and influence grew, *despite* the turbulence that followed Peter the Great's death in 1725. In the 1730s the dominant influence in the formulation of Russian foreign policy was the Westphalian Ostermann, who established an alliance with the Austrian Habsburgs. As the Habsburgs were traditional enemies of Bourbon France, this meant that for most of the eighteenth century France and Russia were enemies too. French diplomatic wiles were therefore used to stir up Russia's other traditional foes, Poland, Sweden and Turkey, against her.

Poland was the first focus for this Franco–Russian antagonism, because the ramshackle Polish constitution allowed both powers to put forward their own candidates for the Polish throne. Russia favoured Augustus III, and her geographical proximity allowed her to intervene effectively and depose the elected Polish monarch Stanislaw Leszczyński. There is an old Polish adage, 'nierzadam Polska stoi' ('the essential thing about Poland is unrule'), and Russia was one of the major beneficiaries of her condition in the last two-thirds of the eighteenth century.

The War of the Polish Succession (1733–5) was barely resolved in her favour when Russia became involved in a second struggle, with the Ottoman Turks in an effort to reverse the effects of the disaster of 1711. Her object was to reclaim Azov, which was the key to the delta of the River Don and with it the whole river system of Southern Russia. This war, from 1735 to 1739, resulted in a Russian victory, but the defection of the Austrians made it a somewhat Pyrrhic one. The Treaty of Belgrade (1739) allowed the Russians to trade on the Sea of Azov, but only in Turkish ships; Azov was also restored to them, but only after its fortress had been razed to the ground. B.H. Sumner describes Belgrade as 'a triumph for French diplomacy',[8] and while it is true that France was able to protect her defeated ally, the Austrian action was more significant. The major priority of the Austrian empress, Maria Theresa, was to win back the lost province of Silesia from the Prussians, and not for the last time in their history the Russians found themselves on the wrong end of Habsburg perfidy.

Angered though she was by Austrian bad faith, the Tsaritsa Elizabeth had a fiercer passion, her hatred of Frederick the Great (1740–86). This meant that, although France changed sides as a result of the so-called 'Diplomatic Revolution' of the 1750s, Russia remained steadfastly anti-Prussian, if temporarily pro-French. Chancellor Bestuzhev-Ryumin remained the leader of the anti-Prussian faction at court, just as he had been at the time of the marriage alliance between Holstein and Anhalt-Zerbst a decade earlier. Meantime, the Grand Duke Peter could only watch impotently, as Russia's hordes began to affect the military balance in Central Europe.

In 1757 Field Marshal Apraksin defeated the Prussians at Gross-Jägersdorf but failed to follow up his victory, and the empress accused him of cowardice. In reality Apraksin had a perfectly valid reason for retreating, which was the lack of adequate supplies, but the overimaginative tsaritsa accused him of conspiring with Bestuzhev and the Grand Duchess Catherine. A plan to court-martial Apraksin was dropped, but he was deprived of his command and placed under house arrest. Meanwhile the pattern of Russian success against the Prussians continued. In 1759 they defeated Frederick the Great once more at Kunersdorf, and in the following year Russian troops occupied his capital Berlin. Frederick was in despair, and contemplated suicide until the death of Elizabeth removed one of his two arch enemies from the scene. (Maria Theresa never forgave him for occupying Silesia in 1740.) Peter III then had the opportunity to indulge his Prussomania by recalling his army and ending the campaign. The Seven Years War (1756–63), as it is generally known, then petered out and Frederick the Great warned his successors 'to cultivate the friendship of these barbarians'. It was a lesson well learnt. Only in 1914 did Prussia, later Germany, find itself at war with Russia again, and the new alignment proved to be fatal for both regimes.

CHAPTER NINE

Catherine the Great
1762–1796

Sophia, Princess of Anhalt-Zerbst, was fifteen-years-old when she left her native Germany for Russia in 1744. A year later she had married the Tsarevich Peter and become the Grand Duchess Catherine, in preparation for her role of being a brood mare for the Romanov dynasty. When her son Paul was born, he was immediately carried off to the tsaritsa's apartments (as indeed were all Catherine's children) while the exhausted mother was left to fend for herself.

In her early years in Russia, Catherine had to put up with her gossipy, interfering mother Johanna, but she was sent packing when the Grand Duke Paul was born, and the daughter proved to be far more adept at acclimatising herself to Russian conditions. She converted to Orthodoxy, and was zealous about her devotions, unlike her husband. She learnt Russian and read voraciously in the difficult years before 1762 when her husband frequently ignored her, and openly preferred his mistress Elizaveta Vorontsova. As an imperial princess Catherine also learnt to dance well and become a crack shot; she was also an excellent horsewoman who flouted convention by not following the usual practice of riding side-saddle, although she was careful to follow convention when the Tsaritsa Elizabeth was around. The relationship with the strong-willed tsaritsa was the key one for the young grand duchess, and Catherine generally managed it well. She tried to moderate her husband's excesses (which included a bizarre episode when Peter drilled peep-holes in the walls of the tsaritsa's apartment) and learnt to take the edge off Elizabeth's temper with the magic phrase 'vinovaty, Matushka' (we beg your pardon, Mama). She was careful to learn all she could from the empress about the art of government, and developed important friendships with men like Chancellor Bestuzhev.

Precisely when Catherine formulated the idea of seizing the imperial throne for herself is uncertain, but she is known to have been appalled by both Elizabeth's sloth and Peter III's fantasising. Catherine was a woman of considerable intellect and a hard worker, and even the eccentric Peter recognised this by allowing 'Madame la resource' (Madam Resourceful) to have a say in the governance of Holstein. It is clear, too, that this ill-fated tsar underestimated both his wife's anger at the way he had treated her, and her capacity to win the loyalty of others.

In government, Catherine's talents had the opportunity to shine, although she could show on occasion the ruthlessness of a Peter the Great. No mercy was shown to Peter III or Ivan VI, or to the small army of imperial pretenders during her reign. She disliked the barbarity involved in quartering corpses, but she did not shrink from the use of the gallows or the knout. It is true, therefore, that there was often quite a wide gap between the tsaritsa's beliefs and her practice.

Catherine 'the Great', a deserved title, shared with Elizabeth a reputation for being a voluptuary. Foreign envoys, particularly the British ones, tended to indulge in wild stories about the tsaritsa's sexual excesses. It is true that, as she grew older, Catherine became more and more involved with young lovers, but none of them, with the possible exception of Potemkin, were allowed to meddle in state affairs. Nothing in her life justified some of the wilder nonsense written about her, both in her own lifetime and subsequently. She was not, as Josef von Sternberg's 1934 Hollywood epic *The Scarlet Empress* absurdly suggested, 'the Messalina of the North' (Messalina was the second wife of the Roman emperor Claudius who was a debauchee in a class of her own). As Professor Alexander points out in his recent biography, Catherine did not have the time for such sexual extravaganzas, and he puts the number of men involved with the tsaritsa at only twelve.[1] Much of the salacious gossip about her private life was the result of male prejudice, so that while Britain's George I, who died two years after Peter the Great, could have two German mistresses who were affectionately known as 'the Elephant and Castle', Catherine was virtually branded as a nymphomaniac. Alexander's verdict on this overblown aspect of the Russian empress' life seems to be an eminently fair one: 'Amid the welter of state duties and court routine she sometimes felt achingly lonesome.

Catherine the Great

A nymphomaniac she was not, but a normal person in an abnormal position.'[2]

What is true is that Catherine was sometimes excessively generous to her lovers. Grigory Orlov received 50,000 roubles for his part in the coup d'etat of 1762, and Potemkin received a gift of 600 souls (male serfs) which suggested a certain lack of consistency in a tsaritsa who claimed to dislike the institution of serfdom.

Catherine II and the Enlightenment

Catherine II was a child of her time, and she liked to think of herself as a philosopher-empress in the tradition of the eighteenth-century Enlightenment. This movement expressed a growing disillusionment with organised religion and a more humane attitude to the government of men. For many years Catherine was a leading exponent of its ideas, and she was in regular correspondence with its foremost writers like Voltaire, Diderot and d'Alembert. As a lawmaker, Catherine also relied on the works of Cesare Beccaria and the Englishman Blackstone, and her 'Instruction' of 1767 to the Russian Law Commission owed much to the ideas of the French political theorist Montesquieu.

Whether Catherine deserved to be called 'an enlightened despot' is another matter, because her schemes tended to founder in Russian conditions. Ideas which were inspiring in books took on another aspect when she tried to put them into practice, and Catherine was never willing to weaken the autocracy in the interests of personal liberty. She never, for example, got to grips with the issue of serfdom, and when Diderot questioned her about its effect on Russian agriculture she replied evasively, 'I know of no country where the worker loves his land and home more than in Russia.'

Diderot was the only one of the major philosophers actually to visit Catherine's court, and he was dazzled by his host who, he claimed, had 'the soul of Caesar, with all the seductions of Cleopatra'. Catherine was less enthusiastic. She was annoyed by Diderot's probing questions and preferred his companion Grimm, a lesser light who became her cultural representative in Paris. It is likely that the trauma of the Pugachev uprising of 1773 had reminded the tsaritsa of Russia's ancient barbarism, and reduced her enthusiasm to reform. The influence of France during Catherine's reign was, in any case, essentially cultural, and her political allies were Britain and Austria (until Anglo–Russian relations worsened in the 1780s). She read Monstesquieu's *De l'Esprit des Lois* (the Spirit of the Laws), with its pro-British bias, but never felt obliged to grant her people any truly representative national forum.

Latterly, in the years that followed the French Revolution, Catherine turned away from her former enthusiasm for intellectual debate. Diderot's famous *Encyclopédie* was banned, and when Alexander Radishchev (1749–1802) published his *Journey from St Petersburg to Moscow* in 1790, with its portrayal of the miseries of peasant life, he was sentenced to death. Although Catherine later commuted his sentence to ten years in Siberia, she had fired the first shots in the long war between tsarism and the Russian intelligentsia. Radishchev, however, was not embittered by his treatment because he recognised that the more liberal atmosphere of Catherine's early years had allowed Russia to start to develop her own distinctive literary tradition.

Prominent in this process was Michael Lomonosov (1711–65), a professor of chemistry who also dabbled in philology and history, but Catherine herself encouraged the writing of more Russian history books. Like Radishchev, Lomonosov had also fallen foul of a tsaritsa in her final reactionary phase, but in his case the culprit was the Empress Elizabeth, who lacked Catherine II's intellectual ability. In the 1790s that ability turned in on itself, and Catherine's later conservatism found its mouthpiece in Prince Shcherbatov (1733–90) who was a leading critic of the whole experience of 'westernisation' in Russia.

Ultimately Catherine's legacy to Russian cultural life was to make it more cosmopolitan. French tutors became the rage (Catherine hired the Swiss-born La Harpe to teach her grandsons) and leading noble families like the Golitsyns and Vorontsovs were as well known in Paris as they were in St Petersburg. French was the established language of court life and diplomacy, and Catherine II might have reflected on the paradox which made her a Russian nationalist, while her empire at its highest levels became more Frenchified.

Church/State Relations

In the years before her seizure of the throne in 1762, Catherine the Great was ostentatious in her loyalty to Orthodoxy and this paid dividends. Peter III's secularisation of church property had provoked a hostile reaction from the Orthodox clergy, but Catherine had no intention of restoring it; she was regular in her devotion both to holy days and large helpings of church property. In this sense she was in the mainstream of enlightened despotism, which was characterised by its scepticism about religious matters. Her fellow monarch Joseph II of Austria, for example, expelled the Jesuits and regulated Church life down to the minutest detail, so that Frederick the Great sneeringly referred to him as 'my brother the sacristan'.

Catherine began by abolishing the Collegium of Economy, which was the state agency involved in the confiscation of church lands, and setting up a commission of enquiry to examine the whole issue of secularisation. This was a typical imperial device, which the tsaritsa often used when she wished to avoid tackling a difficult problem head on. Having temporarily defused the issue, Catherine then restored the Collegium of Economy in 1763.

The Orthodox clergy grumbled about Catherine's ecclesiastical policy, but only the Metropolitan Arseny Matseevich openly criticised it. Indeed, his opposition to secularisation was so well known that he had deliberately been excluded from Catherine's coronation service in 1762. If this snub was intended to intimidate the determined cleric, it had the opposite effect, and the Metropolitan continued loudly to proclaim his opposition to Catherine's church policy. The tsaritsa was particularly irked by Matseevich's statement that 'with us it is not like in England, that one is to live and make one's way by money alone', because it struck a raw nerve. The state would make considerable financial gain from the confiscation of church lands, but Catherine did not care to be reminded of this particular piece of venality. She insisted that 'the liar and humbug' be put on trial, stripped of his position and imprisoned for life in the fortress of Reval, where he was known to the warders as 'Andrey the Liar'. Thereafter the church was to be the pliant instrument of 'the Little Mother'.

Mainstream Orthodoxy was, therefore, dominated by the tsarist autocracy, and in 1764 one million male peasants (known as economic peasants after the Collegium) were transferred to state control. They had to pay taxes to the government rather than to the church, and many monastic houses had to close down because of the resulting loss of revenue. But Russia's spiritual tradition did not die, because 'the Russians are basically devout and they turned to the hermits and the startsy'.[3]

In this tradition were the monk Tikhon of Zadonsk (1724–82) and especially Seraphim of Sarov (1759–1833). Thousands of Russians visited Seraphim's cell in Central Russia to hear the old teachings.

By the end of the eighteenth century a monastic revival was also under way as a result of the influence of Paisy Velichkovsky (1722–94), a monk in the monastery of Optina Pustina near Tula. In the nineteenth century, the reputation of the monastery was so high that it was used as a spiritual retreat by writers like Tolstoy, Gogol and Dostoevsky. It is likely that Catherine, with her German background and humanist tastes, underestimated the traditional piety of the Russian people.

The Pugachev Uprising

In 1773 the tsaritsa was in mid-reign, with a successful war against Turkey drawing to a close (see p. 115), and a large slice of Polish territory already in her hands. If her subjects were known to grumble from time to time, Catherine would have regarded their complaints as nothing more than the usual moans of a semi-barbaric peasantry. She knew, too, that they had a penchant for rallying around pretenders to the imperial throne, and there had already been three such episodes in her reign. The last, in 1772, concerned one Fyodor Kazin (alias Bogomilov), who claimed that 'the tsar's marks' on his chest proved that he was Peter III despite the concrete evidence available that this unfortunate ruler was long dead. The false Peter III got short shrift from the authorities and was speedily knouted, branded and sent into permanent exile. So when another impostor appeared late in the same year claiming to be Catherine's husband, the tsaritsa was not unduly concerned. Particularly as the miscreant was easily captured and taken in irons to Kazan where he was imprisoned.

That sentence should have marked the end of Emilian Pugachev, but it did not. Instead, this illiterate ex-soldier of uncertain origin escaped

Pugachev from a contemporary engraving

from captivity, and reappeared in the summer of 1773 in the Cossack region around Yaitsk. He proved to be an effective demagogue, with an appeal to the Cossacks and the Kazakh nomads of the region. It seems that some of the Cossacks didn't care whether Pugachev was really Peter III or not (there was very little physical likeness) and boasted that they could 'make a prince out of muck'. By October 1773, the uprising was serious enough to warrant imperial attention and Catherine sent General Karr to deal with this 'chief brigand, incendiary and impostor'. His small force was routed by Pugachev, and the tsaritsa was forced to send the more experienced General Bibikov to crush the rebels.

Catherine was afraid that foreign powers (France or Turkey) might be stirring up the Cossack dissidents, but Bibikov could find no evidence of this. It seemed at the end of 1773 that Pugachev had shot his bolt, and Catherine amused herself by getting the court historiographer, Prince Mikhail Shcherbatov, to write a short history about pretenders to the Russian throne. She also set up a commission to examine the reasons for the Pugachevshchina (the dark deeds of Pugachev). This confirmed, rather against Catherine's instincts, that Pugachev was a charismatic leader with a broad appeal to Cossacks, Kazakhs, Bashkirs, and other displaced peasants who had been forced to work in the new metalworks in the Urals. In response, Catherine II sent Pavel Potemkin, the cousin of her lover, to the region on her behalf but he arrived only three days before Kazan was stormed by 20,000 rebels.

Pugachev was clearly far from being finished, and he encouraged the outrages committed by his supporters against the landed aristocracy. They were offered 100 roubles for a dead nobleman or a sacked mansion, and 1000 roubles for ten dead noblemen or sacked mansions. His success in Kazan also sparked off another peasant uprising in the neighbouring region of Nizhny-Novgorod. Catherine was appalled, both by the carnage and that the spirit of her dead husband could attract such popular support. 'European public opinion', she told her frightened courtiers, 'will think we have returned to the era of Tsar Ivan Vasilievich [Ivan IV].' Even more alarming perhaps was the way Pugachev was arousing local chauvinism against her as 'the German, the Devil's daughter'.

After the sack of Kazan Pugachev's luck deserted him, and he suffered three rapid defeats at the hands of the imperial forces. He then crossed the Volga with what remained of his army, cutting a murderous swathe through the towns and villages of its basin. In the interim Bibikov had died, to be replaced by General Peter Panin with the talented Suvorov as his second-in-command.

Nemesis finally caught up with the fake Peter III in August 1774, when his forces were routed at Tsaritsyn (now Volgograd). After the battle the frightened Cossacks trussed Pugachev up and handed him over to the authorities. Catherine was 'filled with joy that the miscreant has come to an end'. Pugachev was then closely questioned, because the tsaritsa could not believe that an illiterate brigand could cause such mayhem, but no foreign involvement could be uncovered. Nor could the authorities find any link between Pugachev and the Old Believers. He was brought to Moscow for trial at the end of December 1774, but the verdict was a formality. All that was at issue was the form the pretender's execution would take, given the tsaritsa's aversion to torture (she wouldn't allow Pugachev to be racked). Since she refused to allow Pugachev to be quartered, a rather ghoulish compromise was worked out: the Moscow police agreed that Pugachev would be beheaded, and then have his hands and feet cut off. He perished before a large Muscovite crowd in January 1775.

Catherine was profoundly shaken by Pugachev's uprising, which reminded her of her own tenuous claim to the crown. She never referred to the Pugachevshchina again, but the experience put some iron into her soul. After the uprising, Henri Troyat notes, 'when reasons of state demanded it she was a hard as nails'.[4]

The Significance of the Pugachevshchina

The major significance of Pugachev's uprising was that it demonstrated that Catherine II did not understand the peasantry, and cared very little about them. 'Wherever you touch it,' she exclaimed rather lamely, 'it does not yield.' Even the coincidence of war and revolt did not alarm the empress sufficiently to make her do something about serfdom. Instead, she went on using serfs as the currency of court favour, and strengthened the bonds between the crown and the aristocracy in her Charter of 1785. By contrast, her fellow 'enlightened despot' Joseph II of Austria made some real efforts to improve the plight of the peasantry inside the Habsburg empire.

The dark masses in the countryside were an alien force as far as the tsaritsa was concerned, and she would have agreed with the statement by the nineteenth-century revolutionary, Chernyshevsky, that 'the mass is simply the raw material for diplomatic and political experiments. Whoever rules it tells it what to do, and it obeys.' What Catherine failed to discern was that Pugachev's revolt, like that of Stenka Razin in the reign of Tsar Alexis, was a genuine reaction against appalling social conditions. While it is true that the peasants were credulous enough to follow a false Dimitry or a reincarnated Peter III, they did expect these figureheads to improve their conditions. Because Catherine chose to ignore this fact (it is hard to believe that she lacked the perception to understand it), her 'enlightenment' in domestic policy was never more than skin-deep. Pugachev's supporters had certainly expected her to extend the scope of Peter III's 1762 reform to them, and she had conspicuously failed to oblige.

Instead, by 1796, the year of Catherine's death, there were over nine million male serfs in private ownership and a further seven million in state ownership. Since female serfs did not count for statistical purposes, this meant that more than 90 per cent of the population were 'in private or state bondage'.[5]

The Charter of Nobility

It was no coincidence that Catherine II began to revise the relationship between the autocracy and the nobility as early as 1775, the year of Pugachev's execution. The reform did not weaken the tsaritsa's authority at the centre, but it did give the nobles their own elected assemblies within each of the empire's *gubernii* (administrative divisions). Authority over local government and justice was also devolved to the nobles, but they themselves remained subordinate to the governors appointed by St Petersburg.

A decade later, Catherine's Charter of Nobility (1785) consolidated the alliance between the autocracy and the nobility which had been developing since the sixteenth century. There was to be no obligation on the nobles to enlist in the army, or serve the bureaucracy, and they were to be exempted from taxation. Members of the nobility who broke the law were only to be tried by a court of their peers, although they had the right to impose any sentence on a serf, short of death.

In fact, as Professor Alexander has pointed out, the 1785 Charter gave the nobility no new privileges but merely defined the status of the nobles more exactly. The reaffirmation of the principle of *voluntary* state service was also made with an extremely significant qualification in article 20. In it, the empress reminded her nobles that their security depended on the security of the autocracy and the realm,

> so therefore at any such time as needed by the Russian autocracy, when the service of the nobility is needed and necessary for the common good then every well-born nobleman is obliged, at the first summons from the sovereign authority, not to spare either labour or life itself for the state service.[6]

In practice, as Catherine well knew, economic realities made it impossible for many members of the nobility to opt out of state service. In 1777, for example, only 16 per cent of the nobility had more than 100 serfs, and a further 32 per cent had less than ten. In this sense, the tsaritsa's reform was only an exercise in granting a right, which economic reality made it impossible to indulge.

More (apparently) limited rights were also conceded to the top categories of merchants and townspeople by the Charter. They shared with the nobility the dubious privilege of having a separately defined legal status.

The Succession

When Catherine II observed the antics of her son, the Grand Duke Paul, in her later years, she might have felt that her murdered husband had come back to haunt her. The relationship between Catherine and her son seems to have been doomed from the start, and this was not entirely Paul's fault. He was removed from his mother's care virtually from birth, at the dictate of the Tsaritsa Elizabeth, and then fell under the influence of his tutor, Nikita Panin, whose attitude towards the coup of

1762 was at best ambivalent. It was from Panin that Paul learnt about the mystery surrounding his father's death, and this knowledge created a rift between mother and son which was never repaired.

On her side, Catherine made no secret of her belief that her son lacked the capacity to rule, and she removed her grandsons, Alexander, Constantine and Nicholas, from his jurisdiction. The resulting bitterness poisoned the Grand Duke's mind for the rest of Catherine's life, although there were some short truces when the relationship seemed to be on the mend. Generally though the Grand Duke's home at Gatchina remained a sort of unofficial centre of opposition to his mother's rule, and he lost no opportunity to complain to foreigners about the way he was treated.

Catherine's Death

In the autumn of 1794 Catherine made her intentions about the imperial succession known to the Council of State. She gave an outline of her son's behaviour over the years and used this evidence to conclude that Paul was unfit to govern and that 'it would be expedient to have his Imperial Highness excluded from succeeding us'. As the Grand Duke's frailties were common knowledge there was no opposition to this move, but Catherine was strangely sluggish about formalising the situation so that her grandson Alexander would be nominated as her heir. Only late in 1796 did she decide that the formal announcement of her decision would be made on 1 January 1797. The delay proved fatal.

Early on the morning of 5 November Catherine had a stroke which deprived her of speech, and she died at ten o'clock the same evening. The evidence suggests that the empress had been deluding herself about Alexander's willingness to succeed. While willing to indulge the grandmother who virtually brought him up, Alexander was known to be very loyal to his parents, although he kept his reservations about the succession a secret from Catherine.[7] Even before the end of Catherine's last day Prussian uniforms were to be seen in the corridors of the Winter Palace, just as they had been in the heyday of her doomed husband.

Foreign Relations

If Catherine II merits the title 'the Great', it is primarily because of her achievements in foreign policy. She came to the throne in the latter stages of the Seven Years War, when only her northern frontiers had been secured, but by the end of her reign Russia had brought about the destruction of the ancient Polish foe, and gained vast territories in the south-east.

POLAND

The weakness of the ancient Polish kingdom had been obvious at the time of the War of the Polish Succession in the 1730s. But it followed its uncertain independent path until 1764, when Russian pressure brought about the election of Catherine II's former lover, Stanislaw Poniatowski. Poniatowski was expected to be a Russian stooge and, as Neal Ascherson says in his recent history of Poland, 'nobody expected much of him.'⁸ However, Poniatowski then proceeded to shock both Poles and Russians alike by attempting to reform the unworkable Polish constitution. He tried to strengthen the power of the monarchy while reducing that of the landed aristocracy, and promised to abolish the subversive 'liberum veto'. This allowed individual members of the Sejm (Parliament) to abort any government measure just by calling out, 'I do not permit'.

Such constitutional chaos in Poland suited Catherine's book, of course, and she responded to King Stanislaw's burst of reformism by encouraging opposition, and particularly the formation of the so-called Confederation of Bar in 1768. The members of the Confederation were reactionary Polish magnates who opposed both Russian interference, and what they took to be the king's collaboration with them. Four years of fighting between the Confederation and the royal forces failed to resolve the issue, and only weakened Poland's capacity to resist further Rusian interference.

A Russo–Polish treaty also placed the Polish constitution under Russian protection and opened the way for the events of 1772, when Catherine II persuaded Austria and Prussia to partition Poland with her. This First Partition of Poland gave Russia 36,000 square miles of former Polish territory with one and three-quarter million people. The White Russian areas of Polotsk, Vitebsk and Mogilev were now incorporated into Catherine's empire.

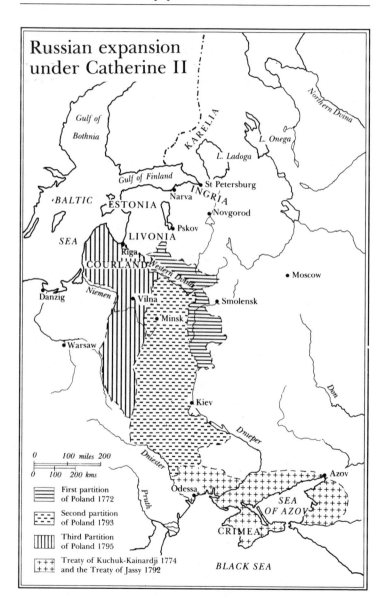

Russian expansion under Catherine II

It was surprising, given the rump state's vulnerable position, that King Stanislaw persevered with his reform programme. But he continued to ask for the restructuring of the constitution, and was the guiding spirit behind the famous 1791 Constitution which owed something to the example of revolutionary France. The new constitution would have replaced the elective monarchy with an hereditary one, and also abolished the unanimity rule in the Sejm. Further reforms would have put the Polish peasantry under legal protection, and made townspeople able to claim the same civil rights as the nobility.

Catherine II regarded this constitution as unacceptable. So did the ultra-conservative nobility who formed the Confederation of Targowice and gave aid and comfort to the Russian invasion of 1792. In this instance, Catherine could persuade only Prussia to co-operate in this act of international piracy, which found the western powers sidetracked by the emergency surrounding the French Revolution. In this Second Partition of Poland, Russia was then able to annex a large slice of the former Grand Duchy of Lithuania.

Polish spirits remained uncrushed. In 1794 the people rose again, under the capable leadership of Tadeusz Kosciuszko (1746–1817), a French-trained soldier who had fought in the American War of Independence. Although the Poles fought valiantly and gained some victories, in the end their revolt was brutally crushed by General Suvorov. The three enlightened despots of Russia, Prussia and Austria then conspired to obliterate the Polish kingdom from the map of Europe in the Third Partition of Poland (1795). A clause in the agreement stated that 'the name or designation of the Kingdom of Poland ... shall remain suppressed as of now and forever'. Catherine's personal role in the destruction of Poland had been quite ruthless. Her claim to have been rooting out 'Jacobinism' in Poland was also a shameless piece of diplomatic cynicism. The passage of time would show that the unfortunate Poles would not 'remain suppressed'.

TURKEY

At home Catherine II showed singularly little interest in the Orthodox Church, but in her foreign policy she adroitly exploited the sympathy of the Orthodox Russians for their co-religionists in the Ottoman Empire.

This was all part of that expansion southwards, which had been severely checked by Peter the Great's disaster on the banks of the Pruth in 1711. So, once freed from entanglements in Central Europe, the Russians took on the Ottomans again in what Frederick the Great unkindly described as a war 'between the one-eyed and the blind'. Yet in its way the Russo–Turkish War of 1768 to 1774 was as decisive as the Great Northern War had been.

In 1769 the Russians occupied Jassy and Bucharest before going on to annex the entire provinces of Moldavia and Wallachia (modern Rumania). Their new naval arm, commanded by the former British admiral Elphinstone, then distinguished itself also by sailing from the Baltic to the Aegean and destroying the Turkish fleet off Chios. But with the Turks at her mercy Catherine II was then distracted by the Pugachevshchina, and the Turks got off relatively lightly. Under the terms of the Treaty of Kuchuk-Kainardji (1774), Turkey was to grant independent status to the Crimea, and give Russia the rather vague role of Protector of Orthodox Christians in the Ottoman Empire. Azov, Kerch and Yenikale were ceded to Russia, and her ships were to have free passage on the Black Sea and through the Bosphorus and the Dardanelles. It was a decisive shift in the balance of power in the Balkans, and one which caused the other European powers to keep a wary eye on the colossus of the North in St Petersburg.

In 1783, less than a decade after Kuchuk-Kainardji, Russia formally annexed the Crimea, and in the next decade the first signs of Anglo–Russian animosity appeared. Its origin was a dispute over the fortress of Ochakov and the small strip of territory around it between the Rivers Bug and Dniester. The British prime minister, William Pitt the Younger, took exception to Russia's seizure of Ochakov in 1791, and Catherine took exception to what she took to be British meddling. Lewd cartoons appeared in the British press about her sexual appetites, and she deliberately cultivated links with Pitt's opponent, Charles James Fox. 'Since Mr Pitt has chosen to drive me from Petersburg,' the ageing tsaritsa remarked tartly, 'he must forgive me if I take refuge in Constantinople.' In reality Pitt was not prepared to fight for Ochakov and Catherine was, although she rejected the American privateer John Paul Jones' plan to attack British ships en route for India (he had entered

Russian service in 1788, so preserving the cosmopolitan nature of the imperial navy).

Catherine's reign was doubly significant because her southern conquests provided Russia both with a granary, and an additional outlet to the sea through the Black Sea ports. By 1793 one-fifth of Russia's cereal exports went through the Dardanelles and were grown in the black earth provinces south of a line marked Zhitomir–Kiev–Tula–Kazan. Whereas the Russian heartland around Moscow had poor soil and severe weather conditions, this rich new agricultural acquisition provided the foodstuffs to sustain a 300 per cent growth in population in the nineteenth century. A further treaty in 1783 with subtropical Georgia gave the Russian empire access to its varying produce.

IMMIGRATION

In 1762 an imperial ukase invited foreigners (Jews apart) to settle in the new lands of the empire, and to do so on specially favourable terms. Most of those who were tempted were Germans, and some 20,000 of them settled near Saratov and Tsaritsyn in the Lower Volga region. The new citizens were sober and industrious, and the forerunners of the ethnic German community in the USSR today.

Conclusion

Catherine the Great's foreign policy was undoubtedly more effective than that of her admitted model, Peter the Great. By 1796 Russia was unquestionably a great European power, and on occasion this power seemed great enough to threaten others. At home, Catherine adopted the rhetoric of a reformer, without ever realising the promise of her early years.

CHAPTER TEN

Tsarism in Crisis
1796–1855

The Reign of the Tsar Paul

The irony of Catherine the Great's life was that she obtained the throne by usurping it from her feeble-minded husband Peter III and then left it to her deranged son Paul (1796–1801). Well before his ill-fated reign began, Paul's hatred of his mother had overflowed into other obsessional behaviour.

His particular obsession was military mania, and like his father before him he became an admirer of all things Prussian. At Gatchina he played toy soldiers incessantly, wearying his guardsmen with his endless drilling. The signs for the new reign were therefore ominous as the Grand Duke's adviser Count Rostopchin (later governor of Moscow during Napoleon's occupation) noted,

> One might think that he was searching for ways of making himself loathed and detested. He thinks that people despise him and seek to avoid him, as a result, he picks on anything, and punishes indiscriminately . . . The smallest delay, the slightest disagreement, makes him lose his temper and he explodes.

Once his mother was safely dead, the new tsar wreaked posthumous revenge on her. One of his first acts was to have his father's body disinterred and placed next to hers in the Hall of Pillars in the Winter Palace. Catherine's body therefore lay on the lying-in-state bed with the skeleton of her murdered husband, under an inscription which read, with gruesome lack of taste, 'Divided in life, united in death'. Every effort was made to discredit the dead empress, even to the extent of nicknaming her favourite dragoon regiment 'Catherine's skirts'.

In fact, Catherine's death removed the last restraint on Paul's excesses, which soon became reminiscent of the Emperor Caligula (who made his horse a consul) at his worst. His egomania was reflected in his statement that 'no one in Russia is important except the person who is speaking to me; and that, only while he is speaking'. During four years of what one American historian has called 'wildly capricious rule',[1] Paul's behaviour became more and more bizarre. Among his more eccentric decisions was the sending out of watchmen with long sticks to patrol the streets of St Petersburg and knock the fashionable French-style round hats off people's heads. These hats, together with top boots and frock coats, were deemed to be examples of republican subversion and as such unacceptable! Woe betide the courtier who appeared at court with his wig insufficiently powdered. He ran the risk of banishment to his country estate, or even to Siberia.

We can only speculate about how long Russia's élite would have tolerated this tyranny before revolting. As it was, Paul's decision to abandon his mother's anti-French policy was to seal his fate. For, like his father Peter III, Paul was susceptible to hero-worship, which in his case meant Napoleon-worship and withdrawal from the war against revolutionary France.

This new foreign-policy orientation proved to be unacceptable to his courtiers, and more importantly to his son Alexander, the heir to the throne. On the night of 23–24 March 1801, a group of guards officers and disaffected courtiers led by Levin Bennigsen (a general of Hanoverian origin) broke into the tsar's bedroom and murdered him. Legend has it that he was strangled with his own silk scarf. Did Alexander know about the conspiracy against his father? It is hard to believe that he did not, but at least one historian is convinced of the traumatic affect which the assassination had on the new young tsar. 'For years thereafter,' writes Curtis Cate, 'he lived under the oppressive fear that he too might suffer the fate that had overtaken his father.'[2]

Alexander I

Whatever dark shadows afflicted Alexander I (1801–25) later in his life, they were not evident at the beginning of his reign. There was intense

Tsar Alexander I

relief in St Petersburg that the despotic Paul was dead, and the handsome young emperor was greatly admired. 'Never', wrote one of the ladies-in-waiting at his court, 'was the start of a reign more brilliant.'

He was certainly well prepared for his task as his grandmother had provided him with a tutor, La Harpe, who had filled the young man with the learning of the eighteenth-century Enlightenment. She, as the last chapter demonstrated, had flirted with the ideas of the Enlightenment but done very little to implement them in Russia. Her grandson attempted more but was increasingly, and ultimately fatally, inhibited by the arch-conservatism of Russian society.

The French War

Alexander was perhaps unfortunate that his early efforts at reform were framed to the backcloth of the French wars. In the latter phase of this struggle (1812–14) Russia was involved in a life-and-death struggle, and in the opening phase (1805–7) the young tsar was a victim of his own youthful inexperience. Alexander loathed the phenomenon of Bonapartism as strongly as his father had admired it. He therefore made the anglophile Voronzov his chancellor and the Polish prince Czartoryski became his foreign minister in 1804. The latter appointment reflected his early 'liberalism' because Czartoryski's avowed objective was to unite all Poland under the tsar's auspices. This explains Alexander's flat rejection of any Franco–Russian alliance, which would have undermined his friend's plans. His distaste for the upstart Bonaparte (who crowned himself emperor in 1804) was encouraged by Czartoryski who remained a considerable influence at the Russian court for another decade.

So it was that Russia joined Austria and Britain in the Third Coalition against Bonaparte, which proved to be such a disastrous failure. Some of this failure can be attributed directly to Alexander himself. He was strongly influenced by the vain and arrogant Count Dolgorukov, who misleadingly described Bonaparte after a visit to the French camp as 'a little figure, extremely dirty and ill dressed', and by his own desire to 'experience and win a battle'. By contrast, Czartoryski, who recommended a retreat until Prussia entered the conflict, recognised that the young emperor 'could not know how to command' and was surrounded by 'young, giddy, ignorant presumptuous men'.[3] The Russian commander Kutuzov, a veteran of Suvorov's campaigns, also recommended caution, but the 28-year-old tsar was determined to strike a blow against Bonaparte. So too was the Austrian emperor Francis II (1768–1835), already shaken by the surrender of his own General Mack with 30,000 men at Ulm in October. The decisive engagement took place at the small village of Austerlitz in Bohemia on 2 December 1805, and the Austro–Russian army was routed by Napoleon, whose own position was endangered by the threat of Prussian intervention. Tolstoy was to write later that nine-tenths of the Russian army at that moment was 'in love . . . with their tsar and the glory of Russian arms' (the battle is beautifully described in *War and Peace*) but it did not save them from defeat. The Russian troops had fought with traditional bravery, but of the 15,000 dead and wounded on the allied side 11,000 were Russians.

Yet Austerlitz was not quite the overwhelming victory that French propaganda made it out to be. While it is true that Austria was forced to make peace in 1805, Russia did not, and in the following year Prussia joined the coalition against Bonaparte. Fatally, however, she did not wait for Russian assistance, and her incompetent generals were heavily defeated at Jena and Auerstadt. Nevertheless Prussian intervention did force Napoleon to fight an unwelcome winter campaign in Poland, during which the Grande Armée came close to disaster at Eylau (8 February 1807). Once again Napoleon's position was perilous, and once again he was assisted by Russian incompetence, although the tsar had given up his dreams of personal command. This time the Russian commander Bennigsen, the ringleader of the plot against Tsar Paul, opted to fight at Friedland with his back to the River Alle and with predictable results: the battle (14 June 1807) cost Bennigsen 11,000 dead and 7000 wounded, one-third of his effectives, and left Alexander I little option but to make peace with France.

Russia now moved into an uneasy phase of alliance with France as a result of the Treaty of Tilsit, signed on 9 July 1807 on a raft in the middle of the River Niemen, which was supposed to be a concession to the tsar's feelings. No one, though, was deceived, except perhaps Alexander himself. Tilsit was an admission that Napoleonic France dominated Europe, even if it pandered to Russian ambitions by containing vague references to Franco–Rusian expeditions against Turkey and British India. Alexander's vanity may have been 'flattered by the privileged treatment he was accorded by the emperor of the French'[4] but Tilsit still placed him in embarrassing tutelage to Napoleon.

It was a situation which plainly could not last. Anti-French feeling was strong in Russia, and was increased by the provisions of the 1807 treaty which forced her to join Napoleon's ill-fated 'Continental System'. This was designed to ruin Britain's economy by closing continental ports to her, but it also severed long-standing Russian trading links with the island empire. The Continental System was deeply unpopular in Russia, and a major cause of the rift which took place in 1812. In St Petersburg further resentment was caused by French behaviour in the so-called 'Grand Duchy of Warsaw', that part of former Austrian and Prussian Poland created by the 1807 settlement.

Marshal Davout, one of Napoleon's senior marshals, had been given the task of recruiting a Polish army there, and it made no secret of the anti-Russian sentiments which had been fiercely expressed as recently as 1791.

The French Marriage

But the grievances were not just on the Russian side. In the war of 1809 in which Napoleon had yet again defeated the Austrians, Russia had been the most dilatory of allies for the French. Her army advanced into Galicia (Austrian Poland) at a snail's pace and just two Cossacks lost their lives in the hostilities! French suspicions that Alexander was responsible for this lethargy were entirely justified.

Further ill-feeling was created by Bonaparte's proposals in 1809–10 for a Franco–Russian marriage alliance. At first the Grand Duchess Catherine, Alexander's favourite sister, appears to have been flattered by the prospect of marrying the master of Europe. But by the end of 1809 she was declaring to all and sundry that she would sooner marry 'a *pop* [author's italics] than the sovereign of a country under the influence of France'. Since a pop was a Russian Orthodox parish priest, the reference was hardly likely to endear her family to the French.

Instead, Alexander prevaricated for a month before sending a negative response on 4 February 1810. Within three days Napoleon had transferred his interest to Marie Louise of Habsburg, and within twenty-four hours of the marriage proposal the Austrian Chancellor Prince von Schwarzenberg had accepted it on behalf of his government. The unfortunate Josephine, who had been unable to provide Napoleon with a male heir, was speedily divorced. The Russians suspected that Napoleon had been negotiating simultaneously with the Habsburgs, but one Frenchman at least was severely disappointed by the Austrian marriage. Armand de Caulaincourt, the French 'ambassador' in St Petersburg, had laboured hard to establish a personal rapport with the tsar. He made little effort to disguise his disappointment from the American minister, on the occasion in May 1810 of a celebration ball for the marriage in St Petersburg. John Quincy Adams, a future President of the United States, wrote in his diary, 'I heard the Ambassador himself

say to someone that he gave the ball because he was obliged to do it – it
gave him no pleasure.'

In retrospect it is clear that Alexander was playing double game as far
back as the Erfurt meeting with Bonaparte in October 1808. He did so,
moreover, with the encouragement of both Caulaincourt and the former
French foreign minister Talleyrand, whom Napoleon had acidly
described as 'filth in silk stockings'. They urged him to stand up to
Napoleon but Alexander said that he was trying 'to gain a breathing-
space, and during this precious interval, build up our resources'. In fact
this advice made a good deal of sense.

Napoleon was perturbed by the fierceness of Austrian resistance in
1809, and the French campaign in Spain (after 1808) was a serious drain
on his resources. Napoleon's biographer Felix Markham has stated that
once he 'had made the choice of the Austrian marriage, Franco–Russian
relations deteriorated rapidly in the course of the year 1810',[5] but he does
so in the context of an alliance which could never have been more than
a marriage of convenience. It was, in the words of another analyst, 'a
beautiful makebelieve'.[6]

The War of 1812

The Russian position was strengthened in two ways before the actual
French invasion in June 1812. First of all, Napoleon's former marshal,
Bernadotte, took Sweden out of the Continental System in April 1812
and over to the side of Russia. Secondly, in May Alexander I concluded
a peace treaty with the Turks, which freed his southern flank from the
threat of attack. On 22 June Napoleon ordered his vast army of 600,000
men across the Niemen after telling his troops that they would
'terminate the fatal influence which Russia for fifty years has exercised
in Europe'. Historians disagree about the level of Napoleon's preparations and their adequacy for Russian conditions. Some, like Felix
Markham, have felt that these were adequate. Others, like Corelli
Barnett, have disagreed, and Barnett has been particularly critical of
Bonaparte's own role.

This criticism is only part of Barnett's general attack on Napoleon's
generalship, so it may be necessary to enter a caveat here. What the

Russian campaign did show was the disadvantages of the French system of living off the countryside, amidst a population that was *actively* hostile. The French faced the same problems in Spain, where the Duke of Wellington noted the effectiveness of the Spanish guerillas.

In Russia Bonaparte got his 'great battle' outside Moscow at Borodino (7 September), but it settled nothing. Once again Kutuzov did not wish to fight, but Alexander was under pressure to force the issue and he decided to give battle. This decision cost the Russians 50,000 casualties and the loss of Moscow, but for Kutuzov possession of Russia's former capital was a secondary matter. 'As long as the army exists,' the old warrior pointed out, 'and is in a condition to oppose the enemy, we preserve the hope of winning the war.'

This assessment proved to be exactly right, and Borodino was to be one of the most Pyrrhic of victories for Bonaparte. He was further undone by two unrelated events, the burning of Moscow and the refusal of the tsar to contemplate surrender. The first is no longer a matter of controversy for modern historians and is known to have been carried out on the orders of the city governor Rostopchin;[8] several hundred Russian incendiaries were later shot by the French for their involvement in it (this whole episode is harrowingly portrayed in Bondarchuk's epic 1960s Russian film version of *War and Peace*). Bonaparte's decision to retreat was not in fact primarily linked to the firing of the city, but to Alexander's refusal to negotiate which was quite predictable. He would have endangered his own throne had he contemplated peace with the 'Antichrist', but Napoleon made elaborate arrangements to contact the Russian court at Kamenny Island.

But these overtures had no result. On 29 September Alexander made a proclamation calling on his people to save Mother Russia which 'in saving itself . . . will save the freedom and independence of rulers and their realms'. There could be no compromise with Bonapartism, and the only surprising feature in this episode is that Napoleon could ever have imagined otherwise. Thereafter, what began as a French retreat rapidly became a rout.

THE RETREAT FROM MOSCOW

The retreat began over the night of 18–19 October 1812, and from the outset the omens were gloomy. The French began by burning some of their own supplies by accident, and Napoleon did nothing to prevent his army from burdening itself with half the riches of Moscow. Worse still, this motley force (French, Italians, Poles, Hessians, Württembergers) had a great army of camp followers, which even included the actors and actresses of the Théâtre Français.

Napoleon's misfortunes began when he allowed himself to be pushed back along the line of the French advance in the summer, and he found their depot at Smolensk half burnt out and lacking the necessary provisions. Snow fell early on 7 November to add to the miseries of the Grande Armée, which was in no way prepared for the privations of the Russian winter. Kutuzov vowed to make the French 'eat horseflesh', and this is exactly what he did.

It would be misleading though to suggest that all was well on the Russian side. Kutuzov's leadership in the retreat was at best sluggish and as much open to criticism as Napoleon's;[9] other Russian leaders, like Bennigsen, still glorying in the partial victory at Eylau, were just incompetent. Otherwise the destruction of Napoleon's army might have been total. As it was, some 30,000 skeletal figures staggered back across the Niemen by the end of the year (figures vary for the number of survivors).

In the heady days of victory over the winter of 1812–13, it would have been surprising if Alexander's head had not been turned by the adulation he had received. For even level-headed foreign observers seemed to lose their sense of proportion and John Quincy Adams wrote that 'there had been nothing like it in history since the days of Xerxes', The real heroes, as so often before (and since), were the common people of Russia – the peasants, whose ferocious resistance to the 'Antichrist' had involved burning Frenchmen alive, and the Cossacks, who had harried and harassed them out of the motherland.

The War of Liberation

The great saga of national resistance was soon replaced by the harsh urgencies of 'realpolitik'. To pursue the war Russia needed money and this was provided by a British subsidy. She also needed allies and the

Treaty of Kalisch (February 1813) gave her one in the shape of Prussia, which had suffered so severely at the hands of Bonaparte in 1806. The Prussians had been the most lukewarm of allies for France in the campaign of 1812, and they were rewarded by promises of territory in the Rhineland and Saxony. Russia as the senior partner in the alliance was to obtain some of Prussia's Polish territories in exchange.

Austria was not to prove so accommodating. Her foreign minister, Metternich, did his best to preserve Napoleonic France, and would have done so had her emperor showed the slightest disposition to compromise. He also remained seriously sceptical about Alexander's long-term aims, and hovered uneasily on the edge of the Fourth Coalition against Bonaparte. In the end Austria only entered the war after a six-week armistice and Napoleon's refusal to accept anything less than France's boundaries as he had fixed them (in August 1813).

Austria's defection made Bonaparte's defeat inevitable. He was decisively defeated in the 'Battle of the Nations' at Leipzig in October 1813, and by the end of the year the British were on French soil after Wellington's victory at Vitoria. It was therefore only a matter of time, although Napoleon's quicksilver brilliance in the campaign of 1814 caused the allied leaders several anxious moments.

When Napoleon finally abdicated in March 1814, he left a Europe seared by a quarter of a century of almost continuous warfare. He also left the Russian tsar as the arbiter of Europe, and his country with a central role in European affairs which she had never enjoyed previously. At the Congress of Vienna in 1814–15 Alexander I was the most feared figure, and his empire was credited with a strength which it did not really possess.

Alexander I and the Peace Settlement

Nevertheless, the settlement hammered out at Vienna did bear something of Alexander's imprint. If he got less of Poland than he wanted, his experiment with 'Congress Poland' showed that La Harpe's influence was not quite dead. Similarly, his lack of enthusiasm for the Bourbon restoration in France resulted in the allied insistence that Louis XVIII agree to a constitutional charter for his people. The worst excesses of Prussian spite (like blowing up the Pont d'Iéna) were also restrained.

By contrast, Alexander's scheme for a 'Holy Alliance' of Christian monarchs has been rightly criticised both at the time and subsequently. Castlereagh, the British foreign secretary, called it 'a sublime piece of mysticism and nonsense' and it is hard to disagree. The tsar's hare-brained scheme for intervention against the revolutionaries in Latin America belonged to the fantasy world to which he increasingly belonged in the last decade of his reign. The only significant long-term achievement of the Holy Alliance was to frighten President James Monroe into making his famous declaration in 1822 warning the European powers to keep out of the New World. Its language, with its reference to the need for Europe's rulers to 'take for their sole guide the precepts of the Christian religion', showed that Alexander had replaced the military mania of his father with a religious mania of his own.

This strange religious mysticism seems to have been a reaction both to the perils of the French invasion and the reformism of Alexander's youth. The latter was effectively ended by the former.

The Speransky Reforms

This was the period when the dominant influence in the tsar's life was Michael Speransky (1772–1839), a man of humble origins but considerable ability, who soon discerned the central problem facing the tsarist autocracy. Writing in 1802, Speransky observed:

> I find in Russia two classes: the slaves of the sovereign and the slaves of the landowners. The first are called free only in relation to the second, but there are no truly free persons in Russia, except beggars and philosophers . . . The interest of the nobility is that the peasants should be placed in their unlimited control; the interest of the peasants is that the nobility be in the same degree of dependence on the throne.

This statement was equally true of Russia half a century later, and stated her greatest dilemma. How could the autocracy tackle the problem of serfdom without endangering the delicate power-sharing mechanism created by Peter the Great and Catherine the Great? Initially at least Alexander I did appear to be willing to address the issue of reform. He surrounded himself with a small group of friends nicknamed the 'Unofficial Committee', of whom Adam Czartoryski (1770–1861) favoured an overhaul of imperial institutions, while Count Paul Stroganov (1772–1817) was against any diminution of the tsar's powers. Spearansky led the reformers and for a while he seemed to be having his way. Separate government ministries were created, although they were still responsible to the tsar alone, and a Council of State was given the task of preparing legislation (this had formerly been done by the Senate). Most radical of all was Speransky's proposal for a duma or parliament, but this proved to be too advanced a concept even for Alexander. Only after the 1905 revolution was Speransky's plan for a duma found in the imperial archives, dusted down, and then implemented!

Speransky also recognised the urgent need for economic reform. He tried, for example, to stop inflation by preventing the printing of extra paper roubles to deal with financial emergencies. He also wished to stabilise the value of the notoriously volatile Russian currency but found it impossible to break old tsarist habits. Alexander I continued to borrow money abroad at very high rates of interest, and to print extra paper money.

Doubtless Speransky would have suggested a solution for the problem of serfdom, but the times were against him. He had powerful enemies at court, like the war minister, Arakcheyev, who saw his reforms as evidence of poisonous western influence, and he was finally undone by the French invasion in 1812. There were malicious rumours that Speransky was 'a French spy', and faced with a national emergency Alexander was unwilling to defend his protégé. Speransky was therefore removed from office, and sadly for Russia his former master drifted slowly, but decisively, into the clutches of reactionaries like Arakcheyev and Golitsyn, the procurator of the Holy Synod.

The Last Phase

Abroad this was the period of the 'Holy Alliance', and 'Metternich's system', a device for suppressing nationalism and liberalism in Europe which had Alexander's complete support. At home it was an era of seances, spooks and cranks, a twilight world of mysticism and holy men.

None was more sinister than Arakcheyev, who was an important influence in the last years. He was, according to one British historian, 'one of the most loathsome creatures'[10] of nineteenth-century Russia, whose most unpleasant exploit was the execution of a whole wood full of nightingales for keeping him awake at night. Nasty and brutish though it was, this action was in itself revealing about Arakcheyev's character, which reached the heights of crankery in his notorious scheme for military colonies in 1819. This crazy plan, which appears to have had the tsar's approval, had the stark simplicity of autocracy run riot: the 'colonists' would double as peasants and soldiers, thus saving money (it was claimed). But peasants resented being made to do military service on a part-time basis, and Arakcheyev fell back on draconian expedients. Those, for example, who unwisely did their washing on the wrong day were rewarded with a sound flogging! Eventually Alexander heard of these excesses and put an end to the scheme.

The other major figure was Prince Golitsyn, the procurator of the Holy Synod. He encouraged Alexander's religious hysteria, and turned a blind eye to the seances of Madame de Krüdener which the unhappy tsar attended. Repression of the universities and a rigorous censorship were the work of Golitsyn's confederate Prince Galitzin, the minister of education.

Poland

Nowhere perhaps were the contradictions of Alexander's reign better demonstrated than in Poland, where the positive influence of Prince Czartoryski seemed at first to bear fruit. But these hopes were to be dashed even in the miniature 'Congress Poland' (only one-fifth of the whole country) which came into existence in 1815. Congress Poland was to be a sort of political laboratory in which freedom of expression, association and worship were to be allowed, together with a separate Polish army and assembly. This was all very impressive on the surface; in reality, Russian influence still predominated and Alexander retained control of the Diet (assembly) by virtue of his position as emperor. His brother Constantine commanded the Polish army, and the special 'Commissioner for the Kingdom', Novosiltsev, interfered incessantly in Polish affairs. The rest of Russian Poland, in any case, remained under direct tsarist control.

The Legacy of Alexander

In one important respect Alexander I was unable to resist the influences unleashed by the Napoleonic Wars *inside* Russia. Russian officers and soldiers had served in France and Germany, and they had been influenced by the ideas of the Enlightenment and the French Revolution. Nothing Alexander or Arakcheyev could do would reverse this process, which caused rumblings of discontent in the army while the tsar was attending the Congress of Troppau in 1820. These had been nipped in the bud, but were a portent of the wider discontent which was to emerge after Alexander's death in 1825. Part of his tragedy was that, as a young man, he would probably have shared the ideals of these dissenters. As it was, his death was an occasion for rejoicing in Russia rather than regret. The hero of Europe in 1812 had by then become the object of international detestation, as Lord Byron's contemporary verdict demonstrates:

> Now half dissolving to a liberal thaw,
> But hardened back where'er the morning's raw;
> With no objection to true liberty,
> Except that it would made the nations free.

The Reign of Nicholas I

There was to be no question of 'a liberal thaw' during the reign of Alexander's younger brother Nicholas I (1825–55). Any remote possibility that Nicholas would consider weakening the powers of the autocracy disappeared in the crisis of December 1825 when tsarism faced at least as great a crisis as that brought about by the French invasion of 1812. It was therefore a much more profound crisis than the palace revolutions of 1762 and 1801, even if the question of the imperial succession was a significant issue for the conspirators.

The Decembrist Conspiracy

The Decembrists were idealists, but they were also revolutionaries influenced by two distinct currents of radical thought. One, formed around the person of Nikita Muravyev, was based in St Petersburg and was known as the Society of the North. It wanted to transform Russia into a British-style constitutional monarchy, with serfdom abolished and equality before the law. On social matters, as Jacques Droz has pointed out,[11] it was quite conservative, and only envisaged giving the freed peasants a small plot of land.

The Society of the South was centred on Tulchin, a small garrison town in the Ukraine, and its leading figure was a Colonel Pestel. Its ideological basis was laid down in Pestel's *Russian Reality* with its far more radical solution for Russia's problems. Pestel was a republican, who hated the concept of monarchy with all the misery it had brought to the Russian people. He was also a devolutionist, who wanted to give areas like the Ukraine far more control over their own affairs. Most radical of all was his solution to the land question. Like Muravyev he wanted to abolish serfdom, but unlike him he addressed the question of *ownership*. His book demanded that half the land in Russia be taken into state ownership and that the other half should be divided amongst the peasants. Foreign relations were dominated by his belief in Panslavism, and he wanted a federal union with Poland where his ideas had considerable influence.

Despite their ideological differences, the two societies had by 1825 succeeded in creating a very big organisation. Most of the members were ex-soldiers, disillusioned by the grim repression of Alexander I's closing years and, as we have seen, inspired by what they had seen in Western Europe in 1813–14. Their weakness was that they had little real contact with the masses and placed too much faith in the Grand Duke Constantine as a putative reforming tsar. Their strength was that they were able to infiltrate important army formations like the Pavlovsky Guards, who were to play a key role in the conspiracy. As one historian has pointed out, it was not an unusual role for them because 'for a whole century, the Guard had done nothing but raise tsars and empresses to the throne, so now why could it not bring about the downfall of tsarism with the help of those which always obeyed a strong hand?[12]

Nevertheless the Decembrists needed a figurehead, and they fixed (mistakenly) on the person of the Grand Duke Constantine. He had been forced to renounce his rights to the succession in 1822 because he had married a Polish Catholic, which meant that the tsar's heir apparent would be his stern, unbending youngest brother, Nicholas. This, the misreading of Constantine's personality, and the knowledge that the authorities were close on their heels in the autumn of 1825, made the conspirators decide to strike early when they heard the news of Alexander's death on 1 December.

The attempted coup was a fiasco. Constantine's repudiation of the throne had been kept a secret (even from his successor), and for three weeks after Alexander's death there was total confusion, with Nicholas proclaiming Constantine as tsar in St Petersburg and Constantine acknowledging Nicholas in Warsaw! For a while this paralysis was duplicated on the side of the new tsar. Nicholas was horrified by the news that his beloved army was in a state of mutiny, but once he had recovered his nerve he made short work of the rebels. Artillery was brought up to break the ice on the River Neva, and finding themselves surrounded the rebels surrendered. The few Decembrists who escaped from St Petersburg were soon rounded up, and five ringleaders (including Pestel) were hanged. A mordant sequel was provided at the execution when the ropes broke. 'Poor Russia,' said another conspirator, Apostol Murayev, 'she cannot even hang decently.'

THE EFFECTS OF THE DECEMBRIST CONSPIRACY

Surprisingly, this idealistic disaster was to have a major influence on modern Russian history. Nicholas I himself was traumatised by the experience, and he personally questioned the conspirators in a vain attempt to understand the nature of their heresy. Subsequently, the slightest deviation towards the modern or the liberal in Russia would awaken the growing anxiety in a tsar who soon acquired the unflattering nickname of 'the Gendarme of Europe'. But it was the place of the Decembrists in the martyrology of Russian radicalism which proved to be most long-lasting. Lenin admired them, as did other revolutionary leaders, and they provided role models for idealists like Chernyshevsky. The revolt against the theocratic rule of Alexander I was also emphasised by the fact that some Decembrists were freemasons, and one noted analyst has summed up the effect of their failure on Russia in the following terms:

> The severity of the punishments meted out, created a gulf between the autocracy, and large section of the intellectuals.[13]

Only when Alexander II became tsar in 1855 were the surviving Decembrists released from imprisonment. The breach with the intellectuals was never really healed.

There was no doubt who was tsar after the Decembrist conspiracy. The moral that Nicholas I drew from this challenge to the autocracy was an absolute one. 'Revolution is at the gates of Russia,' he said, 'but I swear that it shall not enter as long as I have breath in my body.' His regime became a byword for archaic repression and blinkered nationalism.

Mistrust bred inefficiency though. Nicholas trusted no one and therefore took far too much upon himself. The files about the great poet Pushkin bear witness to his insistence on personally interviewing dissidents, and there are stories about the Tsar of All the Russias bursting into schoolrooms and lecturing wretched schoolmasters on their failings!

Nicholas was anxious to know everything about his people, and it was for this reason that he instituted the infamous Third Section of the Imperial Chancellery, which was to evolve into the Okhrana or secret police. Its task, the tsar told its first commander, General Benckendorff, was to be the 'eyes and ears' of the autocracy, but its original brief of information-gathering soon became plain spying and repression.

Afraid then of dissent and revolution, Nicholas tried to mould the Russian empire into a homogeneous, conformist shape. So the motto of the new reign was to be 'Orthodoxy, Autocracy, Nationality', and while the 1990s has its 'glasnost', the 1830s had its 'narodnost' or nationality principle. Loyalty to Church, Tsar and Empire were to be paramount. Those who could not conform to the tsar's image of a good Russian suffered accordingly. Catholic Poles and Lithuanian Uniates were persecuted because they could not accept the Orthodox Church (Baltic Protestants escaped only because Nicholas did not want to upset his steadfast Prussian ally). Autocracy meant absolute acceptance of the authority of the Batyushka; those who could not accept it had only to recall the fate of the Decembrists. Narodnost meant the dominance of Russian language and culture in the empire; when the Poles and Finns tried to challenge this principle they were ruthlessly crushed. Thus, while it was the education minister Count S.S. Uvarov (1786–1855) who invented the slogan 'Orthodoxy, Autocracy, Nationality', it was Nicholas I's myopic determination which gave it life.

EDUCATION

Uvarov himself was the agent of repression in the education system. No longer were students to be allowed to study abroad or to hear lectures on philosophy or literature. Instead they were to wear uniforms while they attended university, and be subject to the watchful eye of the secret police. Only the most privileged could in any case purchase such an education. The lower orders had nothing because, as one celebrated historian has observed, successive tsars held the 'conviction, which actually increased as economic possibilities improved, that the lower orders were best left in ignorance'.[14]

It would be easy to jump to the conclusion that Nicholas was a hopeless reactionary who was blind to the faults of Russian society, but this was not the case. Nicholas identified serfdom as 'the indubitable evil of Russian life' and was prepared to see that the state serfs were better administered, but he was fearful of the political consequences of abolishing serfdom for, if 'the power of the landowner over the serf were removed, what would replace it'?[15] The tsar did not understand how the inefficiency of serfdom affected Russia's economy or register the fact that half of her serf population was privately owned.

Poland

The need for caution in assessing the record of Nicholas I is underlined by his treatment of Poland. Indeed, it was the Polish Prince Lubomirsky who pointed out the contradictions in the tsar's own personality:

> a bizarre mixture of defects and qualities, of meanness and greatness, brutal and chivalrous, courageous to foolhardiness yet faint-hearted as a poltroon, just yet tyrannical, generous and cruel, fond of ostentation and liking simplicity.[16]

The generous side of Nicholas's nature seems to have predominated in the early years, as far as Poland was concerned. It prospered under Lubiecki as finance minister and had been allowed to retain its Diet. Naturally the Poles were not content with this situation. The liberals wanted the Diet to have more power, and the conservatives demanded the restoration of Lithuania and the Ukraine (which had both been part of Poland before partition).

Aspiration took the form of physical force on 29 November 1830 when Polish officer cadets seized the Belvedere Palace in Warsaw and forced the Grand Duke Constantine to flee. This was the signal for a national uprising against tsarism, which lingered on into 1831 as the Poles waited vainly for Anglo-French assistance. Here was a situation tailor-made for Nicholas the soldier, and there were no half-measures. General Paskevich was let loose on the Poles and carried out a so-called 'pacification' of the country. Hundreds were executed; 180,000 were deported to Siberia, and with them went Poland's brief flirtation with self-government. The Sejm (Diet) was abolished, together with the separate Polish army and bank. It was a traumatic episode in Polish history, which led to the phenomenon known as 'the Great Emigration', a flight of Polish intellectuals which represented 'the most extraordinary block of talent ever to transfer itself from one country to another until the Jewish intellectual emigration from Germany and Austria to the United States a hundred years later'.[17]

Interestingly, Nicholas I's father, Tsar Paul, had opposed Suvorov's pacification of Poland in 1791 (mainly to annoy his mother). Contemporaries were to note that as Nicholas grew older he grew more and more like his eccentric father.

THE ARMY

Nowhere was this resemblance more marked than in matters military. Unlike his brothers, Alexander and Constantine, Nicholas had been brought up by his father at Gatchina in an atmosphere of Prussian-style militarism. At the age of three he was made a present of a Guard's uniform, and at twenty-one his obsession with the army was such that his mother warned him lest 'military trifles should interest him more than they ought'.

In 1818 Nicholas was promoted to the rank of colonel in the Izmailovsky Guard Regiment, which later caused Pushkin to quip about 'the execrable sovereign, but distinguished colonel'. As is often the case with those obsessed with military matters, Nicholas was not a good soldier; and his one experience of direct command, in the Turkish War of 1829, was a failure. In tandem with the ageing and promoted Field Marshal Paskevich, he controlled the minutest details of army life, right down to its ridiculous precision goose step.

Foreign Policy

Ironically, in view of his universal reputation as a martinet, Nicholas was more skilful as a diplomat than he was as a soldier. He had, according to a student of Russian military affairs, a 'quick wit and fluent speech in many tongues; he was cunning and devious and he shamelessly flattered the heads of state and their diplomats in the pursuit of his own ends'.[20] He was also cautious and pragmatic when need be. Russia could have taken greater advantage of the revolts of the Ottoman sultan's overmighty vassal Mehmet Ali (1833 and 1839) if another tsar had been on the throne. But Nicholas regarded Mehmet Ali's first revolt as 'a germ of evil and disorder' and sent troops to *save* the sultan from the rebels. The resultant treaty of Unkiar Skelessi (1833) expressed Ottoman gratitude. A secret clause closed the Straits into the Black Sea to foreign warships, and acknowledged the 'predominance of Russia in the affairs of the Ottoman Empire'.

This success, achieved with a minimum degree of force, was undoubtedly a diplomatic triumph for Nicholas, which might have been preserved had Mehmet Ali not tempted fate a second time. This brought about British naval intervention against him, and led to the Straits Convention of 1841. It effectively neutralised the Straits by closing them to foreign warships, but Nicholas recognised that the Russian navy was far too weak to challenge Britain's. This realism disappeared after the tsar's famous visit to Britain in 1844 (leaving a shield at Windsor Castle which could still be seen during President Gorbachev's visit in 1989). Nicholas was already notorious for referring to the Turkish empire as 'the sick man of Europe', which had an ominous ring for British ears.

Cyprus was held out as the bait in exchange for Constantinople, and Nicholas seems to have convinced himself that Britain would accept the partition of the Ottoman empire.

The tsar reverted to his role of universal gendarme as European states were convulsed by revolution in 1848. Russian troops helped to crush the revolt in Hungary in 1849, and the threat of them at Olmütz in 1850 forced Prussia to accept the renewal of Habsburg domination in Germany. Nicholas assumed, quite wrongly, that Austria would show her gratitude by supporting him over the Eastern Question. His loss of touch was also demonstrated by his erroneous conviction that Constantinople had become a refuge for Polish malcontents.

Misunderstanding led to war in 1854, by which the time other influences began to make their mark. One was the French emperor, Napoleon III (1852–70), who had been insulted by the tsar's refusal to address him as 'Brother' (true to form Nicholas I couldn't abide upstarts, and Napoleon had seized power in an 1851 coup). Another was the Franco–Russian feud about the Holy Places in Palestine, which the French claimed should be placed in their custody. Nicholas was also claiming the right to protect *all* the sultan's Christian subjects, whereas the 1774 Treaty of Kuchuk-Kainardji only allowed him to protect the Orthodox ones. This contest was won by the French, but Nicholas was not prepared to accept the decision. Instead he sent the blundering Prince Menshikov to Constantinople; Menshikov's brief was to bully the sultan into agreeing to Russia's demands by a mixture of threats and diplomacy, while the tsar promised all things to all men. Britain was promised Cyprus or Egypt, France Crete, Austria the Adriatic, if only they would agree to the partition of 'the sick man'.

In fact, Nicholas seems to have accepted that France would be hostile, but hoped that Britain would be neutral. In every respect he was proved to have miscalculated. Britain would never accept partition, and her ambassador in Constantinople, Stratford de Redcliffe, completely undermined Menshikov's mission. Worse, Austria was offended by the tsar's patronising tone to Emperor Francis Joseph (1848–1916) and made no response to his overtures. At the last moment Nicholas hesitated, telling Paskevich, 'It is easy to begin war, but God alone knows how to end it.' But the delusion persisted that a military demonstration would overawe the Turks. On 2 July 1853 Nicholas ordered his troops across the River Pruth, into the Turkish provinces of Moldavia and Wallachia.

In doing so Nicholas was the victim of his own propaganda, because his army was in no state to deal with a possible Anglo-French response.[18] The infantry was obsessed with using the bayonet, the artillery inadequate, even though Lord Lucan, who commanded the British cavalry in the Crimea, observed of its Russian counterpart that it was 'as bad as could be, but the Cossacks could be damnably troublesome to an enemy, especially in a retreat'. Sadly for Nicholas, the Cossacks couldn't win the Crimean War unaided.

The Crimean War

Delusions about the attitude of the Great Powers were then followed by short-lived hopes of victory as the Russians annihilated the Turkish fleet in Sinope Bay in November 1853. Unfortunately for the tsar, this action coincided with the last diplomatic feelers put out by his foreign minister, Count Nesselrode, and it enraged the powers. More than anything else the 'massacre of Sinope' precipitated the Anglo–French decision to intervene against Russia. Once they did so, Russian shortcomings were laid bare by

the fortunes of war at the Alma, Balaclava and Inkerman (1854). This was not because the Russian soldiers lacked courage but because they were commanded by incompetents. Bad though Lord Raglan might have been (he had to be reminded that Britain was not fighting France), the Russian commander-in-chief, Prince Menshikov, was even worse. A product of imperial nepotism, he was such a dedicated careerist that 'he never declined an honour, or refused a post, whether it was deserved or whether it was in his power to fulfil its duties'.[19] Insanely, he had also been made Commander-in-Chief of the Black Sea Fleet!

The object of the Allied expedition to the Crimea was the capture of the great Russian naval base at Sevastopol. Here at least the Russians emerged with some credit, because the skill of the great engineer Totleben allowed its defence to be extended into the autumn of 1855. That it was, however, was due to the allied failure to follow up their victory on the Alma immediately. The news from Balaclava broke Nicholas because, as de Grunwald wrote, 'the brilliant insubstantial pageant of his reign had vanished'. He now bitterly regretted that he had not listened to Paskevich and the Tsarevich Alexander and avoided hostilities. On 27 February 1855, he belatedly dismissed the wretched Menshikov, but it was too late. On the morning of 2 March Nicholas died, as much a victim of the war as his troops.

The Arts

The national humiliation in the Crimea should not blind us to the significant artistic achievement of Nicholas's reign. This despite the fact that the shock of the 1848 revolutions finally expunged any lighter shades in the tsar's personality. The cultural flowering of the period was personified in particular by the figure of Alexander Pushkin (1799–1837), the greatest of Russian poets and the most influential. It was Pushkin who gave the Russians a sense of national consciousness in poems like *The Bronze Horseman* (1833), which gives us this image of Peter the Great:

> Ah, lord of doom
> And potentate, 'twas thus, appearing
> Above the void, and in thy hold
> A curb or iron, thou sat'st of old
> O'er Russia, on her haunches rearing.

Pushkin

He also wrote, in *The Captain's Daughter* (1836), a favourable account of the Pugachev revolt of 1773, and subsequently wrote a history of it. Small wonder then that Pushkin was regarded as a subversive in the Russia of Nicholas I. Whether, as has been alleged, his death in a duel was the work of a government agent provocateur is uncertain, but the tsarist authorities had good reasons for wanting to be rid of him, and the death of Pushkin's contemporary Mikhail Lermontov (1814–41) in similar circumstances suggests that there is a case to answer.

All the plays of Nikolay Gogol (1809–52) were written during the reign of Nicholas I, and he had a sharp eye for the absurdities of contemporary Russia. *The Government Inspector* (1836) is a marvellous send-up of the bungling tsarist bureaucracy, while *Taras Bulba* (1834) gives the story of the romantic fighting Cossacks. *Dead Souls*, with its description of the plight of the peasantry, is perhaps Gogol's greatest masterpiece.

The role of this literature of subversion was vital in a society which lacked representative institutions and had to express its frustrations through an amazing galaxy of nineteenth-century novelists and playrights. Yet the literary community itself in the 1830s and 1840s provided a battlefield for the age-old debate about Russia's relationship with the West. One group known as the Slavophiles rejected western influence because it was both individualistic and materialist. Thus men like Khomyakov, the Aksakov brothers and Kireyevsky longed for the restoration of old Russian values and rejected the autocracy. In their view, the Russian Orthodox Church would provide the social unity which the tsarist autocracy had destroyed.

Others looked westwards. The literary critic Belinsky admired western culture, while Chaadayev advocated the adoption of Roman Catholicism. Union with Rome, he believed, would restore the cultural union with the rest of Europe which the Mongols had destroyed. It was Alexander Herzen (1812–70) who memorably described Nicholas I's reign as the 'plague zone of Russian history' but he cannot be labelled either as a Slavophile or a Westerner. Like many Russian writers, Herzen was an admirer of the purity of rural existence, and his novel contribution was to make the link between the *mir* (village) and the evolution of socialist forms. This was to influence the thinking of the Narodniks (populists) of the 1860s and their successors, the Social Revolutionaries.

Herzen's damning remarks about the reign seem to be endorsed by the government's arrest of the members of the Petrashevsky circle in 1849 (although this was the work of the ordinary police rather than the Third Section). Notable mainly for the presence of the young Fyodor Dostoyevsky in its ranks, the circle was little more than a discussion group which hardly represented a serious threat to the authorities. Even subversive thought, however, was not to be tolerated in the grim climate of post-1848 Russia.

Writing in the same year that the Petrashevskyites were arrested, the historian Granovsky expressed in vehement form the despair and frustration of his fellow intellectuals:

> Russia is nothing but a living pyramid of crimes, frauds and abuses, full of spies, policemen, rascally governors, drunken magistrates and cowardly aristocrats, all united in their desire for theft and pillage and supported by six hundred thousand automata with bayonets.

Granovsky went on to say that the 'dead are the lucky ones. If only one could wipe out this intolerable state of things.' It is a severe judgement, yet the gap between the writer and the hated tyrant was not perhaps quite as great as he suggests. Nicholas I was certainly intelligent enough to discern what was wrong with his empire, but his upbringing and philosophy made him quite unable really to address its problems. They in turn were a product of the ideological straitjacket which Peter the Great and his successors had placed around Russia.

CHAPTER ELEVEN

Reform and Reaction – Russia
1855–1894

Alexander II

The war into which the 'Gendarme of Europe' took his native Russia in 1854 left his successor Alexander II (1855–81) with a most unpromising legacy. A contemporary *Punch* cartoon showed the young Alexander pulling on his imperial boots while cannonballs whizzed around his head, and it is a good image. The Crimean War destroyed the myth of Russian military might, but also left the country with serious social and economic problems which Nicholas I had done very little to address.

Alexander II remains an historical puzzle, more like his indecisive uncle Alexander I than his martinet father. He began in a blaze of glory and ended mourned by few as the victim of an assassin's bomb. For some he was the 'Tsar Liberator', for others a reactionary tyrant, while his essential personality remains elusive.

His greatest problem in 1855 was the turbulent state of the Russian countryside. In his father's reign there had been as many as 556 separate peasant uprisings, and while none posed the threat of the Pugachev uprising they were a substantial indicator of rural distress. These risings continued after 1855 and were an additional pressure on the new tsar to make peace as quickly as possible. A small victory over the Turks at Kars in 1855 did something to revive Russian spirits, but did not make Russia's military position any more tenable. The decisive factor here was an Austrian ultimatum at the end of that year which gave the tsarist government some three weeks to accept peace terms. A meeting of the State Council on 15 January 1856 decided that Russia must accept the inevitable or face war with the Habsburgs as well. Nevertheless there was bitter resentment in St Petersburg over Austria's role in the Crimean War, when Nicholas I had saved her from disaster in Hungary in 1849. At the time the tough Austrian Chancellor Prince Felix von Schwarzenberg remarked that Austria 'would astonish the world with her ingratitude'. She was to pay for that ingratitude in 1866.

In the meantime Russia had to accept the neutralisation of the Black Sea and the restoration of the provinces of Moldavia and Wallachia to Turkey. She also lost any special rights to protect the sultan's Christian subjects. Three hundred thousand Russian lives had paid for the collapse of Nicholas I's Near Eastern policy and, as one noted analyst has remarked, 'defeat in 1856 exposed the inadequacy of Russia as rarely before. A social system came to grief as well as a nation.'[1]

It is a paradox, though, that the shattering Crimean defeat may have been a blessing in disguise. For more than a decade Russia abandoned her Balkan pretensions, until the Franco–Prussian war of 1870–1 allowed her to revoke the Black Sea clauses of the Treaty of Paris (1856). During this period she annexed all the territory between the Black and Caspian Seas, and proceeded with the conquest of Turkestan. This was completed when Samarkand was captured in 1868. Alexander's major foreign policy oversight was to permit the sale of the giant territory of Alaska to the United States in 1867, for the very low price of $7.2 million. In the United States at the time this sale was nicknamed 'Seward's Folly' (after the Secretary of State responsible for it), but the loss was Russia's, although the tsar could hardly have foreseen the discovery of vast mineral wealth there.

The Emancipation of the Serfs

The tsar was quite sensible enough, however, to recognise the need for thoroughgoing land reform in Russia. This was admitted in his famous statement of April 1856 when he said, 'It is better to abolish serfdom from above rather than to wait for the time when it will begin to abolish itself from below'. A Reform Commission was then set up to examine the problem, which even the repressive Nicholas had recognised to be 'the indubitable evil of Russian life'. Unsurprisingly, the commission met considerable opposition from the landowning classes. This took formal shape in the so-called Bezobrazov Memorandum of 1860. This put forward the landowners' conviction that any concessions to the peasantry would be fatal to the fabric of Russian life.

It also highlighted Alexander's central dilemma. How could he free the peasants *with* their land without antagonising the landowners on whose support the regime relied? To do so would destroy the basis of the autocracy in Russia, which rested not on the will of the people, but on an alliance of throne, aristocracy and altar. If Alexander wished to take on the landed interest, he would need to enlist the support of the mass of the Russian people as well. This in turn would demand the concession of some form of representative assembly. Faced with such a choice, Alexander II opted to play safe. The imperial ukase of 19 February 1861 freed the serfs from personal slavery, but did not make a free grant of land as well.

The Emancipation Edict, as it is generally known, was in fact made up of a series of ambiguities. Although the serfs were no longer the personal property of the landowners, they had to pay for any land they received. These so-called 'redemption payments' were strung out over a period of forty-nine years and became quite onerous. By 1875 22 per cent of Russian peasants were already in arrears on their annual payments. Thus the peasants felt in some sense cheated by the whole arrangement. Before emancipation they had said 'we are yours, but the land is ours', but now it seemed that they had surrendered their security for the illusion of freedom.

Further ill-feeling was caused by the fact that state serfs received more land on average than privately-owned serfs, and that heads of households were made responsible for the collection of personal taxation. Nevertheless, there was a fundamental shift of power in the Russian countryside, away from the landowner to the *obshchina* or commune. The commune was composed of a series of villages (*mir*) and it now took responsibility for the enforcement of law and order and the movement of persons. In one sense little had changed: a passport system was retained, and the serfs still required permission (this time from the village elders) to leave their villages.

On the face of it the landowners gained most from the 1861 reform. They received more than the current market value of land given to the peasantry, and the level of redemption payments often forced the latter to work for them as wage labourers. Yet in the long run it was the landowners who lost most of all. Many were heavily in debt, and it has been estimated that as much as two-fifths of the money they received from the settlement was used up in settling these. The rest was used as income, and was not reinvested in agricultural improvements in the way the government had hoped. In part the landowners were paying for a lavish life style, which required many to keep expensive town houses in Moscow and St Petersburg where they drank and gambled to excess. But the decline of the landowning class in the closing decades of the nineteenth century was also a result of the peculiarly Russian pheno-menon known as 'Oblomovism', named after the literary anti-hero of Goncharov's novel *Oblomov*, a character of monumental sloth for whom getting out of bed in the morning presented a massive problem! While obviously overstated by Goncharov, this state of inertia and resistance to change proved to be a powerful obstacle to the sort of agricultural reform that Alexander wanted.

So for a variety of reasons the Emancipation Edict of 1861 was 'no solution to the peasant question, it created more problems than it solved, and difficulties piled up in the following years'.[2] Many Russians came to regard the reform as 'the great disappointment'. In fact there is an uncanny historical parallel between the emancipation of the serfs in Russia and Abraham Lincoln's freeing of the black slaves in the USA in 1863. Lincoln (like Alexander) recognised the evil nature of slavery, and that in addition no democracy could exist 'half slave and half free'. He too compromised in the Gettysburg Address by only freeing slaves in the Confederate-held states (a fact that is often forgotten). The black slaves received no land, but their freedom also proved to be an illusion in the bitter aftermath of the US Civil War in the southern states. Their disappointment therefore was as great as that of their counterparts in Russia.

Local Government Reform

The element of compromise in Alexander's reform programme was also evident in the local government reform which he introduced in 1864.

While the *Zemstva* or local councils were an innovation, they had powers which were severely circumscribed. They did have control of local education, health and communications, but their membership was strictly limited to the privileged classes. Nevertheless the existence of the *zemstva* did encourage aspirations about a national assembly or duma. The Moscow province *zemstva* went as far as to petition the tsar 'to complete the structure of the state by convoking a general assembly of elected persons of the Russian land'. Seeing a veiled request for a national parliament in this petition, Alexander II turned it down flat. It was, he reminded the representatives of the *zemstva*, his task alone to rule the Russian lands.

Once again it is possible to criticise the tsar for introducing a sort of 'halfway house' reform. But this is to make assumptions about the attitudes of educated Russians, not all of whom were admirers of western-style democracy. The criticism also ignores the positive aspect of the *zemstvo* reform which created a new class of *zemstvo* administrators who both favoured and encouraged reform. These officials were a powerful influence in the Liberal (or Kadet) party, which played a significant role in Russian politics before the 1917 Revolution.

Law and Education

Education was another area where Alexander II was an innovator, his instrument being the liberal minister of education, Golovnin. A series of reforms in 1863–4 both extended the scope of secondary education and removed the restrictions on subjects like philosophy which had been a feature of the reign of Nicholas I. Students were allowed to travel abroad and no longer had to wear uniforms, although the Okhrana continued to spy on university campuses. Unfortunately for the government, once concessions were made the students wanted more, a common problem for regimes which attempt to introduce liberal reforms. All the same, the Golovnin reforms were an indication of intent, even if they did not satisfy the radicalism of the 1860s. Legal reforms which granted the right of jury trial in Russia for the first time were also implemented. These were based on western models, and showed that Alexander had abandoned the crass anti-westernism of his father.

Where did it all go wrong therefore? In the Russian lands the crucial year was 1866, when a demented student called Karakozov (who believed that he was suffering from an incurable disease) attempted to assassinate Alexander. This event marks a clear watershed in the reign, but one which fits into a melancholy strain in Russian history.

Poland

In 1863 there was another Polish uprising, which lingered on into 1864 and was crushed with the usual severity by a Russian army some 350,000 strong. In this instance a conscious decision seems to have been taken to avoid any flirtations with Polish nationalism which had marked the earlier experiment with 'Congress Poland'. There was, as one writer on Poland notes, no possible compromise between 'the Russian tradition of total, utterly centralised and despotic authority and Poland's history of free speech and limited power'.[3]

The leader of the uprising, Romuald Traugutt, was hanged outside the Citadel in Warsaw in 1864, and the collapse of the revolt was followed by a series of reprisals. Thousands of Poles were sent into exile in Siberia, and a deliberate attempt was made to destroy Polish language and culture. Poles were excluded from important posts and there were forcible 'conversions' to Orthodoxy. None of this destroyed the fierce sense of Polish identity that has characterised that nation through centuries of suffering.

In one area alone did the tsarist regime show a degree of finesse in its treatment of the Polish problem. This was in its handling of the land question, whereby in 1864 Polish peasants were offered full ownership of their land, and an end to the labour duties they had traditionally performed for landowners. Here at least was a subtle attempt to take advantage of the Polish aristocracy's insensitive treatment of the peasantry, which departed from the usual Russian policy of brutal repression. Readers should note in passing the cynical role played in these events by Bismarck's Prussia. An agreement in 1863 provided for the handing over of those rebel Poles who had fled into Prussian Poland.

The Polish revolt, of course, knocks rather a severe dent in Alexander's claim to be 'the Tsar Liberator'. The real issue must be whether it was ever *realistic* to expect Alexander II, in his particular historical context, to be a 'Tsar Liberator'.

Reaction

The effect of Karakozov's attempt on the tsar's life was felt immediately in the Russian heartland, when Golovnin was replaced by the reactionary Count Dimitry Tolstoy. This was a clear signal that the real era of reform was over, although some limited reform did continue into the 1870s. There were, in particular, the army reforms of D.N. Milyutin, which codified Russian military law, created a general staff, and abolished savage punishments like flogging. Their impact in the short run was limited, and in the Russo-Turkish War of 1877 the same breakdowns of supply took place which had bedevilled the Russians in the Crimea.

As it was, Tolstoy rather than Milyutin was in tune with the themes of Alexander's reign after 1866. His 1871 reform banned literature in schools because it was deemed to be subversive, and the teaching of history was also severely restricted. In the following year the time devoted to the natural sciences was also cut back, so that as much as ten hours a week was devoted to handwriting, etching and drawing! Doubtless Nicholas I would have approved. The predominant motive behind all this was fear, because it was among the student population of Russia that opposition to the autocracy was strongest. Tolstoy hoped that state interference could produce future generations of docile students. He had clearly failed to learn from the experience of the previous reign.

Culture and Opposition

The separate themes of culture and opposition under Alexander II have been drawn together in this section of the chapter because they are interdependent. In Russia over the centuries, literature (in particular) has been the main vehicle for opposition to the regime, for the simple reason that no other one has been available. The history of tsarist Russia bears eloquent testimony to the fact that 'the pen is mightier than the sword'. The story of the opposition to Alexander II's government is also the story of a generation gap. It is salutary for us to be reminded of this fact in the 1990s, when generational tensions are frequently treated as if they are an entirely new phenomenon. In fact the parallels with modern times are uncannily precise in some instances.

It was student demonstrations in the early 1860s which forced the hand of Alexander and Golovnin, although on two occasions (1861 and 1863) the University of St Petersburg was closed down. The demonstrations in turn were the result of inadequate financial support from the state, malnutrition, and bad living conditions. But these very practical causes of student discontent were also linked to the idealism of a younger generation in revolt against the heavy-handed repression of Nicholas I. In this context, 1862 was the seminal year when Ivan Turgenev's great novel *Fathers and Sons* appeared (curiously it was conceived while the author was swimming off the Isle of Wight). The hero of the novel is Bazarov, an atheistic freethinker with a touching belief in the ability of modern science to solve all mankind's problems. Bazarov has been described as the prototype 'Nihilist' (although Turgenev (1818–83) always denied this intention) and he seemed to sum up the frustration of his generation with the 'status quo'. It was obvious to contemporaries that the 'Fathers' in the novel's title were the old men who had grown to maturity under Nicholas I.

It was this antagonism to the authoritarian values of old Russia which lay behind the Nihilist movement of the 1860s (from the Latin 'nihil' meaning nothing). The British historian D. Mackenzie Wallace tells us that the Nihilists hoped to:

> . . . introduce a new kind of social order, founded on the most advanced principles of social equality and Communism. As a first step towards the great transformation they had reversed the traditional order of things in the matter of coiffure: the males allowed their hair to grow long, and the female adepts cut their hair short, adding occasionally the additional badge of blue spectacles.

A second writer notes that the young Nihilists were regarded as 'godless, free loving, subversive, treasonous, indecent, dirty, and with menacing hair styles'.[4] The Nihilist phenomenon prompts the reflection that there is little essentially new about the state of the human race.

In the great panorama of Russian history, the Nihilists proved to be less influential than other movements of their period. While *Fathers and Sons* is undoubtedly a great novel, it had less influence on mainstream political development than N.G. Chernyshevsky's *What is to be Done?* which appeared in 1864. If ever there was a model revolutionary it was Chernyshevsky himself, the ascetic idealist who spent much of his life mewed up in the infamous SS Peter and Paul fortress outside St Petersburg. A generation of Russian revolutionaries were to regard him as a father figure, and it was no accident that in 1902 one V.I. Lenin produced a pamphlet with exactly the same title as Chernyshevsky's novel. Chernyshevsky's strongest conviction was that young men of the 1860s were 'new men' who were characterised by their 'cold-blooded practicality, regular and calculating activity, active calculation'.

Unusually for his time he also detected the existence of 'new women', in the person of his heroine Vera Pavlovna who was 'one of the first women whose life has been ordered well'. Women were to have a high profile in the revolutionary movements which appeared in Russia in the last third of the nineteenth century. Most remarkable of all was the way in which Nikolay Chernyshevsky kept faith with the possibility of real change in Russia throughout a life of intense suffering and privation. A flavour of both his suffering and his courage comes across in this letter, written to his wife in 1871 from Siberia (after nine years of imprisonment and exile):

> Poor Russian people, a miserable fate awaits it in this struggle. But the result will be favourable and then, my dear, it will have need of truth. I am no longer a young man, but remember that our life is still ahead of us . . . I can speak of historical events because I have learned and thought much. My turn will come.[5]

There are echoes here of Pushkin's lament 'O God, how sad our Russia is!', but Chernyshevsky recognised the amazing tenacity of his fellow countrymen in this letter. He well deserves the tribute paid to him by the British historian Edward Hallett Carr. 'It was Chernyshevsky,' Carr wrote, 'more than any other one man, who shaped the moral attitudes of two generations of Russian revolutionaries.'[6]

But modern western readers might have reservations about his insistence in 'cold-blooded practicality', which had some gruesome consequences. No one could have been more cold-blooded than Chernyshevsky's contemporary Nechayev, the leader of a revolutionary group called the Avengers. Nechayev was a 'grim fanatic . . . ready to use blackmail, lies and violence to attain his ends',[7] and responsible for the murder of one of his colleagues, Ivanov. Thereafter Nechayev fled to Switzerland, but was extradited back to Russia and imprisoned for life. It has been suggested that Nechayev was the model for Dostoyevsky's hero Peter Verkhovensky, and the novelist did refer to the Nechayev–Ivanov case in a letter dated December 1870. But subsequently Dostoyevsky (1821–81) was to deny that Nechayev was the prototype for Verkhovensky, or Ivanov the model for the novel's victim Shatov. What is beyond doubt is Dostoyevsky's fierce personal opposition to Nechayev's particular brand of revolutionary fanaticism. Although the novelist had been a radical in his youth, and narrowly escaped the gallows in 1848, he thought that 'the strengthening of socialism in Russia was a direct threat to the country's future'.[8] Dostoyevsky's writings are full of references to 'the revolutionary disease' which he believed was the result of the weakness of 'the beautiful souls', the weak-kneed liberals of the 1840s who had fathered a generation of subversives. He would therefore have rejoiced over the fate of Nechayev and his fellow revolutionaries, and in *Crime and Punishment* the fate of the murderer Raskolnikov showed Dostoyevsky's detestation of all political extremism.

Nechayev's fate, however, also discredited the whole cause of radicalism in Russia for, as J.N. Westwood has pointed out, 'many who had been sympathetic to radical thought came to believe that all revolutionaries resembled these cold-blooded conspirators'. Radical youth itself began to search out more peaceful means of reform, and this strain of opposition reflected itself in the *narodnik* or populist movement of the 1870s (see below).

The maverick figure in the history of nineteenth-century Russian literature was Leo Nikolayevich Tolstoy (1828–1910) who has been described as one of the great subversives of the period. Unlike Turgenev, Tolstoy rejected the pretensions of modern science, but he also rejected Dostoyevsky's devotion to the traditional aspects of Russian life

Leo Tolstoy

(especially religion). Tolstoy's belief in the simple virtues of peasant life was reminiscent of Rousseau's 'noble savage', but he had begun his own life as a brilliant, well-travelled aristocrat with every advantage. His later life was ruled by a few simple Christian precepts like 'Judge not lest you be judged', and a simplicity of lifestyle which caused him to give up his own considerable royalties in 1891.

These were the product of the prolific sixties and seventies when *War and Peace* and *Anna Karenina* were written. The former, the best known of Tolstoy's novels, was a powerful polemic against both war and the 'great man' theory of history in which the corruption of Bonaparte is contrasted with the innocence of the central character Pierre Bezukhov (probably based on the novelist himself). Tolstoy shared the populists' central preoccupation with rural life, but unlike them he wished to preserve its traditions.

MUSIC

The nineteenth century was a period of tremendous musical achievement in Russia, associated with the group of composers known as 'The

Five' – Rimsky-Korsakov, Borodin, Mussorgsky, Cui and Balakirev.

Of this five Rimsky-Korsakov (1844–1908) was the most influential, not only because of his own works like *Mlada*, but also because he was able to orchestrate the works of others like Mussorgsky's *Boris Godunov*. Rimsky-Korsakov was scathing about other European music (describing Chopin as 'a nervous society woman') but he did influence non-Russian composers like Ravel.

Mussorgsky (1839–81) has been described by the contemporary Soviet pianist, Viktoria Postnikova, as the most Russian of composers, and he fell victim at an early age to that traditional vice of the Russian aristocrat, drink. He was born in the village of Karevo near Pskov, a desolate barren area, whose flavour comes over perhaps in Mussorgsky's best-known work, 'Night on the Bare Mountain'. A child prodigy who was able to play a concerto at the age of nine, Mussorgsky was profoundly influenced by the folk songs of his region and the music of the Orthodox Church. In later years he became something of a nationalist mystic who described the Kremlin as 'a sacred antiquity' and was deeply affected by his move from St Petersburg to Moscow. After his arrival in Russia's old capital, Mussorgsky declared that 'everything Russian suddenly seems very close to me'.

But the composer still retained his sense of humour and felt no qualms about satirising the Orthodox Church in his piece 'The Seminarist'. It was, therefore, a tragedy for Russian music that Mussorgsky killed himself, in a misguided effort to keep up with the booze-centred lifestyle of his colleagues in the Preobrazhensky Guards Regiment. It was left to Rimsky-Korsakov to arrange 'Night on the Bare Mountain' for posterity.

Borodin was the most remarkable of 'The Five' because he also had an international reputation as a chemist. Indeed he claimed that he could only compose pieces like 'The Polovtsian Dances' when he was too ill to give his lectures on chemistry. By comparison, Balakirev and Cui were little known outside their native Russia.

Peter Ilyich Tchaikovsky (1840–93) was not an intimate of 'The Five' but his output was prodigious and compositions like *The 1812 Overture* and *Swan Lake* are standards at modern concerts. Some Russians thought that Tchaikovsky was influenced too much by western music, but his two greatest operas were based on Pushkin's *Yevgeny Onegin* and *Queen of Spades* and he could be influenced by native folk music as easily as Mussorgsky.

But if Tchaikovsky was something of a loner (he suffered from manic depression), the influence of Mussorgsky can be traced in Stravinsky's *Firebird* and Prokofiev's *The Love for Three Oranges*.

The Populists

The *narodniki* thought that the key to success in Russia was the winning over of the peasantry to political consciousness, and with it the mass support needed to bring down tsarism. Unlike the terrorists of the Nechayev school, they rejected violence and believed that their task was to educate the peasants concerning their role in Russian society. This was the thinking behind the famous 'going to the people' of 1874. It was an extraordinary happening. Some 3000 students and intellectuals went into the countryside, giving practical expression to the populist belief that it was their duty to 'serve the masses'. They were led by two members of the so-called 'repentant nobility', and these men, Lavrov and Mikhailovsky, were working off the accumulated guilt of generations.

But the populists got a dusty reception from the peasantry when they arrived in the villages. Who were these strangely dressed outsiders with their soft hands, asked the peasants? They had obviously never worked a day in the fields in their entire lives, and they became the objects of great suspicion. 'Can the chicken teach the egg?' said the peasants, using the form of an old Russian proverb.

The 'going to the people' was accordingly not a success, although paradoxically it seriously alarmed the tsarist government. Despite the obvious fact that the narodniks had no violent intentions, hundreds of them were arrested by the police in an action which soon proved to be counterproductive. When the government staged a series of mass trials of narodniks in 1875/6, their saintly demeanour only created a favourable impression on outside observers. Nevertheless, eighty of them were found guilty and transported to Siberia, on the spurious ground that they had been 'conspiring' against the regime. Of those whose background has been investigated, it is interesting to note that twenty-eight of the narodniks came from noble families, seventeen were the sons or daughters of priests, five were the children of government officials, five peasants, and three foreigners. It was alarming for the regime to see that so many of these young people were from the privileged classes, but its panicky reaction war characteristic of the drift into repression of the regime in the 1870s. As it did so the populists joined the Decembrist conspirators in the litany of revolutionary martyrs.

In one sense the *narodnik* movement represented Alexander II's last (albeit thin) chance of reaching any kind of consensus with the opposition. Instead, after the mass trial of the populists terrorism reappeared in the form of the 'People's Will', a group who believed that political assassination could bring about the changes they wanted. But the more peaceful tradition represented by the populists still remained, via the organisation known as 'Land and Liberty'. It still focused on the need to win over the peasantry, but its methods were too passive for some of its supporters, who set up the 'People's Will' in 1879. Those who rejected revolutionary violence set up the non-violent 'Black Partition', but it was their rivals who dominated the period between 1879 and 1881.

Meanwhile the shadows began to lengthen for Alexander II. He surrounded himself with reactionaries like the chief of police, Peter Shuvalov, and Trepov, the former governor of Kazan. A notorious case in 1878 involving the latter served to underline the extent to which the tsar seemed to have abandoned the liberal pretensions of his youth. This concerned a young woman called Vera Zasulich, who had seen her radical colleague Bogolyubov flogged on Trepov's orders. Incensed by this action Zasulich then shot and wounded Trepov in full public view. She was put on trial, but to the anger of the authorities the jury refused to convict the romantic young heroine and she was acquitted amid much popular rejoicing. Once again the government responded in a heavy-handed manner, this time by suspending jury trials for all those charged with political offences. At one blow the impact of Alexander's western-style legal reforms was destroyed.

Even the tsar's personal life seemed to be afflicted by sadness and confusion. In 1880 he married his long-standing mistress, Princess Catherine Dolgoruky, but the marriage was not popular at court and damaged his reputation. Increasingly, Alexander's last years were dominated by the attempts by the 'People's Will' to carry out their avowed aim of killing him. On one occasion the imperial train was blown up, on another one of the dining-rooms in the Winter Palace, but eventually nemesis caught up with the 'Tsar Liberator'. On 13 March 1881 a member of the 'People's Will' threw a bomb at his carriage. It missed. The tsar apparently then stepped down to question the captured assassin, while thanking God for his deliverance from death. At this point a second assassin in the crowd cried, 'It is too early to thank God,' and threw another bomb which blew Alexander's legs off. Fatally wounded, the tsar murmured, 'Take me home to die', and expired an hour and a half later.

On the surface it was an inevitable conclusion to a tale of failed hopes and unrealised expectations, but there is a twist at the end of Alexander's story. There was, it seems, a spark of the old reformism left, because Alexander had set up a special reform commission under General Loris-Melikov. This had suggested, among other things, that a duma be allowed and that the Okhrana should be temporarily suspended. It is known that on the very day of his death Alexander II was considering Loris-Melikov's proposals. Was he contemplating yet another turnabout to accommodate the radicals? This question can never be answered but it is one which has continued to intrigue historians ever since. This has not prevented some of them, like W.E. Mosse, from delivering a harsh verdict on Alexander's reign:

> Alexander proved himself not only a disappointing 'liberal' – if indeed that term can be applied to him – but more seriously an inefficient autocrat.[9]

The contemporary French diplomat Maurice Paléologue was kinder in his assessment.

> He was a great tsar and deserved a kinder fate . . . His was not a great intellect but he had a generous soul, very upright and very lofty. He loved his people and his solicitude for the humble and the suffering was unbounded.

It has been observed that Alexander's grandson Nicholas II, the last of the Romanovs, was the wrong man, in the wrong place, at the wrong time. Part of Alexander II's tragedy was that he *seemed* to be, for a while, the right tsar for the times. In this sense he was 'the nearly man' of modern Russian history, more a victim of the expectations of others than of his own.

Alexander III

The reign of Alexander III (1881–94) makes a melancholy sequel to the storms of the previous one. It contained all the evil features of Alexander II's reign without any of the redeeming ones. But from the outset there was no doubt about where this stern, unbending autocrat stood. In an ukase dated 13 May 1881, two months after his father's assassination, Alexander III proclaimed:

> In the midst of our great grief the voice of God commands us to stand bravely at the helm of the state, to trust Divine Providence, with faith in the power and truth of Absolutism.

The assassins of the 'People's Will' were ruthlessly hunted down, and subsequently their leader, Sophia Perovskaya, and four others were executed. The use of terrorism may therefore seem to the modern reader to have been counterproductive, because it was merely followed by even greater repression. Yet writing long after the events of the 1880s, Vera Figner, a member of the 'People's Will', was to deny any link with desperadoes like Nechayev.

> We never thought of forcing upon the majority of the people the will of the minority, and we never planned a government which would bring about revolutionary, socialistic, economic, and political changes by decree. If we had thought so, we would not have called our party the People's Will.

Sophia Perovskaya

The logic of her statement is irrefutable, but the validity of political terrorism as a vehicle for change remained a matter of great controversy in tsarist Russia. It was here particularly that the influence of Michael Bakunin (1814–76), the founder of modern anarchism and co-author with Nechayev of *The Revolutionary Catechism*, was so profound. In Russia, and throughout Europe, the 1890s were characterised by random acts of anarchist violence against political leaders, although in Russia these acts were more usually associated with a mainstream political movement.

Pobedonostsev and Repression

The extremes of repression reached under Alexander III were certainly sufficient to cause desperation. In another attempt on the tsar's life in 1887, one of the conspirators was Alexander Ulyanov, Lenin's elder brother, and his subsequent hanging had a profound effect on the young Vladimir Ilyich. It was a repression, though, which had a coherent philosophy behind it, whereas the repression under Alexander II was a last-ditch response to policies which had failed. The high priest of reaction, even more so than Alexander III himself, was Konstantin Pobedonostsev (1827–1907), the procurator of the Holy Synod, and personal tutor to Alexander and his son Nicholas II. As a walking personification of the values of Old Russia Pobedonostsev regarded parliamentary democracy as 'the great falsehood of our time', and as a cleric he saw the demand for it only as proof of man's fallen nature. Russia, he believed, would be preserved by the old alliance between Tsarism and Orthodoxy, so that 'he saw in state power a divinely appointed means for the conduct of fallen men through a transitory life'.[10]

The interests of absolutism dictated the rejection not just of parliamentary government, but also of a free press, the jury system, and popular education above the primary stage. Thus an 1889 reform sponsored by Pobedonostsev secured the abolition of the 1863 University Statute and the placing of all Russian universities directly under the ministry of education. Bizarre criteria (like the exclusion of the children of washerwomen) were then applied to restrict entry to 'the politically reliable classes'. Lower down the educational ladder, great efforts were made to found more church schools, to counteract what Pobedonostsev regarded as the covert atheism of the state system.

In 1882 the censorship was also tightened, but all Pobedonostsev's best efforts could not destroy the remarkable cultural flowering of the period. Throughout this time, Leo Tolstoy, Anton Chekhov (1860–1904) and Maxim Gorky (1868–1936) were writing their novels and plays.

ANTI-SEMITISM

The nastiest aspect of Alexander III's Russia was its racism. The earlier part of this chapter touched on the policy of 'Russification' in Poland, but its greatest victims were the Jews. Anti-semitism reached virulent levels under Alexander III, although it was not a new phenomenon in Russian history. What was new was the fact that the government of Alexander III enjoyed 'the melancholy distinction of being the first in modern Europe to use anti-semitism as a deliberate instrument of policy'.[11] This campaign was sparked off by the murder of Alexander II, which was conveniently, and wrongly, blamed on the Jews and led, in turn, to anti-semitic 'pogroms' in 1881–2. Persecution of the Jews remained at a constant level, until the climax of 1891–2 when they were expelled from Moscow altogether; they were then forcibly resettled in 'ghettoes' in the interior. It is significant that the most emotive words in the language of anti-semitism derive from this period: the 'ghettoes' and 'pogroms' of tsarist Russia were to populate large areas of London and New York with refugees from such persecution.

The Jews suffered most, but they were not alone. The so-called 'Old Believers' suffered because they refused to do military service. The Protestants and Catholics in the Baltic provinces of Latvia, Estonia and Lithuania were also persecuted. All in the interest of attaining the impossible cultural and religious unity which Alexander III and Pobedonostsev craved.

ECONOMIC POLICY

There was a curious irony in all this as well, because it flew in the face of the other major characteristic of the reign, the industrialisation of the Russian empire. This was masterminded by Sergey Witte (1849–1915), the son of a railway official and the only man of real ability in Alexander

III's government. Under his careful guidance the absence of a middle class in Russia to stimulate industrial development was covered by the institution of what was called 'state capitalism'. This meant that the Russian state provided the finance and planning needed to modernise the economy. Nevertheless a great deal of foreign capital was still needed and, as one commentator has pointed out, 'the encouragement of foreign capital was Witte's special preserve'.[12] French francs in particular flooded into Russia after the 1893 Franco–Russian alliance, and technical assistance was also provided. As a result Moscow became a centre for textiles, St Petersburg for machine-building, the Urals for mining, and Baku for petroleum. The beginnings of the rail network laid down in the reign of Alexander II also helped, and by 1890 Russia had 30,000 kilometres of railway.

Witte was disliked at court because he was a commoner and because he stood for innovation rather than tradition. He was tolerated because he could help to modernise Russia's creaking economy, and through it the military machine, but his economic reforms were resisted at every turn. Whether, as his wife the Empress Maria claimed, Alexander III would have resolved the crisis of 1917 had he lived is very debatable. In most respects he was a throwback to his grandfather, and if Nicholas I was 'the Gendarme of Europe' he was its Cossack.

Foreign Policy

Only in foreign policy can we discern absolute continuity. Once Russia had revoked the Black Sea clauses of the Treaty of Paris in 1870, the old obsession with Constantinople returned, and with it the desire to play the father-figure for all the discontented Slav minorities in the Ottoman empire. This tendency had always alarmed the British, and Anglo-Russian tensions focused on Bulgaria in 1876–8. In fact everyone got it wrong in the crisis over the so-called 'Big Bulgaria', which resulted from Russia's victory over Turkey in 1877. Although the Congress of Berlin forced Russia to agree to reduce the size of the new independent Bulgaria, the Bulgars were never to be the pliant clients that St Petersburg (and London) imagined. Nor were the Russians ever the threat to British India that Disraeli imagined. The buying up of the Suez

Canal shares in 1876 anyway ensured that Britain's land communications with the Raj were secure. It was in other areas of Russia's foreign relations that the 1878 settlement was to prove decisive, because Alexander II was not taken in by Bismarck's claim at the Congress to be 'an honest broker'. Instead he described him as 'a scoundrel' for forcing Russia to give way, and suspected (rightly) that the German chancellor was secretly arranging an alliance with Austria–Hungary. This 'community of blood', as Bismarck called it, appeared to threaten Russian security, and the tsar did not regard the vague-sounding 'Three Emperors' League' of 1872 (Germany, Austria–Hungary and Russia) as an adequate substitute. Although the actual terms of the 1879 Dual Alliance between Germany and Austria–Hungary remained secret, Russian suspicions were not allayed, and to mollify them Bismarck agreed to the signing of the 1887 Reinsurance Treaty.

All Russian policy after 1870 was conducted in the knowledge 'that the leading continental power was Germany',[13] and that Austria–Hungary was an impossible ally. Strong Pan-Slav elements inside Russia itself demanded freedom, not just for the Ottoman Slav minorities, but also for those Slav minorities like the Serbs, Ruthenes, and Slovaks behind the frontiers of the Dual Monarchy. Austro–Russian conflict in the Balkans was therefore inevitable and it would force Bismarck to choose between the two powers. Reluctant though they might be to admit it, the Russians knew that when confronted with such a choice Bismarck would choose Austria–Hungary.

In the end, it was Bismarck himself who caused the final rift in 1888. This was when the Russians approached the German Reichsbank for a loan, and the German chancellor ordered that their request should be rejected. His motives remain mysterious to this day, although fear of growing Russian industrial power could have been one. When Bismarck fell from power in 1890 the Reinsurance Treaty was still intact, but the damage had already been done before Kaiser William II decided to let it lapse. Disenchanted Russia had turned to France for her needed credits, and this financial link led directly to the Franco–Russian alliance of 1893. Even the reactionary Alexander III was prepared to listen bareheaded to the 'Marseillaise' in the interests of imperial foreign policy. The domestic problems which he left were not to be so easily solved.

CHAPTER TWELVE

War and Revolution
1894–1917

Nicholas II

The well-known saying 'Cometh the hour, cometh the man' has, of course, a corollary. There are some men, and women, for whom the times are manifestly out of joint and Tsar Nicholas II (1894–1917) was such a man. Nicholas was weak-willed, negative and of limited intelligence, characteristics which meant that he was easily influenced by those with stronger personalities than his own. To read the tsar's diary, one historian remarks, is to read the diary 'of a nobody, of a man transparently immature and of patently insignificant interests'.[1]

Nicholas was not helped by his upbringing. His martinet of a father gave him no real grounding in state affairs, although the tsarevich was sometimes allowed to attend meetings of the State Council and the Committee of Ministers. Otherwise life consisted of physical pursuits like shooting, cycling, skating and rowing; Nicholas would probably have been much happier as an obscure member of the landed aristocracy. As it was, the young tsar revered his father's memory, which was understandable, but also tried to rule in the same autocratic style, which was not. He was too indecisive to rule in Alexander III's style and sadly for him he did not know it. Thus, although the Dowager Empress Maria had considerable influence over her son in the early years, the tsar's weakness eventually turned to stubbornness in a hopeless attempt to live up to his wife's demand that he 'be a tsar'.

THE TSARITSA ALEXANDRA AND RASPUTIN

Nicholas II was not fortunate in his choice of spouse. By 1891 he had fallen hopelessly in love with Princess Alexandra of Hesse-Darmstadt. At the time she was nineteen while Nicholas was twenty-three, and they were both equally unprepared for the role history had assigned to them. Alix, or 'Sunny' as Nicholas called her, had spent much of her youth in Kensington Palace, under the watchful eye of her grandmother Queen Victoria. Nothing in her life had prepared her for the onerous duties of a tsar's wife. The couple were devoted to each other, with echoes of Victorian bourgeois parlours in the use of nicknames like 'Hubby' and 'Wifey'. But Alexandra was the stronger character, and her insistence on absolute loyalty to the throne cut her husband off from wise counsel, a tendency which grew stronger as the reign drew on.

After her husband, the tsaritsa's other obsession was religion. She had been reluctant to give up the Lutheranism of her youth, but once persuaded she adopted Orthodoxy with all the enthusiasm of the convert. This enthusiasm reached rather manic proportions when the Tsarevich Alexis was found to be suffering from haemophilia, the incurable blood disease which affected many European royal families because of the practice of intermarriage between them. Given the tsaritsa's deeply religious nature, this disaster convinced her that her son's condition was in some way a judgement on the whole family. It also made her an easy victim for the most famous of the *startsy*, Grigory Rasputin.

'Our Friend', as the doting tsaritsa called Rasputin, was a country priest of uncouth habits and unrestrained sexual appetites. This in itself was a remarkable testimony to his influence over Alexandra, who was a rather prudish product of Victorian court life. But its kernel was Rasputin's mysterious ability to stem the internal bleeding which was the most dangerous of the tsarevich's symptoms. The nature of this ability has long been a matter of controversy. One obvious explanation is hypnosis, but hypnosis cannot cure haemophilia, and Rasputin's biographer, Alex de Jonge, doubts if the *starets* ever had the capacity to hypnotise. What he did have was the power to dominate and provide the imperial couple with a link, however tenuous, with the peasant masses from which Rasputin had sprung. 'He was one of the very few persons who appeared before them at their personal invitation, and not in order to fulfil some aspect of imperial protocol.'[2]

Despite Rasputin's considerable reputation for womanising, there is no real evidence that his relationship with the tsaritsa was in any way a sexual one. Nor did he aspire to political influence, although he was often credited with doing so. Common and disrespectful to the aristocracy as he was, he was hardly likely to be popular at court.

The Government of Russia

Nicholas II had been so dominated by his father that the continuity between the two reigns is unsurprising. Pobedonostsev remained to protect the autocracy from the evils of the modern world, and Witte remained to attempt exactly the opposite, the modernisation of the Russian economy. Another paradox was created by tsarist Russia's alliance with republican France in 1894, but it is unlikely that Nicholas ever queried any policy initiated by his father.

Latterly Nicholas II was well served by Peter Stolypin, prime minister from 1906 to 1911, who alerted him to the unpopularity of Rasputin and the tsaritsa. Unfortunately his good work was often undermined by others like Plehve, the reactionary minister of the interior. The tsar's lack of judgement meant that he was likely to be unappreciative of the efforts Stolypin and Witte while grateful for the advice of the mediocre when it reflected the views of his wife.

THE LAND QUESTION

By the turn of the century the biggest problem facing the imperial government was the crisis in the countryside, which was reflected in a series of measures forced upon the government in the 1890s. First of all, it was evident that many peasants were hopelessly behind with their redemption payments, and these were cancelled altogether in 1899. The peasant and noble land banks were also amalgamated in 1896, and the new land bank was able to make loans at 4 per cent interest. The bank was able to acquire land in its own name, which it could then sell back to the peasantry.

The other major problem was 'land hunger'. Between 1877 and 1905 the average size of a peasant holding went down from 35 acres to 28, and the black earth provinces of European Russia were overworked. One solution was the traditional one of migration to the east, and the government encouraged this by setting up the Siberian Resettlement Bureau in 1896. The settlements were made along the route of the Trans-Siberian Railway, and three-quarters of a million people moved eastwards between 1896 and 1900. Siberia's new-found importance was acknowledged in an imperial ukase of 1900 which abolished its status as a penal colony, although offenders continued to be sent there. The autocracy continued to show its legendary inefficiency, however (1500 people had died in 1894 when a stand collapsed at Nicholas II's coronation), and the new settlement was badly organised. Some of the frozen new settlers abandoned their holdings and went home.

FINANCE AND INDUSTRY

Witte was well aware of the crucial importance of the agricultural sector in the Russian economy, but he was also aware of the political pitfalls associated with attempts to reform it. The landed aristocracy was opposed to reform, as was the interior minister, Plehve, and Witte was unwilling to sacrifice his career on the altar of agricultural interest. Witte concentrated therefore on the currency reform which he deemed to be essential if the notorious instability of the paper rouble was to be counteracted. His solution was to amass large gold reserves, by stimulating grain exports and placing high tariffs on foreign goods. Simultaneously he obtained large loans from Russia's ally France, and was able to achieve full convertibility of the rouble into gold at the beginning of 1897. Four good harvests between 1893 and 1896 materially assisted his achievement.

But there was a price to pay for all this. The peasantry were paying heavy indirect taxation on staple products like sugar, tea and vodka, while the high level of grain exports caused food shortages at home. The gentry, increasingly impoverished since the 1860s, also suffered because Witte's industrialisation drive needed a large labour force, which in turn needed low bread prices to survive. Only large landowners, using the most up-to-date methods, could survive in such a low bread-price regime and many smaller landowners were ruined. The bad harvest of 1897 resulted in a big rise in land sales which bankrupted many of the gentry, who were bought out by urban bourgeoisie and richer peasants.

THE MINORITIES

Nowhere was the Russian chauvinism of Nicholas II and Pobedonostsev more evident than in their treatment of the empire's racial minorities. In its draconian shortsightedness, it probably outdid the *narodnost* of Nicholas I half a century before.

FINLAND

Early victims of 'Russification' under Nicholas II were the Finns, who had been granted the status of an autonomous grand duchy within the empire in 1808. In 1898 the provocative appointment of Bobrikov, an extreme Russophile, as governor-general began the process of alienating the population which culminated in revolt in 1905. This included imposition of the Russian language, the disbandment of the separate Finnish army, and the appointment in 1899 of Plehve as secretary for Finland (a position normally given to a Finn). Russian legislation, against precedent, was also imposed and Finland lost its separate postal system.

ANTI-SEMITISM

The most deplorable example of government-inspired racism under Nicholas concerned the Jews, the traditional scapegoats of a poorly educated and credulous population. Both Alexander III and Nicholas II were rabid anti-Semites, and government-sponsored anti-Semitism produced its own backlash in the Jewish community. A 1905 secret police report from the Siberian military region showed that out of 5246 people under political surveillance, 1676 were Jews. (Significant revolutionary figures like Trotsky, Zinoviev and Rosa Luxemburg were Jews.) However, although there were isolated pogroms between 1881 and 1903, it was the events of the latter year and the government's disreputable role in them which do much to explain the political radicalism of the Jewish community.

They began at Kishinev in Bessarabia on Easter Day 1903 after a mendacious campaign against Jews in the local press. Stories circulated about ritual murders of Christian children by Jews, which were widely believed, and the local Jewish community was attacked. Many of them were killed including women and children, while the police stood by and did nothing. Only on the second day did the police intervene to end the pogrom. International opinion was outraged by the news, and the tsarist government was forced to dismiss the provincial governor and condemn the attack. Most suspect of all, however, was Plehve, now minister of the interior with overall control of the police force. He is known to have ordered the authorities in Kishinev not to move against the rioters lest the local population be 'inflamed' against the government. And he kept his job. A second less serious pogrom followed in August 1903 at Gomal in White Russia.

There is little doubt that the covert encouragement of anti-Semitism in tsarist Russia, presumably part of a misguided attempt to distract the population's attention from other ills, was completely counter-productive. It alienated foreign opinion, and was a recruiting agent for radical and revolutionary groups. The ideal of 'revolutionary justice' in the Jewish community also accelerated the flow of funds into the coffers of opposition parties. Some Jews voted with their feet and emigrated.

Despite the devastating evidence of 1903, a major caveat needs to be entered where anti-Semitism is concerned. It was not a Russian preserve, as the Dreyfus case in France in the 1890s underlined. Within months too of the end of World War II, with all that involved for European Jewry, there were pogroms in Poland where anti-Semitism was a traditional force in the countryside.

THE OPPOSITION

What Dostoyevsky had termed 'the revolutionary disease' grew apace during the reign of Nicholas II. It was now to be influenced by a foreign (though Jewish) implant, which the tsarist authorities did not take seriously and which cynics suggested they could not understand anyway.

Marxism had been brought into Russia by a translation of *Das Kapital* (Capital) in 1869, two years after the original version had been published, in German. Its influence was only felt slowly. This was because its message, though idealistic and methodical, appealed in the first instance to the students and intellectuals: by 1887, when the desperate terrorism of the 'People's Will' was the most obvious threat to tsarism, *Das Kapital* was the most popular book among Russian students. Conversely, the early Marxists had little contact with the masses, despite Marx's selection of the industrial proletariat as the instrument of revolution. It was precisely because Russia was so socially backward that Marx wrote off her revolutionary potential, because most Russians were peasants and lacked 'class consciousness'. In the 1880s and 1890s the tsarist authorities seemed to share Marx's reservations, allowing Marxist literature to circulate freely. The Marxists were known to oppose the random terror of the 'People's Will', and their half-baked discussion groups seemed to the Okhrana to be essentially harmless.

The first really important Marxist organisation was the 'Emancipation of Labour' group, which was set up by G.V. Plekhanov who is often credited with being the 'Father of Russian Marxism'. He was perhaps too dogmatic a Marxist to adapt readily to Russian conditions. Another watershed was the merging together in 1895 of some twenty Marxist discussion groups to form the 'Fighting Union for the Liberation of the Working Class'. It was led by two key revolutionary figures, Lenin and Martov, both of whom were involved in organising Russia's first real strike, by the textile workers of St Petersburg in 1896.

Serious rifts soon appeared in the ranks of the Marxists. To begin with they had a twofold strategy: a long-term one to bring about the destruction of capitalism via socialist revolution; and short-term to destroy the tsarist autocracy and establish some form of democracy. The second strategy also included very pragmatic aims, such as the achievement of an eight-hour working day.

THE RUSSIAN SOCIAL DEMOCRATIC PARTY

These two strategies were fused together in 1903 to form the Russian Social Democratic Party (RSDP), but the unity proved to be illusory. There were serious differences between Lenin's supporters (the future Bolsheviks) and Martov's (the Mensheviks). Lenin wanted a tightly disciplined, totally dedicated revolutionary party, while Martov favoured a much larger 'mass' party, which could take in 'hangers on' as well as activists. These views were to prove incompatible.

THE SOCIAL REVOLUTIONARIES

The old populist tradition of the 1860s was represented by the Social Revolutionaries (SRs), also known as the Peasant Party. This was what made them different from the Marxists who rejected the peasantry as an instrument of revolution. They also believed, like the 'People's Will', in the use of political assassination as a weapon against the autocracy, and were prepared to co-operate with the bourgeois liberal opposition while the Marxists were not. The Social Revolutionaries also accused the Marxists of wanting 'concentrated bureaucratisation'. It was an accusation which the passage of time was to prove all too accurate.

THE LIBERALS

The constitutional wing of the opposition to Nicholas II and his government was represented by the Liberal (or Kadet) party. The term 'Liberal' covered a multitude of sins in tsarist Russia. On the left were radical neo-socialists, and on the right were conservative *zemstvo* board leaders who wished somewhat optimistically, to point Tsar Nicholas in the direction of a constitutional monarchy. The latter grouping did not even demand a duma, but merely pleaded for more consultation between the tsar and his people. They were led by D.N. Shipov, the chairman of the Moscow *zemstvo* board, while the more radical Liberals were led by the historian P.N. Milyukov. Later on a distinctive group of *zemstvo* officials (rather than board members) formed a more radical group called 'the Third Element', who wanted a universal primary education system and the abolition of the separate legal status of the peasantry.

GOVERNMENT REACTION

In the long run, the survival of the Romanov dynasty depended on a cohesive response to the various strands of opposition in Russia. Clearly the constitutional liberals were the most attractive allies for the regime. In 1899, therefore, the then minister of the interior, Goremykin, who had some *zemstvo* experience, made an important concession to the *zemstvo* liberals by proposing to extend the *zemstvo* system to Lithuania, White Russia, the Western Ukraine and the Lower Volga.

Surprisingly, this initiative was opposed by Witte. In a memorandum to the tsar called 'Autocracy and Zemstvo', he put forward a curiously ambiguous argument whereby *either* the autocracy should be replaced by constitutional government, *or* local government should cease to be elected. Witte was obviously sitting on the fence for reasons linked to his own insecure position at court. His priority was his industrial modernisation programme, and to get it through he needed the help of the influential Pobedonostsev. To do so, he denounced the *zemstvo* Liberal demand to control primary education, because he knew that Pobedonostsev wished to keep it under clerical control. He also distrusted regional opinion, which he believed would side with the agrarian interest against his industrialisation plans. So he persuaded the tsar to reject Goremykin's plan and to sack him. Thereby the finance minister created difficulties for himself, because in 1902 he needed *zemstvo* support against the reactionaries.

Witte's canny ploy also had its effect on the attitude of the Liberals. The radicals were disillusioned by the government's tactics, and in 1902 they brought out their own newspaper *Osvobozhdenie* (Liberation) to challenge it. The editor, Peter Struve, subsequently joined the 'Third Element' in 1904 to found a new party called 'The Union of Liberation'. Its platform included demands for a secret ballot and the restoration of Finnish rights. But the Union still rejected revolutionary violence.

THE PEASANTRY

The great threat to Russia's social fabric was a peasant uprising. Normally passive and unquestioning, as the populists found to their cost, the peasants could pose a serious threat if they felt that their livelihoods were in danger. This was exactly the situation reached at the turn of the century in the Ukraine, where the peasants had been reduced to subsistence farming. In 1901 nearly 100 manor houses were burnt in the provinces of Poltava and Kharkov alone, and the tsar was frightened into appointing a special conference to look into the problems of agriculture. Witte, now fully alerted to these problems, was to act as conference chairman. A 58-volume report emerged in 1903 which recommended the abolition of corporal punishment, tax reform, and the end of separate class representation in the *zemstva*. Its most important result was the abolition of the collective responsibility for taxation which had been vested in the village commune (a result of the 1861 reform). Witte's influence was significant here but his power was on the wane.

Foreign Affairs 1894–1905

In 1905 crises in domestic and foreign affairs achieved a rare coincidence in Russia. The latter was the result of a new far eastern emphasis in policy, although in 1894 Russia did make her crucial alliance with France which pledged both sides to help each other in the event of war.

The focus for Russian policy in the Far East was Manchuria, where the expansion of the Trans-Siberian railway brought the Russians into conflict with the emergent power of Japan. Both powers also had interests in Korea, where Russian ministers like Plehve had commercial investments in timber. Russian admirals also wished to obtain another warm-water port to supplement Port Arthur, which they had obtained in 1898 after pressure on the Chinese. This was a particular snub to the Japanese, who had annexed Port Arthur after defeating China in the Sino–Japanese war of 1894. Russian ships which had been allowed to winter in Japanese ports lost this facility thereafter.

There was also a personal and racial tinge to Russian policy. In the faintly absurd 'Willy-Nicky' correspondence Kaiser William II (1888–1918) encouraged the gullible Tsar Nicholas to see himself as the protector of western civilisation against the 'Yellow Peril', and accorded him the meaningless title of 'Admiral of the Pacific'. In his memoirs Witte accused the kaiser of being 'the author of the war' of 1904–5, and William did have a tendency to refer to the Japanese as 'little yellow monkeys' in official correspondence.

Unfortunately, Tsar Nicholas was naive enough to fall for the kaiser's blandishments and his racial stereotyping. So did other members of the tsarist establishment who should have known better, although Witte consistently opposed a forward policy in the Far East. In the prevailing atmosphere of tension over Manchuria and Korea, the Japanese in 1902 sensibly made an alliance with Britain (the British had already trained their navy).

The Russo-Japanese War

By 1903 the Japanese realised that the Russians were not going to accommodate them over Port Arthur and Korea, and that as time passed Russia's numerical superiority would become an increasingly crucial factor. At that time the only rail link with the Far East, which had a gap around Lake Baikal, was the immensely long Trans-Siberian railway.

The military therefore argued for a sudden knockout blow against the Russian Pacific fleet at Port Arthur, before the Russians could make use of their superior numbers. Treaty restrictions dating from 1856 prevented Russia from using her Black Sea fleet, and the Baltic fleet would have to sail round the world to affect the issue.

On the Russian side there was grotesque overconfidence reflected by the fact that just one officer on the army staff was allocated to do intelligence work on the Japanese. Popular illustrations showed Russians crushing the Japanese pygmies with ease. They were due for a rude awakening. In February 1904 the Japanese broke off diplomatic relations and launched a surprise torpedo attack on the Pacific squadron inside Port Arthur. This attack crippled part of the Russian squadron and bottled up the rest inside the harbour, where it remained for the rest of hostilities. The advantages of geography then allowed the Japanese to send troops across the Yellow Sea to the hinterland of Port Arthur and lay siege to it.

After a lengthy siege, and considerable Japanese losses, Port Arthur fell in January 1905, an event which was to have considerable internal effects in Russia as well. Some weeks later the Japanese also won the great land battle of Mukden in Manchuria, which effectively ended Russian involvement there.

What followed seemed to underline history's propensity for repeating itself as farce. The Baltic fleet, thrown desperately into the scales in an effort to save Port Arthur, left port so hurriedly that the painters were still on board. Every old tub that would float was sent, together with officers who were manifestly incompetent. En route, the Russians managed to create quite a serious diplomatic incident when they fired on British trawlers off the Dogger Bank in the North Sea, thinking that they were Japanese warships! The British then honoured their treaty with Japan by closing the Suez Canal, which forced the unfortunate Russian admiral, Rozhdestvensky, to sail around the Cape. The Russian warships were laden down with bunking coal, which was supplied to them by German liners although the 'Admiral of the Atlantic' (as the kaiser called himself) avoided direct involvement in the fighting.

Given that Rozhdestvensky's destroyers had been quite unable to hit a stationary target on gunnery practice, the sequel was to be expected.

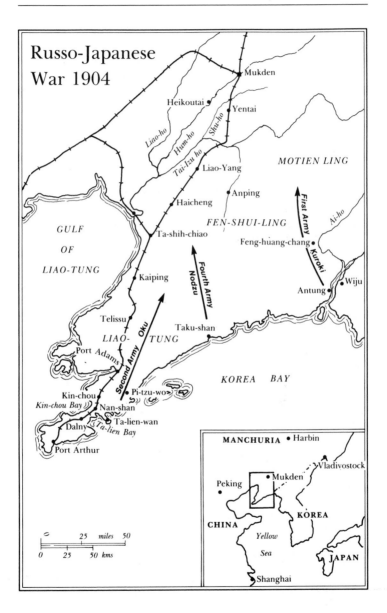

Russo-Japanese
War 1904

Mukden

Heikoutai

Yentai

Liao-ho

Hun-ho

Shu-ho

Tai-tzu ho

Liao-Yang

MOTIEN LING

Anping

Haicheng

FEN-SHUI-LING

First Army

Ai-ho

Ta-shih-chiao

Feng-huang-chang

GULF

OF

LIAO-TUNG

Kaiping

Fourth Army

Nodzu

Kuroki

Antung

Wiju

Telissu

LIAO-

TUNG

Oku

Taku-shan

Port Adams

Second Army

KOREA   BAY

Kin-chou

Kin-chou Bay

Pi-tzu-wo

Nan-shan

Ta-lien-wan

Dalny

Ta-lien Bay

Port Arthur

25   *miles*   50

0   25   50 *kms*

MANCHURIA   • Harbin

Vladivostock

Peking

Mukden

KOREA

CHINA

Yellow

Sea

JAPAN

Shanghai

When the Baltic fleet arrived in the Straits of Tsushima, one historian tells us,

> Rozhdestvensky confined himself to just two orders, the first of which caused 'mystification and dismay' while the second caused 'a state of chaos'. The complete destruction of the Russian fleet followed, much as Rozhdestvensky knew it would.[3]

Tsushima was perhaps a metaphor for the tsarist system, that strange mixture of blunders and ruthlessness. It took place six months after Port Arthur had fallen.

This strange war ended equally strangely with American intercession. Indeed, President Theodore ('Teddy') Roosevelt won himself the Nobel peace prize in his role as peacemaker. Under the terms of the Treaty of Portsmouth (New Hamphire), Russia gave up Port Arthur, left Korea, and evacuated Manchuria. The balance of power in the Pacific was significantly altered, and with it the myth of European invincibility was ended.

The 1905 Revolution

The news that Port Arthur had fallen proved to be just the catalyst that the various discontented fragments of Russian society needed. On 22 January 1905 (9 January by the old-style Julian calendar in use in Russia) a large crowd of demonstrators, many of them from the great Putilev engineering works in St Petersburg, converged on the Winter Palace where they mistakenly thought their 'Little Father' Nicholas was in residence. In fact he was staying at Tsarskoe Selo outside St Petersburg.

The demonstration was led by a mysterious figure, Father George Gapon, the organiser of the Union of Russian Factory Workers, who may have been an Okhrana double agent. A petition to the tsar, signed by 135,000 people, asked for modest concessions like improved wages and working conditions, and the granting of a duma elected by secret ballot. The management of this peaceful demonstration rested with the minister of the interior, Svyatopolk Mirsky, and the Grand Duke Vladimir, a member of the royal family. What happened on this notorious 'Bloody Sunday' in 1905 is still controversial, although at least one modern historian declines to believe that it 'could possibly have been an accident'.[4] As the crowd approached the Winter Palace volleys of rifle fire rang out from the awaiting troops, and at least 100 people were killed and another 3000 wounded. The news of this quite unprovoked horror spread rapidly throughout the empire.

What is the explanation for 'Bloody Sunday'? The coincidence of a printing strike in St Petersburg may have prompted a hardline reaction by the authorities, but the suspicion remains that the tsar was personally involved. His diary entry for that evening read 'God, how sad and grim', reflecting perhaps the reaction of the devoted family man. But this was the same tsar who had tactlessly taken his wife to a reception at the French embassy on the evening of the disaster at his coronation in 1894. The shadow of his autocratic father also hung over him, and he had sworn to preserve the empire in the manner his father had done.

Historians have rightly pointed out that there were not one but several interlinking revolutions in 1905. As the news of 'Bloody Sunday' spread through Russia's towns and cities, the whole of Nicholas II's vast empire was paralysed by strikes; by the end of the year two million workers were on strike. Peasants attacked landowners' property and set up a Peasants' Union to co-ordinate their efforts. There was a mutiny on the *Potemkin*, the flagship of the Black Sea fleet. Even the imperial ballet refused to dance! Strong as the protest movements were in the Russian heartland, they were stronger in the lands of the ethnic minorities in Finland, the Baltic states and the Caucasus. In Russian Poland troops had to be called out to deal with strikers in Lodz.

In the revolutionary moment, the revolutionaries were caught napping. Lenin and the RSDP were taken by surprise, although SR assassins accounted for the Grand Duke Sergey Alexandrovich and Count Shuvalov, the military governor of Moscow. Liberal constitutionalists formed a 'Union of Unions' which doctors, teachers, engineers and lawyers flocked to join. Milyukov, the historian, emerged as its leader.

The only advantage that Nicholas II had in this emergency was the elemental and spontaneous nature of the protests. His first response was to panic. In March, acting on Witte's advice, he issued a manifesto which reaffirmed the autocratic principle, but this made the situation worse.

By August he was willing to concede a duma, but not on the basis of universal suffrage. In October the whole of St Petersburg went on strike again, and during it the Soviet (or council of workers) appeared with Trotsky as its deputy chairman. These soviets then spread rapidly to other towns and villages all over Russia.

This radical development proved, in fact, to be the beginning of the end for the revolution, but in the short run it forced Tsar Nicholas to give way. On 30 October the tsar issued the so-called 'October Manifesto', which seemed to make Russia into a constitutional monarchy. A duma was to be set up, based on a very wide male suffrage, and the people were to be accorded civil rights and liberties. Again the crucial influence was that of Witte, brought back in the emergency to save his master's neck. The tsar said that 'there was no other way', but he and Witte saw the October Manifesto merely as a device to buy time. 'I have a constitution in my head,' said Witte, 'but as to my heart I spit on it.'

This example of *realpolitik* was to win the day because the aims of the professional middle classes had been achieved by the manifesto. Unlike the soviets they were now prepared to call off their agitation, and when the St Petersburg soviet tried to call another general strike in November, it failed. The ringleaders were arrested, and an uprising by the Moscow soviet in the following month was crushed. What the autocracy had conceded it could now claw back again.

In January 1906 the October Manifesto was reversed by the new 'Fundamental Law of the Empire', whose first article referred to the 'supreme autocratic power' of the tsar. Once again Nicholas II laid claim to the right to make war, control the Orthodox Church, and dissolve the Duma at a moment's notice. Constitutional government was further weakened by the tsar's control over the appointment of ministers and the military budget. Then, far from being grateful to Witte, Nicholas dismissed him.

The Emergence of Bolshevism

Leon Trotsky (whose real name was Lev Bronstein) called the 1905 Revolution 'a dress rehearsal for the real revolution of 1917'. But some of the major players in the October 1917 Revolution were not even on stage in 1905. Lenin certainly had to rewrite his revolutionary script to accommodate the unpalatable fact that the peasantry, far from being 'reactionary', had attacked the landowners. The result was a distinctive Marxism–Leninism which gave the peasants a revolutionary role and conceded (which Marx had not) that backward Russia might achieve socialism before the advanced west.

The formal split between Lenin's followers, the Bolsheviks (or majority in Russian), and Martov's Mensheviks (minority) occurred at the Prague Conference of the RSDP in 1912. Trotsky, the hero of 1905, remained a revolutionary maverick. He couldn't stomach Lenin's authoritarianism, what he called 'Bonapartism', and remained outside the Bolshevik Party until the eve of revolution. Meantime, in 1912 Lenin founded the party newspaper *Pravda* (Truth) from exile, and inside Russia the Bolsheviks inspired a serious strike in the Lena goldfield. Lenin also moved from exile in Paris to Cracow in Austrian Poland to be nearer to his homeland. The First World War when it came was attacked as an 'imperialist war'. Lenin predicted that the capitalist powers, including Russia, would destroy themselves and create the stage for socialist revolution. Other Bolsheviks, like the youthful Stalin, disagreed and rallied to the national defence.

The Failure of the Duma

The weakness of the Duma, was soon demonstrated. The First Duma lasted only seventy-three days because it had the temerity to put forward a reform programme. This included a political amnesty, universal suffrage, and the abolition of the death penalty. Additionally the ministers were to be responsible to 'elected representatives of the people'. Predictably, these demands were declared 'inadmissable' by Tsar Nicholas, and subsequent dumas proved to be just as impotent.

The Stolypin Reforms

Peter Stolypin was appointed minister of the interior in 1906, and in June of that year became prime minister. Like Witte, Stolypin was unpopular at court, partly because he warned Nicholas II against Rasputin's excesses. Despite this, during his period in office (1906–11) Stolypin was able to offer the only serious solution during Nicholas' reign to the central problem of agriculture. His strategy was to use agrarian reform as a buffer against revolution and so win over the peasantry to the side of the Romanovs. He began by abolishing communal land tenure, and by 1915 half the farms in European Russia were held by hereditary tenure. The peasants were also encouraged to increase the size of their holdings with big loans from the Peasants' Land Bank.

Land hunger continued to be a problem, and Stolypin encouraged the process of 'internal colonisation' (people settling in Siberia). His difficulty was that primitive technology and a rising rural population made progress slow, and his reforms did not quieten the general level of discontent. He was quite prepared to be repressive and this ambiguity in his policy made him few friends: his reforms made him suspect in the eyes of reactionaries, while the liberals resented the repression. In the end, Stolypin was a victim of his own policy, and in 1911 the double agent Bogrov shot him dead at the opera. The connivance of Rasputin is suspected but not proven; it is certainly true that the *starets* had reason to resent the prime minister, who constantly urged his exile.

Stolypin was cut down before he could see his policies through, and historians have speculated about whether his effort to win over the peasantry could have saved the dynasty (which celebrated its 300th anniversary in 1913). Had war been avoided it could perhaps have been saved, but the Stolypin reforms did have an adverse side. Those poorer, less efficient peasants who didn't benefit drifted into the towns and 'formed a rootless and unstable element',[5] prominent in the wave of strikes before 1914. The crucial factor really seems to be whether Nicholas II *would* have conceded the creation of a constitutional monarchy with really democratic institutions. The evidence suggests that he would not: he did not take the Duma seriously, and one of his last diary entries before the overthrow of his family referred to 'a fat ass' the Duma had sent to him in a final attempt to urge reform (it was Rodzianko, the president of the Duma).

Russia and the Coming of the World War

From 1871 to 1890 Russian foreign policy was dominated by a feeling of insecurity which demanded membership of the Bismarckian alliance system. Once Bismarck, with his awareness of the need for a Russian link, had gone in 1890, relations between Berlin and St Petersburg worsened quite rapidly. Kaiser William II was a young man in a hurry, who might encourage Russian pretensions in the Far East but certainly preferred the Habsburgs to the Romanovs in Europe.

Despite Russian blundering in the Far East after 1894, the Franco-Russian axis remained intact. Indeed, the 1905 disaster against the Japanese made imperial Russia more dependent on her republican ally. It also brought about a marked improvement in Russo–British relations through French auspices. In 1904 Britain and France had agreed an 'entente cordiale' which patched up colonial differences, and in 1907 Russia and Britain did likewise. There was no military agreement, but Russian and British spheres of influence in Persia were recognised, as was the unaligned status of Afghanistan. A Triple Entente (France, Russia, Britain) therefore faced a Triple Alliance (Germany, Austria–Hungary, Italy), but the British had signed no military pacts with anyone.

THE BOSNIA–HERZEGOVINA CRISIS

One immediate consequence of tsarist Russia's humiliation against Japan in 1905 was a redirection of her attentions to the Balkans. Her need for some sort of diplomatic success then made her the victim of what, in modern parlance, would be called a 'sucker punch'. In 1908 the then Austro–Hungarian foreign minister, Aehrenthal, innocently suggested that his country should annex the Turkish provinces of Bosnia–Herzegovina (modern Yugoslavia), which had actually been administered by Vienna since 1878. In exchange Russia should achieve her age-old dream of acquiring Constantinople, and her foreign minister, Izvolsky, jumped at the idea. He should have known better.

While Britain might tolerate a Russian presence in northern Persia, she had not abandoned her opposition to seeing Cossacks in Constantinople. Even France, Russia's ally, showed no great inclination to fight for the Dardanelles, particularly as the kaiser said that Germany would appear like 'a knight in shining armour' at Austria–Hungary's side in the event of conflict. Aehrenthal was, of course, perfectly aware of what the reaction of the other powers to his nefarious plot would be. So should Izvolsky have been, but Aehrenthal got his blow in first and annexed the provinces before Russia had a chance to act. As it was, Izvolsky's naivety brought Russia a second humiliation in three years. Yet Vienna's triumph was likely to be short-lived because Russia could not contemplate a third humiliation of this sort.

SMALL WARS AND A GREAT PROGRAMME

St Petersburg's immediate reaction to her Bosnia–Herzegovina setback was to press ahead with a massive rearmament drive known as 'the Great Programme'. It certainly alarmed the Germans, although Russia was only on the sidelines during the colonial crisis over Morocco in 1911. On paper the Great Programme seemed threatening: Russia's peacetime army would be two million men, three times bigger than Germany's; she would have 122½ infantry divisions to Germany's 96, and over 8000 field guns to her opponent's 6000. But, as one British historian has pointed out, 'beneath this weight, there was not much muscle',[6] because generals made the wrong choices (like putting their field guns in static fortresses).

In some respects the chaos in the Balkans in 1912–13 now seems like shadow boxing before the holocaust to come. Russia's protégé Serbia, a small, energetic Slav power, challenged both Ottoman Turkey and Austria–Hungary with her pretensions, as both had large and clamorous Slav minorities within their borders. Serbia had potential allies in Greece, Rumania and Bulgaria, powers equally anxious to take advantage of growing Ottoman weakness following the 'Young Turk' revolution of 1908. The First Balkan War (1912–13) was won by the Balkan League against the Turks, whose European territories virtually disappeared. Then Bulgaria became greedy about her share of the spoils, and in the Second Balkan War of 1913 she was punished for attacking her former allies. Turkey even managed to win back some of her lost territory.

As Bulgaria was a client state of Germany and Austria–Hungary, this result was greeted with satisfaction in St Petersburg, even if it did nothing for the general stability of Europe. Two facts were ominously significant. A war party in Vienna under Chief of Staff von Hötzendorff wanted to teach the Serbs a lesson, and Russia could not, and would not, allow her small Slav ally to be destroyed.

The War and the End of the Romanovs

The domestic problems referred to earlier in this chapter also created some support for the idea of a war against Austria–Hungary which would rally the nation to the 'Little Father', and when war did come in August 1914, it did just that. Nicholas II and his advisers would have done better to recall Plehve's foolish preference for 'a small, victorious war' in 1904, which had also seriously backfired in the face of the dynasty.

Russian entry into the war came because of Austria–Hungary's declaration of war on Serbia for her alleged implication in the assassination of the Archduke Franz Ferdinand (heir to the Habsburg throne) on 28 June 1914 at Sarajevo. Claims by Germany that Russia helped to precipitate general war because of her partial mobilisation on 29 July do not stand up, because she only put herself into the state of war readiness demanded by the vast size of her forces. The evidence suggests, by contrast, that Russia played a moderating role by advising Belgrade to accept an Austro–Hungarian ultimatum which would have virtually obliterated Serbian independence.

Russia's obligations under the terms of her alliance with France were clear-cut. Within fourteen days of mobilisation she was obliged to put two army corps, about 300,000 men, into East Prussia. The object of this move was to take the strain off her French ally who would bear the weight of the German attack under the notorious Schlieffen Plan. This obligation was met, much to the surprise of the Germans, when two corps under Generals Rennenkampf and Samsonov crossed the border into East Prussia. A minor victory was won at Gumbinnen, to be followed by catastrophic defeats at Tannenberg and the Masurian Lakes which put an end to the Russian intervention in Germany. It never happened again but it had served its purpose. Two German armies had to be switched away from the Battle of the Marne, which Germany lost, and General von Hindenburg had to be taken off the retired list to deal with the emergency. As the Schlieffen Plan was designed to knock France out of the war in six weeks, it can be argued that the Russian invasion of East Prussia was decisive.

Of course, it showed up the usual tsarist deficiencies. Messages were sent out in clear rather than in code (so the Germans had prior knowledge of Russian intentions), and no allowance was made for the different gauges of German railways. General Rennenkampf was accused (absurdly) of being a German spy, and Samsonov shot himself in despair in an East Prussian wood. But he had served his country and their allies well, and legends about Russian weakness had been exaggerated. Kochan and Abraham point out, quite rightly, that 'the tsarist Russian state entered the war in fairly good order'.[7]

Other exaggerations concern Russia's capacity to arm and supply herself. While the failed Gallipoli landings of 1915–16 prevented a link-up between the western democracies and Russia, this failure was by no means as catastrophic as it has often been painted. Research by Professor Norman Stone in the 1970s[8] showed that the tsarist autocracy was able to supply itself with shells quite adequately, and the most serious problems concerned transport. The disruption of the railway system in Russian Poland early in the war adversely affected the whole system, which never really recovered.

Otherwise, a sort of general pattern could be discerned. When faced with the Austro-Hungarian forces the Russians did well, helped perhaps by the unreliability of their fellow Slavs in the enemy forces. But when sizeable German forces were involved, as at Gorlice in 1915, the Russians came off second best. In part this was a matter of leadership, which was not assisted by the tsar's decision to move to Stavka (High Command) and take over supreme command himself. Nevertheless it remains true that in General Brusilov the Russians probably had the best general of the war, and one of the very few who was not obsessed by massive artillery bombardments and frontal bayonet attacks. Brusilov won striking successes in 1916, but Stavka did not have the reserves or the capacity to exploit them properly.

Russian losses were appalling (perhaps upwards of five million) but proportionately not as bad as those of France on the western front, and accounts of the imminent collapse of the Russian army in 1916–17 have been distorted. Gross inefficiency and cowardice are characteristics more properly attributed to the Rumanian army, where high-ranking officers were allowed to wear rouge. Their ill-advised intervention in

1916 wasted valuable Russian resources, and ended in final German occupation of their country.

The February Revolution

By the beginning of 1917 war-weariness and heavy losses had affected the soldiers' spirits, but the army was still a cohesive fighting force. There was resentment against the tsaritsa, Rasputin's alleged influence, and to a degree against the tsar himself although the old belief in the essential goodness of Batyushka died hard. The people could not have known that Nicholas, dominated as ever by his wife, was ending his letters to her 'your poor weak-willed hubby'. Tsar Nicholas was certainly in no position to learn about the food shortages in Petrograd (thought more patriotic than the German sounding Petersburg), given the optimistic drivel which Alexandra fed him from the city.

In December 1916 Rasputin was murdered by Prince Felix Yusupov, a relative of the imperial family, and some friends who had found his

'Russia's Ruling House' a contemporary caricature

pretensions intolerable. The circumstances were quite extraordinary. Rasputin was invited to a party and duped into eating a considerable number of cakes filled with cyanide. Then, while a gramophone played 'Yankee doodle dandy', the conspirators waited for the massive dose of the poison to kill him as it would have any normal mortal. When the cyanide didn't seem to be working, the conspirators panicked. Yusupov then shot the *starets*, and the conspirators began to celebrate when, to their horror, he revived, telling the prince that he would 'tell the tsaritsa'. A second volley of shots was needed to dispatch Rasputin, whose body was then dropped into the Neva.

A rough translation of Rasputin into English comes out as 'the disreputable one', and popular history has attempted to link him intimately with the fall of the Romanovs. This is almost certainly an illusion. Rasputin's biographer believes that 'most of his misdeeds were no more than errors of judgement, and much of his so-called influence was based on bluff'.[9] The *starets* was a convenient scapegoat for the failings of the autocracy when the real answer lay elsewhere.

Most crucial in the short term was the presence in Petrograd of a garrison of 300,000 raw conscripts, who were affected by the discontent in the civilian population over bread shortages (a result of a breakdown in the chaotic supply system). The turning point came on 26 February 1917 when a mutiny took place in the Pavlovsky regiment of the Imperial Guard, and spread the following day even to the Semyonovsky regiment which had brutally crushed the 1905 Moscow uprising. By the end of 27 February 'the tsarist garrison could scarcely be said to exist'.[10] Nicholas II continued to live in a fool's paradise at army headquarters. When he tried to return to his capital he could find no loyal troops, and he learned that all his ministers had been arrested by a 'Provisional Committee of the Duma'. There was a general strike in St Petersburg and soldiers' soviets were being set up on the 1905 model.

On 2 March Nicholas abdicated in favour of his brother, the Grand Duke Michael, but this could not save the dynasty. A Provisional Government was set up and, seeing the hopelessness of the situation, Michael himself abdicated on 3 March. Political prisoners were freed, and on 8 March Nicholas II was arrested at Mogilev. Three hundred years of Romanov autocracy were over.

CHAPTER THIRTEEN

The Evolution of the Communist State
1917–1924

The fall of the Romanov dynasty in February 1917 (March by the new style Gregorian calendar) was followed by the setting up of the so-called Provisional Government under Prince Lvov. It immediately made clear its determination to stay in the war on the side of the Western democracies, and its appearance was greeted with satisfaction in London, Paris and latterly Washington (the USA joined the western side in April 1917). The collapse of tsarism removed the embarrasing link with an autocracy which shared none of the principles of the other Entente powers.

Lenin's return

In April 1917 another event took place in Petrograd which attracted little attention in the outside world, although it was the occasion of some jubilation in the Bolshevik fraternity. This was the return to Russian soil of Lenin, by kind permission of the German High Command which had allowed him to travel from his last place of exile in Zurich across German territory in a sealed train. In the strictly short-term perspective of the German warlords, Lenin was to be sent to Russia like 'a virus' (to quote Winston Churchill) to subvert the Russian war effort after the demise of Nicholas II. He was to do this all too effectively, but Field Marshal von Hindenburg and General von Ludendorff were not to be the beneficiaries.

Once home Lenin propounded his own distinct view of the war, which wasn't shared by all his colleagues. These 'April theses' demanded an immediate end to the war, confiscation of private land, the destruction of the bureaucracy, the army and the police, and the cession of all state power to the workers' soviets. The last point was the crucial one. The soviets had reappeared in February 1917, although initially they endorsed the Provisional Government. Lenin's strategy was to undermine this co-operation, and he produced two telling propaganda slogans, 'Bread, Land, and Peace' and 'All Power to the Soviets'. There was to be no Bolshevik co-operation with the bourgeois constituent assembly.

Lenin understood the underlying war-weariness of the Russian people whereas the Provisional Government did not. But in the early months of the life of the Provisional Government the Bolsheviks could only harass it.

A notable instance of this was in May 1917 when Foreign Minister Milyukov, the old Liberal leader, sent the Allied powers a note stating the Provisional Government's intention to stay in the war while retaining the old tsarist war aims. When the news of the 'Milyukov Note' reached the streets of Petrograd, there were Bolshevik-instigated protests and the foreign minister was forced to resign.

The new government moved perceptibly to the left, with Alexander Kerensky as prime minister and five other moderate socialists in it. By one of the ironies of history, Kerensky's father Fyodor had recommended the young Lenin for admission to the University of Kazan in 1887, despite the fact that his elder brother was implicated in a plot to assassinate Tsar Alexander III.

The Collapse of the Army

Under increasing pressure from the Bolsheviks, the Provisional Government ran into acute difficulty when its military optimism proved to be ill-founded. While Kerensky's rhetoric had inspired the revolutionary troops, grizzled German veterans proved to be less impressed by 'Mr Persuader', as Kerensky's admirers nicknamed him. The vaunted Brusilov offensive in July 1917 failed to make the predicted advances, and it was then, *not* in the winter of 1916–17, that the army's morale began to collapse. Officers were shot, loyal troops were attacked by mutineers, Bolshevik agitators were everywhere. Rank and file soldiers did not become Bolsheviks but they wouldn't fight for the Provisional

Government either. Here lay the seductive appeal of Lenin's 'Bread, Land and Peace'.

DISRUPTION IN INDUSTRY AND THE COUNTRYSIDE

The Provisional Government also began to lose the battle in the factories and in the countryside. Trade union membership doubled between February and October 1917, and the rank and file unionists began to show themselves to be more radical than the leadership. Factory committees were set up in Petrograd, which soon fell under Bolshevik control and began to expel the owners and managers.

Political change was not limited just to the towns. In the countryside as well the peasants saw their opportunity and seized the land. This action was not the work of the Bolsheviks because the peasants were represented in Parliament by the Social Revolutionary Party, but it put the SRs in a considerable dilemma. They were supporters of the Provisional Government, but their natural supporters were now apparently acting in an anti-social way. But when the SR minister of agriculture, Chernov, ordered the peasantry to stop their acts of violence, he was ignored. This was the crux of the SR dilemma. To support the Provisional Government meant losing the support of the mass of the peasantry. To oppose it would encourage anarchy in the countryside.

Coup and Counter Coup

Sensing the disintegration of Kerensky's government, the ordinary Bolsheviks became restive. In July 1917, against the advice of the leadership, an attempt was made to overthrow the government in Petrograd which failed. Kerensky ordered the arrest of Trotsky and other leading Bolsheviks, and Lenin was forced into hiding in Finland. Kerensky denounced Lenin as a 'German spy', a claim which, given the circumstances surrounding the Bolshevik leader's return, had some force.

The Bolsheviks were saved from embarrassment by a right-wing attempt to undermine the revolution under the former tsarist chief of staff, General Kornilov. Whether Kornilov wanted a restoration of the monarchy or a military dictatorship is uncertain, but Kerensky's attitude towards his attempted coup was at best ambivalent. There is no clear evidence that Kerensky favoured Kornilov but Lenin accused him of 'Bonapartism', and the Provisional Government was only preserved by the decisive action of the workers. Railway workers refused to transport Kornilov's men to Petrograd, and the Bolshevik Red Guards, a militant militia, mobilised in Petrograd.

The other major effect of the Kornilov episode was that it frightened the Mensheviks and the SRs into unwilling alliance with the Bolsheviks. Russia was now ripe for a further revolution as the major historian of the Bolshevik Revolution has pointed out: 'In the country, as the self-demobilised soldiers returned to their homes, land hunger grew more acute and peasant disorders and the ransacking of estates grew more frequent.'[1]

BOLSHEVIK DIVISIONS

In September 1917 Lenin, still in exile in Finland, wrote letters to the Central Committee of the Bolshevik Party urging the use of force against the waning authority of the Provisional Government. In early October he came to a committee meeting in disguise and forced through a vote to enable the Bolsheviks to prepare for an armed uprising. Even then Zinoviev and Kamenev, the major opponents of the use of force, circulated a letter protesting at this decision. Lenin put the alternatives starkly.

> The position is clear. Either a Kornilov dictatorship or a dictatorship of the proletariat and the poorest state of the peasantry. We cannot be guided by the mood of the masses: that is changeable and unaccountable. We must be guided by an objective analysis and estimate of the revolution. The masses have given their confidence to the Bolsheviks and ask from them not words, but deeds.

This statement with its reference to the 'changeable and unaccountable' masses was a classic repetition of what Lenin had said in his 1902 pamphlet 'What is to be Done?'. The Bolshevik party was the 'vanguard of the proletariat', the guide of the blind revolutionary potential of the masses who groped about in the autocratic and bourgeois darkness. Put simply, the masses could not be trusted to achieve revolution alone. Nor were they ever to get an opportunity to give a free opinion under the Bolsheviks.

THE BOLSHEVIKS STRIKE

By now military preparations were being made, despite the protests of the Kamenev–Zinoviev faction, and in the early morning of 25 October (7 November by the Gregorian calendar) the Bolsheviks made their assault under Trotsky's leadership. The support of the sailors at the Kronstadt naval base also meant that they had the assistance of the cruiser *Aurora*.

In the event, naval assistance was hardly required as the Provisional Government could only find some officer cadets and a regiment of women soldiers who were prepared to fight for it. The Red Guards 'stormed' the Winter Palace and arrested the members of the Provisional Government, although Kerensky escaped in a car loaned by the US embassy (this gave a key to his future fate – to be reproduced as 'living history' at academic seminars in American universities). That afternoon Lenin was able to announce the triumph of the 'workers' and peasants' revolution'. (Some years later the director Eisenstein commemorated the storming of the Winter Palace, with cinematic overkill, using some of the original participants.)

THE CONSOLIDATION OF BOLSHEVISM

Despite its success, the position of the Bolshevik government was precarious. It had seized control of Petrograd (to be renamed Leningrad) and Moscow but its writ hardly ran anywhere else in Russia. The West was hostile, and there were strong counter-revolutionary elements inside Russia. Even potential political allies like the SRs and Mensheviks were alienated by Lenin's contemptuous rejection of representative democracy. In fact the Bolsheviks' popular base was weak, as was shown by the elections to the Constituent Assembly in December 1917 when they only won 101 seats out of 707. This was Russia's last freely contested election until 1990.

There were liberal concessions like the abolition of capital punishment, but they were rapidly reneged upon in the emergency which faced

Lenin and his colleagues. As early as 20 December 1917 Lenin authorised the setting up of the All Russian Extraordinary Commission (Cheka), the forerunner of the KGB, with the object of 'combating counter-revolution and sabotage'. By a baffling paradox, its first head, the Polish communist Felix Dzerzhinsky, was also put in charge of the ministry for children (a square is named after him in Moscow).

To a limited degree the use of terror by the Bolsheviks could be justified by events because Lenin was seriously wounded by the SR assassin Fanya Kaplan in August 1918. The political case for terror after a socialist revolution had in any case been put forward by Karl Marx as long ago as 1848:

> After the cannibalism of the counter-revolution there was only one means to curtail, simplify and localise the bloody agony of the old society and the bloody birth pangs of the new, only one means – the revolutionary terror.

Lenin himself said, 'We have never renounced terror, and cannot renounce it,' and his party had only rejected the use of random individual assassination of the SR genre. Kaplan's attempt on Lenin's life was followed by a 'red terror' in which 500 victims, some ex-tsarist ministers, disappeared.

The External Threat

On 5 April 1918 Japanese forces landed in Vladivostok, allegedly to protect their citizens (there were hardly any) and property, but in practice to use Russia's problems as an opportunity to seize the vast province of Siberia. The Japanese were motivated therefore purely by greed. In May the Czech Legion, made up of former prisoners of war from the old Austro–Hungarian army, clashed with Bolshevik forces when they were about to be evacuated from Vladivostok. Their motive was to draw the attention of the Allied powers to the cause of Czechoslovak independence. Encouraging noises from the Allied powers persuaded the Czechs to move westwards towards the Volga, while the Japanese moved along the Trans-Siberian railway towards Lake Baikal.

The motives behind the intervention of the western powers in Russia were more complex. Britain and France were outraged by the defection of their former ally, which the new commissar for foreign affairs, Trotsky, had announced as a new foreign policy which rejected territorial annexations and would consist of issuing 'a few proclamations'. After this, Trotsky told enraged western diplomats, he would 'shut up shop', after disclosing the details of tsarist Russia's secret diplomacy! The French were also provoked by the refusal of the new Bolshevik regime to honour its considerable debts, although these were contracted by the capitalist government of the 1880s and 1890s.

The British found Bolshevism ideologically objectionable, but not to the same extent as their American allies who saw themselves as taking part in a crusade against this new atheistic plague. 'I can conceive of no more frightful calamity,' US Secretary of State Lansing warned his fellow countrymen, 'for a people than that which seems about to fall upon Russia.' Russia, said Lansing, was 'a seething cauldron of anarchy and violence'. The British foreign secretary, A.J. Balfour, that silver-tongued operator, adopted a more moderate tone, saying of the Russians that 'we have no desire to intervene in their domestic affairs'. The effect was very much the same, however. British troops landed at Murmansk (to seize control of an arms dump of weapons sent to the former government) and Archangel. The Americans landed forces in the Far East and the French sent their navy to the Black Sea.

The Treaty of Brest Litovsk

The Bolsheviks also had problems on another front, the liquidation of hostilities with imperial Germany. Here Trotsky adopted a strategy which he called 'no peace, no war', which meant not fighting the Germans while hoping that they would be defeated in the west by the democracies. Not surprisingly the Prussian military caste did not trust the Bolsheviks, but this did not help Lenin and Trotsky very much. The major beneficiaries were the British and French, who were saved from the full weight of a renewed German attack while sizeable forces were kept back in the east.

Meantime the Germans called Trotsky's bluff by threatening to resume a full-scale advance on the eastern front. Trotsky knew that the

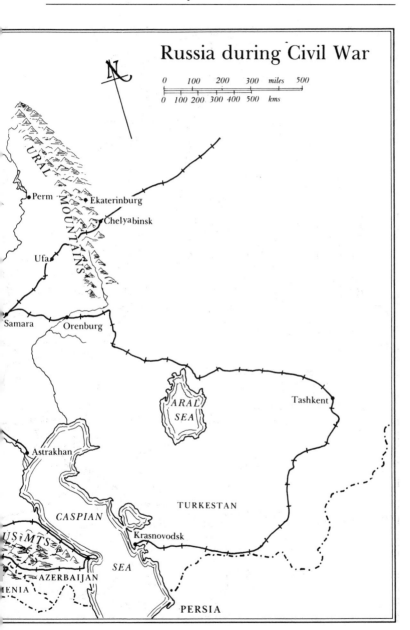

Russia during Civil War

infant Red Army was in no position to combat this. The result was the Treaty of Brest Litovsk of March 1918, which was every bit as punitive as the Bolsheviks must have feared. Russia lost about one-third of its population and industrial capacity, but the Bolsheviks had no option but to sign the treaty. It was an indication of what would have followed from a complete German victory in the First World War, which they were denied by their defeat in the West in the summer and autumn of 1918. This fact was conveniently forgotten by the German nationalists who complained so bitterly about the Treaty of Versailles after 1919.

The Whites

Beset by foreign enemies, the minority Bolshevik government was also at war with a ramshackle coalition of internal ones as well. In December 1917 the former tsarist general and anti-Bolshevik commander-in-chief, Alexeyev, received a large sum from the French, and a general promise of further Allied assistance against the new pariahs of the international system. His supporters were generally known as 'the Whites' to distinguish them from 'the Reds', and should not be confused with the racial grouping known as the White Russians. Subsequently Admiral Kolchak became the nominal leader of the various White armies, but he was based in Siberia and the Whites suffered badly from a lack of co-ordination. Thus Yudenich in the north-west made a drive for Petrograd in 1919, but was not supported by Denikin in the Caucasus or Wrangel in the Crimea. Nor did the White armies co-ordinate their activities with the various foreign armies.

There is no doubt that the White leadership also made a serious tactical blunder in 1918 by stating that Russia must return to its pre-war frontiers. This immediately alienated those national minorities which opposed Bolshevik centralism, but not at the price of a return to tsarist-style chauvinism. It is also probably true that, in a civil war notable for its atrocities, the Whites marginally outdid the Reds in the balance of terror, and managed to alienate mass support in doing so.

The End of the Royal Family

An important factor in White calculations was the Romanov family.

'Nicholas Romanov', as the ex-tsar had now become, had hoped for a foreign refuge but his cousin, King George V of Britain, would not take him, and no one else was willing to oblige either. So Nicholas and his family were moved from one temporary refuge to another, until they finished up in the Siberian town of Ekaterinburg. (The fickleness of the times was demonstrated by the fact that the large former sailor who had carried the Tsarevich Alexis around (lest he fall dangerously and bring on an onset of haemophilia) defected to the Bolsheviks.)

The Bolsheviks feared that Nicholas and his family would remain a focus of opposition. A decision was therefore taken to shoot the entire family, although who made it is still uncertain – the evidence that Lenin was responsible is not conclusive. Nevertheless the affair remained shrouded in mystery for years, because of the legend that the youngest of Nicholas II's daughters, the Grand Duchess Anastasia, had somehow survived the massacre. It is now generally accepted by historians that the woman who claimed to be the Grand Duchess was an imposter.

The international outrage which greeted the news of the murder of the Romanovs needs to be seen in the context of the protesters' refusal to offer the former imperial family a refuge. The world was also to become wearyingly familiar with Bolshevik ruthlessness.

THE NATIONAL MINORITIES

The chaos surrounding the Bolshevik Revolution offered an excellent opportunity for the resentful national minorities of the old tsarist empire to seek to achieve their independence. The Finns achieved permanent independence with German help in 1918, followed by the Baltic republics of Estonia, Latvia and Lithuania. The Ukrainians, with their distinctive religion and culture, also saw their opportunity in an alliance with the Whites who, as indicated above, foolishly insisted on adhering to Russia's 1914 frontiers. Although a separate Ukrainian republic existed for a brief period during the civil war, it was destroyed by the Bolsheviks and with it the hopes of Ukrainian nationalism.

The Russia–Polish War

Russia's emergency was always Poland's opportunity, and Poland in

1919–20 was in a vengeful mood. Encouraged by the Allies, its new hero, Pilsudski, invaded the Ukraine, and, in May 1920, Kiev fell to him. But the Ukrainians remembered their old suspicion of the Poles and failed to rise in Pilsudski's support. He was therefore forced to retreat with Trotsky's new Red Army in hot pursuit. This retreat continued up to the gates of Warsaw when Pilsudski, advised by a French military mission, counterattacked. Warsaw was saved by this 'Miracle of the Vistula', and the Red Army was forced to retreat as quickly as it had advanced. The territory gained was speedily lost, and in the Treaty of Riga (1921) further Russian territory was lost, which gave Poland, wedged between embittered powers on both sides, an illusory security.

The defeat of the Red Army in Poland in 1920 had another wider significance. For Lenin and his colleagues believed that international proletarian revolution was essential if the new Soviet state was to survive. None of the Bolshevik leadership expected to survive *without* socialist revolutions in the advanced industrialised states as well. In 1918–19 things looked hopeful.

It was self-evident, therefore, that with the defeat in Poland communist internationalism had suffered a serious setback. Neither Lenin nor Trotsky abandoned the belief that international revolution would come, but the first priority had to be the survival of the Soviet state itself.

The Red Army crossing the ice at Kronstadt

The Causes of the Bolshevik Victory

On the face of it, the clear-cut victory of the Bolsheviks in the Russian Civil War defies logic. In 1917–18 they were beset with such an array of internal and external enemies that their eventual victory seems quite improbable. Closer analysis suggests otherwise. Firstly, the Bolsheviks had a decisive and able leadership, which was prepared to be quite ruthless when the occasion demanded. Lenin provided the crucial element of political will, and Trotsky was 'the organiser of victory' (the phrase used about the French revolutionary Lazare Carnot in 1793–4). This political tandem provided a cohesiveness never approached on the other side.

The blunders of the Whites have already been outlined, and one study states that the main reason 'for the success of the Bolsheviks against their White and nationalist opponents was that they promised to satisfy the demands of the peasantry'.[2] Misleadingly, the Bolsheviks also promised to protect the rights of the national minorities, a promise which Stalin was flagrantly to breach. Lesser, but significant, importance needs to be attached to the failure of the foreign intervention. Domestic opposition in Britain and France made intervention unpopular and their troops were withdrawn in 1919.

As one historian of the Russian Civil War notes, 'the Bolsheviks who everyone in the West hoped would be swept away in the Civil War, emerged from it with their hold on power consolidated by victory'.[3] In view of the fact that in North Russia the British general, Ironside, commanded a motley force of 30,000 Britons, Americans, Canadians, Italians, Russians, Finns, Poles and Serbs, the failure of the intervention was likely almost on grounds of mutual incomprehension! The only positive achievement of the Allied intervention was to bring about the short-lived independence of the Baltic Republics.

THE KRONSTADT MUTINY

Domestic priorities were pressed by the failure of the Bolshevik policy of so-called 'War Communism' which had involved forcible seizure of food stuffs in the countryside and worker occupation of factories.

This last aspect caused chaos and a mutiny at the great naval base at Kronstadt against falling living standards.

The response of the government was draconian. In an operation under the overall control of Trotsky, troops were led over the frozen ice against the mutineers by the future Red Army Marshal Tukhachevsky. Hundreds of men died, and hundreds more were shot by the secret police afterwards. The mutiny 'revealed the bankruptcy'[4] of war communism and will always place a question mark against Trotsky's claim to be more humane than his arch rival Joseph Stalin. The claim may be just, but Trotsky showed no mercy to the Kronstadt mutineers who were publicising the complaints of many workers.

THE NEW ECONOMIC POLICY

The dead mutineers at Kronstadt achieved one victory from their graves: Lenin abandoned war communism, although he was careful to underline that he had only adopted a short-term compromise. Shortly after the mutiny he admitted that the failures on what he called 'the economic front' were far more serious than any threat that had come from White generals. Their cause was the 'system of distribution in the villages and the immediate application of Communist methods in the towns' which had caused a crisis in production.

Having conceded that war communism was 'a mistake', Lenin went on to put forward his theory of 'State Capitalism'. This would operate what became known as the 'New Economic Policy', a compromise which allowed a degree of private enterprise. Peasants would be allowed to have private plots and grow food for profit, and small businesses would be tolerated in the towns. But transport, heavy industry and banking would remain under state control, hence the phrase 'State Capitalism'. Tragically, the NEP came too late to save many of the 25 million people that *Pravda* disclosed to be suffering from famine. Despite the work done by the American Relief Association five million Soviet citizens starved to death in 1921–2.

Nor did the NEP concede any degree of political liberty in the new Soviet state. The infallibility of the communist party, to give the Bolsheviks their modern name, was to remain the central tenet of Russian lives until modern times.

THE CHURCH AND THE LENINIST STATE

The Russian Orthodox Church could hardly expect to thrive in a communist state based on Marx's slogan that 'religion is the opiate of the masses'. Under Kerensky the church had been favoured with a sympathetic procurator in the ex-premier Prince Lvov, who set up a council of state, and his successor Kartashev then created the post of minister of religion. In November 1917, the patriarchate was restored and Tikhon, metropolitan of Moscow, was elected, but his hope that the church could be kept out of politics proved to be an illusion. Lenin himself had written scathingly of religion as 'one of the forms of spiritual oppression which everywhere weigh upon the masses of the people crushed by continuous toil for others by poverty and loneliness'.

In January 1918 the Russian church was disestablished and its buildings and properties confiscated. Clerics who protested were killed, as were members of the laity who tried to keep icons or religious relics (it became a criminal offence to smuggle icons into the USSR). If the regime expected to kill off religious practice in Russia it failed, because 300,000 people attended Tikhon's funeral in 1925. But the lot of the church did not improve under the ex-seminarian Joseph Stalin.

Lenin's leadership and personality

The overwhelmingly male leadership of the Bolshevik party was still dominated by Lenin himself. Totally dedicated and ruthless as he was in matters political, Lenin presented the model for that twentieth-century paradox, the revolutionary with a largely unknown human touch. Only rarely did he allow his emotions to surface, but when they did so the impression left on colleagues was strong. In 1920 Inessa Armand, an old party comrade and member of the Bolshevik Central Committee, fell seriously ill with cholera and died. At the funeral Angelica Balabankov, whom Lenin had just severely rebuked for criticising Bolshevik excesses in the Ukraine, wrote of her party leader: 'I never saw such torment; I never saw any human being so completely absorbed by sorrow.' The suggestion is of a man who had buried natural humanity, like his hero Chernyshevsky, in the paramount interest of the party.

Lenin, according to his biographer David Shub, was 'a dictator without vanity', a man who enjoyed practical jokes and the company of children.[5] Historians will continue to debate whether Lenin's iron fist in government was forced upon him by the dictates of circumstance.

Culture under Lenin

Marxists had very deterministic views about the place of the arts in a socialist society. Lenin criticised Tolstoy for abandoning social realism in favour of 'parsondom' and complained about the 'middle-class sentimentality' of Charles Dickens. On the other hand, he attacked what he called the 'isms' of the twenties like futurism and surrealism saying that it was nonsense to 'worship the new'. Shub describes the Soviet leader's artistic tastes as 'unperceptive and conventional', and he regarded modern poetry as decadent.

But under Lenin there was a considerable degree of artistic freedom compared with what followed. This was true in the sense that a debate was *allowed* between artists about what their role should be in the socialist state. One group, known as the 'Constructivists', believed that the arts should have a socio-political purpose. They were represented by the poet Mayakovsky, the designer and producer V.E. Meyerhold, and the artist K. Malevich. This trio joined together in 1918 to produce a pageant called 'Mystery Bouffe', which pursued the theme of proletarian triumph over capitalism. In the same stream was the journal *Proletkult* (Proletarian Culture), which tried to involve the working class in cultural activity.

Lenin

A second grouping, known as the 'Fellow Travellers', was comprised of non-communists who were generally in sympathy with the aspirations of 1917. The phrase was Trotsky's, and he regarded them of necessity as a short-term phenomenon. The survival of Soviet culture in his view was dependent on the success of the planned economy. 'Art', wrote Trotsky, 'needs comfort, even abundance. Furnaces have to be hotter, wheels have to move faster, looms have to turn more quickly, schools have to work better.' Among the 'Fellow Travellers' were the novelist Sholokhov, author of *Quiet Flows the Don*, the poet Yesenin and the satirist Zamyatin, whose *We* (1920) had Orwellian echoes.

An important new cultural form in the Leninist period was the cinema, which Lenin himself declared to be 'the most important of the arts'. Soviet cinema made a sizeable contribution to the early history of the genre in this period through classics like *Battleship Potemkin*, directed by Sergei Eisenstein, and the film version of Gorky's novel *Mother*, directed by V.I. Pudovkin. In the musical field the talents of Dimitri Shostakovich were beginning to flower in the early twenties, and he produced his first symphony in 1926.

Tragically, the dead hand of the Stalinist dictatorship began to fall on the artistic community even before the decade was out. As early as 1925 the poet Yesenin committed suicide, to be followed in 1930 by Mayakovsky, the Bolshevik loyalist. Then the surrealist painters Marc Chagall and Kandinsky were driven into exile together with Zamyatin. It is certain that Lenin, like Trotsky, would have been appalled by the banal government-inspired art of the next thirty years.

Foreign Relations

The Bolsheviks, generally regarded as the 'black sheep' of Europe, had not even been invited to participate in the peace settlement of 1918–19 or to join the League of Nations. This isolation continued after the withdrawal of the Allied forces of intervention and the defeat by the Poles in the war of 1920–1. Only one other European great power was in a similar position, and some sort of Russo–German understanding was probable like the old one between St Petersburg and Berlin. In 1922 the then Bolshevik foreign minister, Chicherin, engineered the Treaty of

Rapallo, which increased Soviet–German commercial ties and included a (secret) agreement about German military training facilities on Soviet territory. In return the Reichswehr (German army) agreed to train the Red Army, and high-level links continued between the two armies until the Nazi period.

This agreement between the two pariahs of the international system infuriated the western democracies. They were also antagonised by the activities of the Comintern (or Communist International) whose task was to inspire communist revolutions abroad. The British in particular became oversensitive about the alleged activities of this organisation, now headed by Grigory Zinoviev, the sceptic of October 1917. The most glaring example of anti-Bolshevik hysteria during this period was the celebrated case of the 'Zinoviev letter'. This notorious forgery, probably the work of British intelligence, alleged that Zinoviev had been encouraging communist subversion in Britain. It probably cost the Labour party the 1924 general election in Britain.

CHAPTER FOURTEEN

Russia under Stalin
1924–1953

Lenin's last years were marked by a background, but nonetheless real, struggle for power. The last of his three severe strokes on 9 March 1923 left him partially paralysed and suffering from aphasia. Somehow he struggled on until January 1924, but during this whole period his entire vocabulary consisted of a few words like 'Lloyd George' and 'conference'. When he did eventually die on 21 January 1924, a German specialist was asked to preside at the autopsy. He was amazed to find that Lenin's brain had shrunk, in 'its material composition', to about a quarter of the size of a normal cerebral mass. The Russian Professor Rozanov remarked that 'the amazing thing was not that the thinking power remained intact in such a sclerotic brain, but that he could live so long with such a brain'.

Lenin's Last Testament

Even in this disabled condition, however, Lenin was well aware of the power struggle that was going on around him. He also had serious reservations about both Stalin and Trotsky, the leading contenders for his own position. These emerged in his last will and testament. Trotsky, though, recognised to be 'the most able' of the party leaders, was, in Lenin's view, guilty of 'too far-reaching a self-confidence and a disposition to be far too much attracted by the purely administrative side of affairs'. Lenin was also worried that the differing qualities of the two leaders might 'quite innocently lead to a split'.

A fortnight later Stalin's suitability for his position was under greater scrutiny. In the postscript to the testament, written on 4 January 1923, Lenin wrote:

> Stalin is too rude, and this fault, entirely supportable in relation to us Communists, becomes insupportable in the office of General Secretary. Therefore I propose to the comrades to find a way to remove Stalin from that position and appoint to it another man who in all respects differs from Stalin.

On the face of it, this hostile letter should have dealt a fatal blow to Stalin's ambition to become Lenin's successor. It did not, of course, because four days later Lenin suffered his last, and ultimately fatal, stroke.

Joseph Stalin was an immensely relieved man on 21 January 1924. He performed the eulogy at Lenin's funeral, but was subsequently highly embarrassed when Lenin's comments about him were read out at a session of the Politburo. Ironically, in view of what happened later, Stalin's face was saved on that occasion by Lev Kamenev, who reminded his colleagues of 'Comrade Stalin's' invaluable services to the party. The fact that Kamenev was so easily believed underlines the importance of the key factor in Stalin's later success, his deceptive personality. That it should have deceived anyone as intelligent as Trotsky or Zinoviev seems puzzling, especially as others had already sensed his lurking ambition and ruthlessness.

The key to Stalin's success seems to have lain, to a degree, in his *un-Russianness*. He was, of course, a Georgian (his real name was Djugashvili) but his quiet pipe-smoking image made him quite untypical of either race. This did not, however, fool Bazhanov, his private secretary, and secretary of the Politburo from 1923. He quoted Lenin's original and mistaken assessment of Stalin, 'We don't need an intelligent man there – let us send Stalin', which was based on his belief that Stalin was entirely loyal. Stalin's poor educational background also caused others to underestimate him and not take him seriously as a rival. His picture of Stalin on the eve of power was quite different. He was

> a poor and boring speaker with a deliberate, dry and humourless style. Stalin's main characteristics were cunning, malevolence, political ambition and a pathological desire for power; he entrusted to no man his inner thoughts and *was strangely out of place in a land where everyone talked too much*. When he spoke he used words to conceal his thoughts; one could not know

by his words whether he had thoughts or not. He was sly, the simple down-to-earth mentality of the peasant taking the place of intelligence. [author's italics]

This portrait of Stalin in the twenties is quoted at length because it contains a high degree of authenticity. It is in several respects damning, but also immensely revealing. Stalin had the slyness of the former tsarist agent, the obstinacy to wear down more able opponents, and mundane intellectual powers which would not alarm the rank and file party members. No one would ever accuse him of being 'too clever by half'. This gave him an immense advantage in the struggle that was to come.

It is a paradox that it should, because in every respect Leon Trotsky was the 'swan' to Stalin's 'ugly duckling'. Some problems were not of Trotsky's making. He joined the party, as we have seen, only just before the Revolution; he was a Jew and an intellectual. These were disadvantages which Trotsky's reputation as founder of the Red Army and foreign minister should have allowed him to override. But he did not suffer fools gladly, and he didn't care who knew it. There was also resentment in the party about the years before 1917, when Trotsky had accused Lenin of 'incredible bombast'. Most fatal of all was the way in which he allowed himself to be deceived by the apparent friendliness of a man who lacked his own glittering talents. Stalin used the vehicle of ideological debate to destroy Trotsky, but beneath the niceties of communist dogma was the thrust for the jugular of a political rival.

The Struggle for Power

The chosen battleground was the future of the infant Soviet state, just recovered from years of famine and civil war. Stalin was the proponent of the concept of 'Socialisms in One Country', Trotsky favoured 'Permanent Revolution'. In reality there was little enough to choose between them; what mattered was the *interpretation* Stalin made of Trotsky's views. These were, in essence, the same as Lenin's: only if there were revolutions in the advanced western countries could socialism (or communism) survive in the USSR. Thus revolution, according to Trotsky, was a 'permanent' ongoing process.

Stalin, by contrast, stressed the need to establish socialism in the USSR first, while encouraging its devolopment elsewhere. At no point did he actually challenge the need for revolution abroad. Nor did Trotsky underestimate the importance of a firm foundation for socialism at home. The issue was *timing* not commitment. But Stalin knew differently: Comrade Trotsky was 'a warmonger' and a 'wrecker' who would drag an exhausted Soviet Union back into the struggles of the early 1920s. Stalin was aided in spreading this slander by Grigory Zinoviev and Lev Kamenev, who were both envious of Trotsky and unaware of the danger posed to them by their cunning ally. This 'Triumvirate', as it was known, forced Trotsky out of the leadership. In January 1925 he lost his crucial post as war minister, and shortly afterwards his position on the Politburo itself. Strangely, Trotsky aided his own downfall because of his own loyalty to the Communist Party. The party, he said, was 'in the last analysis always right', and as General Secretary Stalin represented the will of the party. The treacherous recipient of such loyalty was to use this excessive trait in the Old Bolsheviks again in the 1930s.

It was characteristic of Stalin that he was not satisfied just with the disgrace of his rival. Trotsky was deprived of his party membership, and in 1929 he and his family were expelled from the USSR altogether. He then drifted from country to country, France, Turkey and Mexico, everywhere followed by the agents of his implacable enemy. Finally, in 1940 Stalin's agent Mercader lied his way into Trotsky's house in Mexico City, and murdered him with an ice-axe. By then Stalin had created a society in which it was possible to regard Mercader as a hero.

Trotsky's death did not prevent him from playing a central role in Stalinist mythology in the forties and fifties. Although removed from history books in his role as founder of the Soviet state, Trotsky had already been given another one to play – as arch-villain, unperson and enemy of the Soviet state. There was a contradiction here: how could such an apparently mediocre person pose such a serious threat to the Soviet state? But threat he was, especially in the 1930s when the 'Trotsky fascist fiends' were the centrepiece of all Stalin's propaganda. In the Stalinist paradise Trotsky played the role of devil; in the meantime his reputation was clinically destroyed by Stalin's henchmen.

There was a certain justice in the fact that Zinoviev and Kamenev, who had conspired to bring about Trotsky's fall, were themselves brought down by Stalin. Once again Stalin's drive to power was thinly disguised behind an ideological debate, and once again he outmanoeuvred his rivals. This time the Soviet economy provided the scenario for the destruction of those who became known as 'Left Bolsheviks'. They were unwise enough to be right, but at the wrong time. Lenin had introduced the New Economic Policy in 1921, and famine and war had forced him to compromise, but he had never intended the NEP to be permanent. In 1925–6 Zinoviev and Kamenev felt that the circumstances were right for the NEP to be abandoned, and for the Soviet Union to collectivise its farms and begin a massive drive to industrialise the economy.

There was nothing heretical about what Zinoviev and Kamenev were saying, as it had always been accepted that the Communist Party must control 'the commanding heights of the economy' – but Stalin denounced them as 'wreckers'. In doing so he had the unwitting help of Bukharin, Rykov and Tomsky, the so-called 'Right Bolsheviks' (although such labels need to be used with some care). Nikolay Bukharin, in particular, was the apostle of the NEP, saying that industrialisation should proceed at 'a snail's pace'. He was still at this stage, in Lenin's words, 'the darling of the party', and it suited the General Secretary to go along with him for the moment. Zinoviev and Kamenev followed Trotsky down the road of disgrace, expulsion and anonymity, they were allowed to remain in the Soviet Union but their days were numbered, and counted off by Stalin. All too late Kamenev had warned his colleague that Stalin was 'the new Genghis Khan'.

Whether Stalin was ever really convinced by the arguments of Bukharin must remain open to question. Circumstances forced him to abandon the Rightists, for by 1928 the conditions of 1921 had reappeared in the countryside. The richer peasants, or 'kulaks', were hoarding grain, and the people in the great cities of the USSR were starving. In this crisis Stalin was forced to abandon his usual cautious, ponderous decision-making process and act quickly. The NEP was abandoned, and in October 1928 the First Five Year Plan was introduced. The USSR was now to modernise its economy at breakneck speed.

The First Five Year Plan

What followed was far from masterly, and has raised serious doubts about Stalin's competence as a ruler. On one level, he had proved himself a most effective destroyer of political opposition; on another, he was to prove himself an economic illiterate of the first order. The modernisation drive was to proceed at such an unrealistic pace that it soon proved to be unworkable. The responsibility for this is Stalin's alone. He set impossible production targets, and then blamed subordinates when they were not reached. Tractors were produced in great numbers for peasants who could not drive them. Worst of all, in his impatience and dogmatic arrogance, Stalin instituted a reign of terror against the unfortunate kulaks. They had profited from the NEP and were now labelled 'class enemies'. Stalin's new motto was 'We must smash the kulaks' and he let the sinister OGPU (secret police) loose on them. The result was catastrophe. Some kulaks were forced on to the new collective farms, many others were slaughtered. Yet others burnt down their holdings and killed their livestock in protest. Historians can only estimate the number of kulaks who perished in this campaign, in which the authorities were undoubtedly assisted by the envy of the less well-off smaller peasantry.

The first tractor

Various explanations have been put forward for Stalin's behaviour during these years. One is that he suffered a form of nervous breakdown as his unrealistic targets were shown to be unattainable (and it was during this period that his wife Nadezhda Alliluyeva committed suicide after a violent row with him). This explanation does at least contain a hint of the truth because of the paranoid streak in Stalin's personality. This paranoia was not full-blown in the late 1920s but it was certainly well developed. Trotsky, Zinoviev and Bukharin could not be tolerated, not because they were *wrong*, but because they were *enemies*. When transposed to the wider field of international relations, this mistrust embraced a neurosis about the capitalist West. The USSR must industrialise rapidly because otherwise the capitalists would destroy her. Stalin placed Soviet weakness in its historical context in 1931 as he warned that

> To slacken the pace would mean to lag behind; and those who lag behind are beaten. We do not want to be beaten . . . old Russia was ceaselessly beaten for her backwardness. She was beaten by the Mongol Khans, she was beaten by Turkish Beys, she was beated by Swedish feudal lords, she was beaten by Polish–Lithuanian Pans, she was beaten by Japanese barons, she was beaten by all – for her backwardness.

This statement would have been reasonable enough as a justification for a modernisation programme of the Witte or Stolypin type. What characterised Stalin's Five Year Plans was their ruthless bloodletting, which cannot be justified by the appearance of the fascist threat after 1933. In 1928 Adolf Hitler was a little-known German politician, and the immediate capitalist threat to socialism in the USSR had ended with the civil war in 1921. Yet there was a reckless adventurism in the First Five Year Plan which seemed out of character as far as Joseph Stalin was concerned.

At all events, Stalin perceived that his plans were going wrong as early as 1930. In that year, his article 'Dizziness with Success' characteristically laid the blame on overenthusiastic subordinates. But production targets were cut back and some of them were met. By the end of 1930, 55 per cent of Russian peasants had been collectivised, and this figure was to reach 90 per cent by 1936.

In his Second Five Year Plan (1933–7), Stalin placed greater emphasis on industrial production, and considerable progress was made so that (for example) coal production trebled between 1929 and 1938. Suspicion of the West was even temporarily laid aside as foreign technicians were allowed in to help with the modernisation of the Soviet economy. One of them was the American John Scott, who helped with the construction of the massive showpiece steelworks at Magnitogorsk. He has left us with this picture of the hardships endured by Soviet workers in those days:

> This was the Magnitogorsk of 1933. A quarter of a million souls – Communists, Kulaks, foreigners, Tatars, convicted saboteurs and a mass of blue-eyed Russian peasants – building the biggest steel combinat in Europe in the middle of the barren Ural steppe ... Men froze, hungered and suffered, but the construction work went on with a disregard for individuals and a mass heroism seldom paralleled in history.[2]

To encourage the toiling masses Stalin's propaganda machine created 'heroes of Soviet labour'. One of them was Stakhanov, who was declared to have exceeded his production target many times over. Released from the mines as a result of his heroic efforts, Stakhanov was then a victim of one of the bizarre twists which are so typical of Soviet history. In the

The working hero – Stakhanov

1950s, after Stalin's death, Khrushchev was boasting to foreigners about Stakhanov's exploits. He was then irritated to find that Stakhanov no longer worked in the mines. So the ageing hero was ordered back to the Ukraine, where he died in hardship some years later. Another strange episode during this period also demonstrated that Stalin swallowed his suspicions of western capitalists only with the greatest difficulty. In March 1933 six engineers from Metro–Vickers, a British engineering company which had supplied the Soviet regime with advisers, were arrested on 'wildly exaggerated charges of espionage and fabricated charges of sabotage'.[3] After a show trial two of the engineers were sentenced to short prison sentences. The British government retaliated by placing an embargo on Soviet imports. This was lifted in July 1933 when the engineers were released but the Metro–Vickers trial was an ominous sign of things to come.

The Purges

The origin of this terrible period seems to lie with the asassination of Sergey Kirov (who had succeeded Zinoviev as the local party boss in Leningrad) in 1934. He was by all accounts an attractive personality, who had the temerity in that year to get more applause at the Party Congress than Stalin himself! It has been suggested, from more than one source, that this may have been Kirov's undoing. He was shot dead in December 1934, in circumstances that were to say the least suspicious: the guards had disappeared from outside his office, and it transpired later the assassin Nikolayev had been detained a few days earlier while carrying a weapon. After the assassination there was a spate of deaths involving minor figures associated with Kirov. Such evidence has convinced commentators like the British historian Robert Conquest that Stalin knew of, and connived at, 'the plan to kill Kirov' – a death which would, of course, remove a potentially dangerous rival. This theory seems to fit in with what we already know about Stalin's personality, so devastatingly summed up by Alexander Solzhenitsyn in this passage from *The First Circle*:

Distrust of people was the dominating characteristic of Joseph Djugashvili;

it was his only philosophy of life. He had not trusted his own mother, neither had he trusted God, before whom as a young man he had bowed down in His temple. He had not trusted his fellow Party members . . . He had not trusted his comrades in exile . . . He had never trusted his relatives, his wives or his mistresses. He had not even trusted his children. And how right he had been![4]

It is an attractive and convincing thesis, but there is an alternative view. Isaac Deutscher, a veteran Marxist and Stalin's biographer, has argued that Stalin did not plan Kirov's murder but merely *used it* as an excuse to instigate the Purges. Nikolayev was accused of belonging to the Zinoviev faction in the party, and Stalin was then able to purge the so-called Left Bolsheviks, Kamenev and Zinoviev. Either theory is acceptable as explanation for Kirov's death. What is not in dispute is how the assassination was used by Stalin as a 'raison d'être' for the show trials of the thirties. Even here, though, there is a mystery. Why did Stalin wait for two years before staging the trials of the Zinovievites? Was it cool calculation, or sadistic delight in the isolation of his intended victims? A mixture of both perhaps, but there does also seem to be a link with foreign policy. In March 1936 Hitler reoccupied the demilitarised zone of the Rhineland and the Western allies did nothing. Stalin was certainly alarmed by the fascist threat to the USSR, and may have decided to liquidate his internal enemies first. Throughout his period in power he was haunted by the fate of Nicholas II, who had been brought down by a combination of internal and external enemies.

Whatever his motives, Stalin began the trial of the so-called 'Sixteen' in July 1936; the chief defendants were Kamenev and Zinoviev. This show trial was followed in 1937 by that of the 'Seventeen', in which the major defendants were Radek and Pyatakov. The Right Bolsheviks were tried in 1938, although by this time Tomsky had already committed suicide. In between were the trials of leading Red Army commanders who were deemed to be suspect; they included Marshal Tukhachevsky, the commander-in-chief and a hero of the civil war – in all three out of five Red marshals were purged, together with 40 per cent of the officer corps. In every case the defendants were charged with the same bizarre mixture of offences: plotting to murder Stalin, conspiring with Nazi Germany or Japan, wrecking the economy, communicating with Trotskyites, etc. In every case also the accused religiously confessed all their crimes in open court and were executed for their 'crimes'.

The term 'trial' in this context is in any case rather misleading: in 1938 the Finnish communist, Aino Kuusinen, was recalled to Moscow to be purged (this was common practice in Stalin's day) and a Soviet prosecutor told her:

> In bourgeois justice the prosecutor has to prove that the accused is guilty, but under our system the accused has to prove that he is innocent.

Kuusinen goes on to tell a rather morbid joke about Soviet justice under Stalin:

> The Soviet principle is illustrated by the joke about a rabbit which escaped from the Soviet Union into Poland, explaining that it did so because all camels in the USSR were to be shot. 'But you aren't a camel.' 'No, but how can I prove it?'[5]

Aino Kuusinen's personal experience demonstrates another important point about the Purges. Moscow exerted rigid control over foreign communist parties, and many foreign communists were purged during this period. But so were the lower echelons of the Soviet Communist Party. Of the members of the Central Committee of the Party in 1934, 70 per cent were to be dead by 1938. Between 1934 and 1938 1.5 million party members were purged. A whole generation of able young communists were sacrificed to satisfy Stalin's blood lust. The loss of their military equivalents was also to cost the USSR dearly in 1941.

At the time the psychology of the Purges was deeply puzzling to foreign observers. How could such distinguished Old Bolsheviks as Zinoviev and Bukharin be guilty of such outrageous crimes? They weren't, in fact, but Stalin played on their loyalty as party members. The accused knew they were doomed, but were persuaded that their confessions were in the interest of the world communist movement.

This is one explanation, but there is also a more sinister one, the use of physical and psychological torture by the secret police. The NKVD, as the secret police was now called, perfected one particular technique which was nicknamed 'the conveyor belt'. This involved the use of a team of interrogators to break a prisoner's spirit. The method was primarily psychological, although prisoners were given beatings; some effort seems to have been made to cover these up, at least in the major cases. But the use of 'sleep deprivation' and a carrot-and-stick form of questioning seem to have been more common. Prisoners would be confronted by a sympathetic, kindly interrogator and then by two hostile ones who would threaten them. They in turn would be followed by sympathetic officers, and so on until the prisoner, worn out by loss of sleep, would be ready to sign anything.

Aino Kuusinen's personal experience gives us a good idea of what the 'conveyor belt' must have been like:

> At the first few interrogations Zaitsev was all smoothness and flattery; then, as this failed, he laid several traps for me and finally thrust an astounding document across the table – an elaborate indictment of many pages against Otto Kuusinen, my husband and Stalin's friend. Zaitsev ordered me to sign it, as I was the person who knew most about Otto's criminal anti-Soviet intrigues. I told him without hesitation that there was not a word of truth in the charge and that I would not sign. He then switched to a persuasive tone once more, but finding it useless, began to utter fearful threats, including that of torture. He shouted at me that they knew for certain that Kuusinen was a British spy, to which I retorted, 'If you are so sure of it, why do you need my signature?'[6]

Although she does not mention it, a team of interrogators was used with Aino Kuusinen, and the reader will note the blend of persuasion and threats used by Zaitsev. By such methods was the socialist motherland protected from its alleged enemies.

While Stalin could not tolerate opposition, he also craved praise, and he encouraged a thoroughly mendacious and overblown personality cult in which he became the 'great leader and teacher'. History and literature were the main victims of this cult of leader worship, as the past was massaged to suit Stalinist pretensions. Thus the official history of the Soviet Communist Party (1938) deleted all reference to the contribution of men like Trotsky, Zinoviev and Bukharin to the 1917 Revolution; Trotsky even disappeared from official photographs of the day. Conversely, Stalin's role in central events like the civil war was grossly distorted.

SOCIALIST REALISM

Literature was afflicted by the perverse doctrine of 'socialist realism' imposed by Stalin, which insisted that poems, novels and plays reflected the realities of ordinary Soviet life. Some, like Maxim Gorky, tried to accommodate Stalin's megalomania, although even he was disenchanted by the time of his death in 1936. Others, like Boris Pasternak, wrote in secret and awaited better times. A third, more heroic group, represented by the poet Osip Mandelstam, confronted the Stalinist system and suffered accordingly (Mandelstam died in a labour camp). 'Stalin', the exiled Trotsky wrote bitterly, 'is collecting dead souls for lack of living ones.' (All Russians would have picked up the reference to Gogol's nineteenth-century novel *Dead Souls*.)

The visual arts suffered equally badly. Hideous murals were commissioned to commemorate the achievements of socialist labour, while abstract artists like Kandinsky were banned. The cinema was dominated by grotesque eulogies of Stalin's achievements. Everywhere the dead hand of Stalin's dictatorship throttled creative and artistic life in a way which had not been possible in tsarist times.

On the whole the physical sciences fared better. The physicist Peter Kapitsa was allowed to go and do research work with Rutherford in Cambridge. But even in this sphere there were exceptions: the famous Soviet aircraft designer Tupolev was purged in the thirties (although Aino Kuusinen saw him in Moscow in 1964 bedecked with medals).

Even music wasn't safe from Stalin's mania for regulation. At the end of the Stalinist period Prokofiev and Shostakovich were producing music to order, so that the peasants could listen to it as they worked in the fields. There were strange stories about the dictator bullying the composers into singing Georgian folk songs in the Kremlin! But farce, as so often in the Stalin era, masked tragedy. His persecution and bullying undoubtedly ruined the health of the highly nervous and introspective Shostakovich.

Foreign Policy

Before 1941 the USSR was cut off from the outside world by its ideology. In part this was deliberate, because of the need to build the socialist system, but it was also a reflection of traditional Russian suspicion of the West. The conduct of Stalin's foreign policy had to reflect this known antagonism, while hoping that the West would ultimately accept the seriousness of the fascist threat.

Western ignorance of the USSR was unfortunately paralleled by Stalin's ignorance of western conditions. He was responsible for the woefully misguided policy between 1928 and 1934, when foreign communist parties were told to destroy the 'social fascists' (i.e. the socialists). This had particularly tragic consequences in Germany in the early 1930s, where the communists should have been in alliance with the social democrats against Nazism. Worse still was the way in which Stalin forced the German communists into an ideological strait-jacket. He decreed that fascism was 'the last stage of capitalism', to be followed by a socialist takeover; so it was the duty of the German communists actively to assist Hitler into power. The results are well known: within a month of Hitler's appointment as chancellor in January 1933, the German communist party was outlawed and its membership decimated. Elsewhere Stalin was equally blinkered. He was convinced, for example, that Mao Zedong's communists could not succeed against Jiang Jieshi nationalists in China.

All this indicates that Stalin was something less than a genius in his conduct of Soviet foreign policy. Yet he did show a capacity to learn from earlier mistakes, even if it was an overdue reaction to the advent of Hitlerism. From 1934 onwards, through the agency of his Jewish foreign minister Maxim Litvinov, he adopted a policy of 'collective security'. This involved trying to create an anti-Hitler front with the West, and brought the USSR into the League of Nations in 1934. In 1935 defensive agreements were signed with France and Czechoslovakia, while Soviet military assistance was given to the Spanish republicans in their civil war against Franco's nationalists.

There seems little reason to doubt Stalin's commitment to collective security because it was clearly in his interest to safeguard the USSR from the fascist threat. He remained suspicious of Western intentions, but the lack of commitment seemed greater on the other side. France did not ratify the defence agreement, and the British remained resolutely sceptical about the USSR's value as an ally. In this context the military purge of 1937–8 played into the hands of anti-Soviet appeasers in the British government. It was undoubtedly pleased to be bombarded with a stream of pessimistic reports from Colonel Firebrace, the British military attaché, about the fighting abilities of the Red Army. Neville Chamberlain, the British prime minister, also believed that the Poles were 'a great virile nation' and a more reliable military ally than the USSR.

This is not the place for a detailed analysis of the tortuous negotiations surrounding the Munich pact but certain points need to be made. Under the terms of its 1935 treaty with the Czechs, the Soviet Union was not obliged to defend them *unless* France honoured her 1925 treaty with the Czechs first; France did not honour her commitment. Soviet troops would have had to cross Poland if they were to help the Czechs against a German attack; it was well known that such permission would not be forthcoming. At best the Red Army would have had to be airlifted into Czechoslovakia. Were Stalin's intentions honourable? Soviet and pro-Soviet western historians have always claimed that they were but most western historians have taken some convincing. Christopher Thorne cites the evidence of a German observer at the time of the Munich crisis who saw in Moscow 'no preparations that suggested Russia . . . meant business'. Thorne goes on to point out that

> Stalin himself later told Churchill that he had not been ready to fight even defensively in 1939, an obvious excuse to offer, but one which the Finnish campaign and the extent of German penetration in 1941 would seem to bear out.[7]

Whether or not Stalin ever really intended to fight for the Czechs,[8] the failure of Britain and France to do so brought about a fundamental review of Soviet foreign policy after Munich. At the Eighteenth Communist Party Congress in March 1939 Stalin warned that the USSR would not 'be drawn into conflicts of warmongers who are accustomed to have others pull the chestnuts out of the fire for them'. But these warning signals were not picked up in the West. Although an Anglo–French mission was sent to the USSR in the summer of 1939, the British particularly behaved in such a way that it was not taken seriously: they sent their delegation by sea (it took three weeks to arrive) and included no one of consequence. Obvious deductions were made by Stalin and his new foreign minister, Molotov, which were strengthened by the Anglo–French failure to get the Red Army free passage through Poland and Rumania. On 23 August 1939 the world was astounded to hear that the USSR and Nazi Germany, who had in Stalin's words been 'pouring buckets of filth' on each other for years, had signed a non-aggression pact. It contained a secret clause concerning the partition of Poland which was in fact to take effect some three weeks later.

The signing of this Nazi–Soviet pact opened Stalin, both at the time and subsequently, to serious charges of cynicism and duplicity. He defended himself by saying that the pact was, in effect, a Soviet Munich, designed to buy time for rearmament. Critics point out that he used the time bought (August 1939 to June 1941) to gobble up not just eastern Poland but the Baltic Republics of Lithuania, Latvia and Estonia as well, and they stress that nothing can justify the ideological volte-face Stalin made in doing a deal with fascism. From a Soviet perspective the pact does not require justification because it was the obvious corollary to treacherous Western attempts to sell out the Soviet Union to the Nazis. The USSR also faced a Japanese threat in the Far East, where there had been fighting in 1938 and 1939. Only in 1941 did Stalin learn from his master spy in Tokyo, Richard Sorge, that Japan would strike at Britain and the USA rather than at the Soviet Union.

What this debate does illustrate is the total lack of trust between the USSR and the West, which (with the possible exception of the period 1941–5) has been a feature of its entire history.

Stalin and World War Two

The other major area of controversy concerning Stalin's foreign policy relates to the German attack on the USSR on 22 June 1941. Here at least the evidence against Stalin seems to be extremely damning because, in Solzhenitsyn's words 'In all his long, suspicion-ridden life he had only trusted one man . . . This man was Adolf Hitler.'[9] Although there were tensions between Germany and the USSR between 1939 and 1941 (over the annexation of the Baltic Republics in 1940), this statement is essentially true. Stalin adhered to the letter of the Nazi–Soviet pact, even when all the evidence suggested that Hitler was about to attack the USSR.

In his study of Stalin's war leadership Col. Albert Seaton has chronicled the 'Alice in Wonderland' sequence of the last few weeks before the German attack. In early June Ambassador Maisky was warned in London about a possible German attack, and there were frequent violations of Soviet air space by German aircraft. Yet on 14 June Foreign Minister Molotov told a subordinate that 'only a fool would attack Russia'. A week later the 'fool' did attack, and even then Stalin refused to believe the evidence of his own eyes. Even after the attack began he still apparently regarded the invasion as a provocation by German generals. He ordered the Red Army to keep off German territory, and air activity was also to be restricted. The concentration of Soviet armies in the border areas (in sharp contrast with the strategy adopted in 1812) also proved to be disastrous. It is therefore difficult to disagree with Colonel Seaton's remark that 'Stalin alone was responsible for the heavy losses of 1941 and 1942'.[10] Suffice it to say that Stalin, deeply shaken though he was by the German attack, recovered his nerve and placed himself at the head of the Soviet war effort. More will be said later about him as a war leader, but the most intriguing aspect of this period was the way in which he summoned up the spirit of Old Russia to deal with the emergency. Stalin, the ex-seminarian, reopened the churches and encouraged the clergy to preach resistance to the Nazi invader. He made radio broadcasts directly to the Soviet people (previously unheard of). He sanctioned the making of a series of patriotic films like *Ivan the Terrible* and *Alexander Nevsky*, with its famous sequence on the ice showing the defeat of the Teutonic knights (both these were made by the great director Sergie Eisenstein, who had also been responsible for the far more revolutionary *Battleship Potemkin* and *October*). No longer were the tsars of Old Russia to be examples of reaction and corruption, but of heroic resistance to the foreign invader. In fact Stalin himself always showed a curious reverence for Russia's past, although this had never been acknowledged in public.

SOVIET REVERSES

Nevertheless Stalin's conversion to old-style patriotism did not save his armies from terrible initial reverses in the summer and autumn of 1941. The Wehrmacht rapidly overran the Ukraine and was welcomed with open arms by local separatists who detested Stalin far more than they disliked the Nazis. Millions of Red Army soldiers fell into the clutches of an enemy who regarded them as subhuman and used the USSR's failure to sign the Geneva Convention as an excuse to butcher them. While Russia's ancient capital of Kiev fell in the south, Leningrad was invested by German and Finnish forces in the north, so beginning the longest and most heroic siege of the war. Ultimately, the only factor that saved Stalin from complete disaster was Hitler's inability to decide whether Moscow, Leningrad, or the oilfields of the Caucasus should be his prime objective. The attack on the central front was halted and when it resumed in late autumn the rains soon turned Russian roads into muddy tracks. The early onset of wintér in November 1941 then caught the Germans by surprise, because in their over-confidence they had come to the USSR without adequate winter clothing.

As the temperatures dropped German soldiers died of frostbite in their iced-up vehicles, and although advanced elements of the German army got into Moscow's suburbs they were soon driven out again by Soviet factory workers using any weapon which came to hand. Blitzkrieg (lightning war) had met its match.

Stalin's Counter Offensive

It was at this moment in Soviet fortunes that the information supplied by the masterspy Richard Sorge proved to be of priceless value. Sorge had told his master in the Kremlin that Japan would strike southwards against Pearl Harbor, and in that same week Stalin launched a massive counter-offensive against the Germans before Moscow with fresh divisions from Siberia. These hardy soldiers were both used to fighting in sub-zero temperatures and expert skiers, and their frozen enemies were soon driven back. Only Hitler's order that the German army must stand and fight to the last man saved his army from a disaster equivalent to the one that had overtaken the Red Army in the summer. But the immediate threat to Moscow was removed, never to reappear.

FURTHER GERMAN SUCCESSES

The coming of spring in 1942 saw the pattern of German victories in 1941 repeated. This time the major objective was the Caucasus and German forces reached the Maikop oilfields, only to find (predictably) that the Russians had sabotaged the oilwells. In the north the siege of Leningrad continued, with its lice-ridden, starving citizens sustained in their desperate resistance by supply convoys over the frozen Lake Ladoga. Hundreds of thousands died from German bombardment, bombing and starvation before the Red Army was able to raise the siege in 1944.

STALINGRAD

Despite the overall pattern of German advances in the year 1942, Hitler allowed himself to become involved in one fatal diversion. This was when his obsessive hatred of Soviet communism demanded that he capture the city of Stalingrad (now Volgograd) although it had no real strategic value.

So it was that the quarter of a million men of the German Sixth Army become bogged down in a bitter street-by-street battle for Stalingrad which raged throughout the winter of 1942–3. Ultimately, the besiegers became the besieged as the Red Army in turn threw a cordon around the city, and the German situation gradually became hopeless. Only Hitler, by now the inhabitant of a half-crazed Wagnerian fantasy world, was out of touch with reality and ordered the doomed Sixth Army to do 'its heroic duty to the last man'. His attempt to bribe its commander von Paulus by promoting him Field Marshal failed, and on 1 February 1943 Paulus surrendered to his Soviet counterpart Rokossovsky with 90,000 men. They were all that was left of the 250,000 who had begun the siege the previous autumn, and for the first time in history a German field army had been forced to surrender.

Military historians have generally agreed that the Stalingrad surrender marked the decisive turning point of the war. The Red Army had drawn Hitler's teeth and Germany was henceforward in no position to win the war in the East.

KURSK

If his generals accepted this reality, Hitler did not and in the summer of 1943 he launched another great offensive around Kursk under the code-name 'Operation Citadel'. But this battle too (still the greatest tank battle in history) resulted in a German reverse which demonstrated, once and for all, the superiority of the T34 tank.

Fragile German reserves were used up at Kursk, and as the war went on Soviet superiority in both men and material became more and more marked. Although important Western assistance came to Russia via the Arctic route to Archangel, the Soviet forces were largely reliant on native efforts. Here at least Stalin had decided wisely in moving Soviet war production east of the Urals.

German explanations for their defeats centred on the primitive stoicism of the average Red Army soldier, especially those from Soviet Asia. General von Manteuffel, for example, told a British military historian that

> The advance of a Russian army is something that Westerners can't imagine. Behind the tank spearheads rolls on a vast horde, largely mounted on horses. The soldier carries a sack on his back, with dry crusts of bread and raw vegetables collected on the march from the fields and villages. The horses eat the straw from the house roofs – they get very little else.

But the Red Army's success also owed a good deal to the insane genocidal Nazi policy in Russia, which alienated even those Ukrainians, Cossacks and White Russians who hated Stalinism (although some did fight on the German side). Countless Soviet civilians were massacred behind the German lines.

The Final Victory

Once the Germans were cleared off Russian soil the Red Army rolled over the frontiers of Eastern Europe. Poland was liberated although there are still accusations that Stalin deliberately held back and allowed the Polish Home Army to be destroyed, in what was allegedly a premature uprising in Warsaw in 1944. Whatever the truth of the matter it suited the Russian dictator's book that the strength of the non-communist Polish resistance was virtually destroyed in the process. Meanwhile a Polish communist government was set up by the Russians in Lublin.

Budapest was liberated by the Red Army early in 1945 and Russian spearheads reached into the northernmost parts of Czech Bohemia. Once the Red Army crossed the Oder only Berlin remained, but the capture of the German capital in May 1945 was to cost a million men in the face of desperate Nazi resistance. The hero of the Battle of Berlin (which ended with the symbolic hoisting of the hammer and sickle on the former Reich Chancellery building) was Marshal Zhukov, who had ironically been trained by the Germans in the early twenties.

The price paid by the Russian people for victory was immense. European Russia had been devastated and 7 million Russians had died on the battlefield. Estimates put the number of civilian dead in what Russians came to call the 'Great Patriotic War' at a further 20 million. Its legacy was to haunt the Soviet Union for many years to come.

When D-Day came in June 1944 the efforts of the western allies were still downplayed by Stalin. By 1944 Stalin had become a warlord of some confidence and ability. Rude and abusive as he sometimes was to western visitors, he was very much in control. He kept in daily contact with all the fronts and impressed everyone with his faultless memory and grasp of technicalities. By the end of the war Stalin, unlike his rival in Berlin, had learnt not to interfere with competent generals like Zhukov. Overall political control remained absolute nonetheless, and Stalin could still be enraged by unfortunate individuals like General Susloparov (who made the mistake of signing the Reims surrender document without clearing it with the Kremlin first). His years in power had given Stalin a presence and authority which more than made up for any intellectual deficiencies.

The Origins of the Cold War

These deficiencies became more obvious from 1948 as Stalin entered his seventies, but no one dared to question his authority at home. Helped by another Georgian, Lavrenti Beria, as NKVD chief, the dictator rapidly reimposed the pre-war repression. Prisoners of war were suspect because of contacts with the West, Cossacks were slaughtered for collaborating with the Germans, and foreign communists were purged in the old style. A veiled criticism in a letter home was enough to get the young Alexander Solzhenitsyn incarcerated in a labour camp.

The post-war settlement favoured the USSR, as Stalin took advantage of the death of Roosevelt and Churchill's defeat in the 1945 general election. The Labour prime minister Attlee found that, despite Bevin's boast that 'Left could speak to Left', relations with the USSR began to worsen. President Truman, initially sympathetic, also came to distrust Stalin's long-term intentions. Much has been made of Churchill's famous 'iron curtain' speech at Fulton, Missouri, in 1946, but subsequent research has thrown some doubt on the origins of the Cold War. The 'frozen' nature of East–West relations after the late 1940s makes this a matter of crucial relevance for analysts of the period today. Did Stalin intend to overrun a vulnerable Western Europe as part of an overall Communist plan for worldwide domination? At the time the evidence seemed convincing. Between 1945 and 1948 Poland, Hungary, Bulgaria and Rumania had effectively fallen under Soviet control. Early in 1948 Czechoslavakia was the victim of a Communist coup d'état, in the course of which Jan Masaryk (the only non-Communist in the government) was found dead in mysterious circumstances. In May of that year the USSR cut off all communications with the Western zones of the city of Berlin. Although the blockade was called off in 1949, in that year the USSR exploded its first atomic device, much to the surprise of the Americans. In 1950 the Korean war broke out, and it was widely believed that Stalin was behind Kim Il Sung's attack on the South.

Closer analysis of the Cold War suggests that it is not as watertight as contemporaries believed. At Yalta in 1945 Stalin accepted that Greece lay in the British 'sphere of influence', and he did not help the Greek communists in their civil war with the royalists. During the Berlin blockade Soviet air controllers continued to work, so allowing Allied aircraft to maintain the famous 'airlift'. When the North Koreans crossed the 38th Parallel in June 1950, the Soviet representative was absent from the Security Council and could not veto the sending of UN forces to Korea. This hardly backs up the idea that there was collusion between Stalin and Kim Il Sung. The view of the historian A.J.P. Taylor is perhaps close to the truth:

> There are many who think that in 1945, Stalin and his hordes wanted to sweep right across Europe. In my opinion, and I am entitled to my opinion

as others are, this was not the case. Soviet policy wanted security – the defeat of Germany and then the building up of a ring of satellite states which would ensure Soviet Russia's security.[11]

STALIN'S DEATH

Joseph Stalin died in March 1953, sphinx-like to the last. In death as in life he was surrounded by mystery. Rumours of a new purge were widespread, and he already believed (latent anti-Semite as he was) in a conspiracy of Jewish doctors to poison him. According to Khrushchev he already intended 'to finish off' both Molotov and Mikoyan, but death prevented him from doing so. In this atmosphere it is scarcely surprising that stories circulated about the circumstances of Stalin's death. Khrushchev told the American diplomat Averell Harriman that Stalin died three days after a paralysing stroke. Other versions have Beria strangling him or administering poison. Whatever the truth, his spirit continued to hover uneasily over his country.

Stalin's legacy remains a central issue, in a country where historical truth itself is an issue. The very ambiguity of people's reaction to him, both in the 1950s and today, underlines this point. For Milovan Djilas, the Yugoslav communist, Stalin was 'the greatest criminal in history', while Khrushchev admitted that, while he 'fought barbarism with barbarism, he was a great man'. The mixed feelings of the average Soviet citizen are best expressed by the great poet Yevgeny Yevtushenko, who said that when Stalin died 'we wept sincerely with grief, but also perhaps with fear of the unknown'. They are understandable. Those Soviet citizens born in the twenties and thirties had known no other world than the one Stalin had fashioned for them. They were to be shocked by later denunciations of Stalin, because many of them had the touching and naive belief in an individual leader that a totalitarian system can create. As recently as 1987 Konstantin Simonov wrote about how

> I knew that terrible things were happening in 1937/8; many innocent people were imprisoned, but I kept telling myself that Stalin had nothing to do with all that, it was all the fault of Yezhov and the NKVD. I thought Stalin did not know.[12]

But there has been anger too, as reflected in the Georgian film *Repentance* and in the demand for a memorial to the slaughtered innocents of the 1930s. Yevtushenko also recognised the evil force which Stalin represented when he wrote in 1962, 'Triple the guard beside his grave so that he will not rise again and with him the past'. It was to exorcise this past that Nikolay Bukharin's widow sought the posthumous rehabilitation of her husband, which the Soviet government granted her in 1988.

CHAPTER FIFTEEN

The USSR since Stalin

The Stalinist Succession

Because the Soviet Union had no mechanism for appointing a leader, Stalin's death, like Lenin's in 1924, was followed by a succession crisis. But once he was dead another characteristic of his dictatorship died with him: with one exception, no other Soviet leader was to be executed in the years after 1953, and there were to be no more blood purges.

The exception was Lavrenti Beria, the sinister head of the KGB. Although Georgi Malenkov secured the posts of prime minister and general secretary, Beria still exercised immense power, which was felt to be a threat to the other members of the Politburo. Even Malenkov, who owed his position to Beria's support, feared him, but the latter's fall was more directly linked to his radical policy suggestions. One was that East Germany (or the German Democratic Republic) should be sacrificed because it was too much of a liability. Even allowing for the embarrassing seepage of GDR citizens to the West this was heresy at the height of the Cold War, and it gave Beria's anxious colleagues an excuse to eliminate him.

According to Nikita Khrushchev, then the most junior member of the nine-man Politburo, Beria's colleagues subjected him to four hours' questioning just after the failed uprising by East Berlin workers in June 1953. They then decided that it would be too dangerous to let him go free, and Khrushchev later described how he and his colleagues 'came to the unanimous decision that the only correct measure for the defence of the Revolution was to shoot him immediately. This decision was adopted by us and carried out on the spot.' Doubts have been expressed about this version of events, but Beria was never seen alive again after the meeting with his colleagues.[1] Beria's death removed Stalin's most zealous henchman, but it remained true that all the party leaders had been tainted by their association with him. The new leadership would have to distance itself from Stalinism if the USSR was to make any progress in the crucial sphere of economic policy.

MALENKOV'S REFORMS

General Secretary Malenkov was aware of this and made a genuine attempt to introduce thoroughgoing reform in 1954–5. But he was hamstrung at every turn by a party bureaucracy which had waxed fat under the inertia of Stalinism. The crucial factor for Malenkov was his attempt to improve the wretched living standards of the workers by increasing the production of consumer goods. Stalin had not cared a whit for the quality of life of the Russian workers, and his Fourth Five Year Plan continued to reflect his obsession with armaments and heavy industry.

But lessons had been learnt from the Stalin period and its deadening 'cult of the personality'. Power in the USSR was now to be exercised by a 'collective leadership', and it is true that since Stalin's death no Soviet leader has been able to achieve the sort of dominance which the dead dictator had in the 1940s and 1950s.

THE CULTURAL THAW

Although many people in the cultural community would have endorsed the ambivalent feelings of Yevtushenko about Stalin's death, the event did mark an important watershed in the cultural history of the state as well. In 1954 Ilya Ehrenburg's *The Thaw* exactly expressed the writer's relief that Stalin had gone, but also 'condemned the vaunted "New Soviet Man" as a self-seeking toady, and the approved social realist artist as a barely talented hack'.[2] Vera Panova also attacked the apparatchiks who made up the top echelons of the Soviet Communist party in her novel *The Seasons*, while Leonid Zorin's play *The Guests* expressed the new spirit in Soviet theatre.

MALENKOV'S FALL

Malenkov's failure to achieve the much-vaunted improvement in consumer goods production led to his fall from power in February 1955. Another factor was a fundamental difference of opinion in the Politburo about nuclear weapons, which Malenkov accurately described as 'a danger to world civilisation' which would bring about the destruction of both capitalism and communism.

This gave the rising star in the Politburo, Nikita Khrushchev, the opportunity to attack Malenkov, although it is clear in retrospect that Khrushchev agreed with most of what Malenkov had been saying. At a meeting of the Central Committee of the Soviet Communist party early in 1955 Khrushchev used coded language to attack 'theoreticians', but names were unnecessary because everyone knew who he was talking about. A further scathing reference was made to views 'which in their day were preached by Rykov, Bukharin and their kind'. Malenkov could see which way the wind was blowing, and he tendered his resignation on the rather absurd ground of lack of experience. He had been completely outmanoeuvred by Khrushchev in a struggle which was strongly reminiscent of the Trotsky–Stalin struggle in the twenties. Once again the abler, but more politically naïve, man lost out to the accusation that he was deviating from the party line on defence and foreign policy. Khrushchev, according to his biographer, displayed 'qualities as a fly politician better than any other episode in his career'.[3] One of those qualities was undoubtedly a low peasant cunning.

The USSR under Khrushchev

KHRUSHCHEV'S PERSONALITY AND BACKGROUND

Nikita Khrushchev, like Stalin, was of peasant stock. He was born in 1894 in the village of Kalinovka in the Ukraine. This was an important factor in Khrushchev's career because he was seared by his experience of poverty and famine in his native province. His first wife died there in 1921 during the terrible famine. Afterwards Khrushchev climbed steadily up the party hierarchy, which was a remarkable achievement for a man who only learned to read and write properly after the civil war.

Khrushchev's loyalty to the party underwent its severest test between

1938 and 1948 when he was sent back to the Ukraine. First of all, on Stalin's instructions, he purged the Communist party, and then he played a leading role in organising the defence of Stalingrad which earned the respect of soldiers who usually resented political interference. In 1949 Stalin recalled him to Moscow to a senior position in the Party Secretariat. He then became the Party expert on agriculture, and cleverly managed to saddle Malenkov with the blame for a serious harvest failure in 1953 which forced the USSR to cut its grain exports.

Stalin and Khrushchev were as different as chalk and cheese. Where Stalin was secretive, paranoid and ruthless, Khrushchev was warm, friendly and volatile. Despite his lack of education, he was nobody's fool and possessed a lively interest in the outside world which his mentor never showed. It is hard to imagine Stalin going to Hollywood and watching the can-can as Khrushchev did. Or many other members of the Soviet government banging a shoe on a table at the United Nations to interrupt a Philippine delegate who was attacking some aspect of Soviet policy (he did the same thing to British premier Harold MacMillan). Characteristically, Khrushchev apologised the next day, saying: 'I am a young parliamentarian; he is an old hand. Let us learn from each other.' On another memorable occasion he lectured a green Vice-President Richard Nixon in Moscow on the virtues of socialism, which he claimed would enable the USSR to have a better standard of living than the USA.

Nikita Khrushchev

In this instance he also rashly predicted that it would be able 'to wave bye-bye' as the capitalists watched in amazement. In these moods Khrushchev could be truculent and insensitive (he once told Western reporters that Foreign Minister Gromyko would sit on a block of ice if he, Khrushchev, ordered it), and his need to hog the limelight angered colleagues on the Politburo. This endangered his position, because he never wielded absolute power in the way that Stalin had done.

ECONOMIC POLICY

Khrushchev's survival depended on the effectiveness of his economic strategy, which was broadly similar to Malenkov's. There was one important difference, however. Malenkov, like Stalin before him, gave agriculture a low place on his list of priorities, whereas Khrushchev regarded its reform as essential. Unlike his predecessors he also had a real understanding of the Soviet people's demand for a proper diet. This down-to-earth approach is well represented by a statement which he made during this period.

> I do believe that what counts more than anything else is practice. Marxist theory helped us to win power and consolidate it. Having done this we must help the people to eat well, dress well and live well. You cannot put theory into your soup or Marxism into your clothes. If, after forty years of communism, a person cannot have a glass of milk or a pair of shoes, he will not believe that communism is a good thing, no matter what you tell him.

Typical of Khrushchev's populist style, it upset party theoreticians, and sounded remarkably similar to the 'right wing deviationism' propounded by Rykov and Bukharin which got them executed in 1938.

Khrushchev's reformist programme for Soviet agriculture began to operate long before Malenkov's fall. The harvest failure of 1953 was caused in Khrushchev's eyes by two factors: the lack of arable land, and the failure to grow more profitable crops (he pointed to the success the Americans had with maize). The first weakness could be remedied by his 'Virgin Lands' scheme, which involved putting more land under cultivation in Siberia and Kazakhstan. Khrushchev himself had grown maize successfully in the Ukraine and there was little active opposition to this proposal in the Politburo. The Virgin Lands scheme was another matter, and no member of the Politburo was prepared to back him.

Khrushchev now seemed to be in a vulnerable position, but he turned the tables on Malenkov by revealing that he had fiddled the agricultural production figures for 1952, which had the effect of doubling them. Nevertheless, since the production figures for 1953 were bad, Khrushchev had to shift the battleground to an area where Malenkov was weak. The irony here was that both he and Malenkov agreed about the need to produce more consumer goods, which posed the additional question of how it was to be funded. Stalin's 'smoke-stack' industries were both inefficient and costly to run, but Malenkov was stuck with them because he needed the support of traditionalists on the Politburo like Molotov and Kaganovich. They also opposed Khrushchev's agricultural reforms, but would never agree to the dismantling of heavy industry. Malenkov was left therefore with the attractive but dangerous option of cutting defence spending. If he did not, his drive to boost consumer goods production would never get off the ground.

The evolution of the H-bomb in the mid-fifties seemed to offer him a way out of his dilemma. Malenkov argued that the possession of such a terrible weapon would deter any attack on the USSR from the West. The corollary was that conventional forces could be cut back, and the savings invested in other parts of the economy. Although Malenkov was forced to accept the party line and state that *only* the capitalist system would be destroyed by war, Khrushchev sensed his opportunity. In June 1954 Khrushchev made a speech in Prague denouncing Malenkov's doctrine of 'peaceful coexistence' with the West and boasting about the Soviet Union's H-bomb. As Bulganin, Molotov, Kaganovich and Vorshilov had already indicated their opposition to the Malenkov line, the general secretary was doomed. Khrushchev merely administered the coup de grâce in his later speech to the Central Committee.

Malenkov had gambled and lost, but his successor as general secretary was to take even greater risks. Malenkov himself survived his disgrace, and kept his position on the Politburo. Soviet leaders could expect to live out their natural span for the first time in thirty years.

INDUSTRY

Khrushchev's industrial programme benefited from energy resources which were not available to Stalin. Large deposits of natural gas had been discovered in Siberia, and by 1961 the USSR was second only to the USA as an oil producer. Huge pipelines carried the crude oil westwards to European Russia and the satellite states of Eastern Europe (production reached an annual figure of 243 million tonnes in 1965).

During this period the USSR also initiated a programme to upgrade low-quality iron ore, and Stalin's great showpiece at Magnitogorsk was given the largest blast furnace in the world. Further evidence of Soviet technical development came when the first sputnik (space satellite) was launched in 1957. This was followed by another scientific first when Soviet space scientists put the cosmonaut Yuri Gagarin into orbit in 1961. These impressive achievements seem to have gone to Khrushchev's head when he tried to reform what was still a backward economy in other areas.

AGRICULTURE

Khrushchev certainly thought big, particularly in agriculture, his own special sphere of interest. Huge collective farms were created by merging together several smaller ones, and he established 50,000 of them with an average acreage of 37,000 hectares. This was a tribute both to his agricultural expertise and to his tenacity in pushing his policy in the Politburo. No one else had his experience and knowledge, and once he became general secretary in 1955 agriculture received a priority it had never been given before. In his usual down-to-earth manner he underlined its importance. 'What sort of a leader is it,' he asked, 'who can't provide cabbages?' His reforming zeal ensured that the super collectives were producing almost one-fifth of Soviet grain within two years.

Khrushchev's control of agricultural planning and his innovative role in the industry did, of course, leave him very vulnerable if anything went wrong. The Virgin Lands scheme did provide another 225 million hectares under cultivation in Soviet Asia, but it was then sabotaged by nature when the top soil blew away (the fate that befell the American farm states in the 1920s and 1930s). Funding problems also arose later because of Khrushchev's desire to win the space race with the USA and outnumber its missile system.

DeStalinisation

Khrushchev's greatest achievement was undoubtedly his exposure of Stalinism. This was part of a process which started after Stalin's death and then halted for a period in the autumn of 1954. Many political prisoners were released from the labour camps, along with thousands of former Red Army soldiers whose only crime was to have been taken prisoner by the Germans.

The real turning came when Khrushchev made a six-hour speech to a secret session of the 20th Party Congress in February 1956 in which, to the amazement of the delegates, he launched a devastating attack on the former dictator and his policies. Stalin was described as a 'mass murderer' and a 'bungler' who had allowed his country to be taken by surprise when the Germans attacked in 1941. All this to an audience of Soviet Communist delegates who had been taught to see Stalin as an almost godlike figure.

For Khrushchev personally the speech represented a considerable gamble because Politburo colleagues like Molotov and Voroshilov were still unrepentant Stalinists. He himself had been a Stalinist for years, but his speech contained no hint of repentance about his own brutal role in the Ukraine. Nor did it contain any hint that there was anything seriously wrong with Marxism–Leninism; all the mistakes of the 1930s were attributed to Stalin's pathological 'cult of the personality'. This provided a convenient escape route for all those who had been intimately involved in Stalin's crimes. Many government apparatchiks were only too happy to blame Stalin for everything, because serious questions could have been put to them about their own behaviour before 1953. This unwillingness to come to terms with the Stalinist Terror is absurdly evident in the memoirs of the long-standing foreign minister, Andrei Gromyko, who fails to mention Khrushchev's 1956 speech at all (although he gives quite a lot of space to the former Soviet goalkeeper, Lev Yashin, and the current Argentine soccer prodigy, Maradona!).

THE 'THAW' IN THE ARTS

Under Khrushchev, the second phase of the cultural thaw began. Khrushchev himself is said to have read the manuscript of Alexander Solzhenitsyn's *One Day in the Life of Ivan Denisovich* (which described the author's eight-year term in a labour camp) before authorising its publication. He also allowed the young poet Yevtushenko to travel freely in the West, where his controversial *A Precocious Autobiography* was published in 1963. In it he denounced the careerists and apparatchiks who gained privileges by sheltering under the banner of the Soviet Communist party.

Khrushchev evidently had doubts about his concessions to the artistic community, and this ambiguity was shown when he warned them in 1962 that 'peaceful coexistence in the sphere of ideology is treachery to Marxism–Leninism'. The major victim of this indecisive attitude was the poet and novelist Boris Pasternak, who had not been published in Russia during the Stalin period. Pasternak seems to have expected that his novel *Doctor Zhivago* would be published in the Soviet Union and he also sent a copy of his manuscript to an Italian communist publisher. The novel was a great success in the West and Pasternak was awarded the Nobel Prize for Literature in 1958, but far from welcoming the prestige this gave to Soviet literature, the Soviet authorities prevented him from going to Stockholm to collect his prize. They also banned the book's publication in Russia and expelled Pasternak from the Writers' Union. He died in 1960, never to profit from the great success of his book in the West, where it was also made into a film.

Pasternak's experience showed up the flaws in Khrushchev's relatively liberal attitude towards the Arts. Criticism of Stalin was allowed, but Pasternak had set his novel in the period of the 1917 Revolution and the Civil War and did not always show the Bolsheviks in a favourable light. In view of the almost divine status given to Lenin in Soviet history, Pasternak may have been guilty of naivety in expecting that his novel would be passed by the Party as fit for publication in the USSR.

Soviet intellectuals tended to sneer at Khrushchev as a *muzhik* (peasant), but the older generation of artists and writers did recognise that progress had been made under him. The easing of the Cold War also brought about the rehabilitation of some western literature, so that the works of Kafka and Ionesco were translated into Russian although puzzlingly the work of others like Proust and Joyce remained taboo.

At no stage did Khrushchev permit criticism of his own behaviour, although he pressed ahead with his campaign against Stalin. The most symbolic act in this campaign of de-Stalinisation was the removal of Stalin's corpse from the mausoleum in Red Square where he had lain with Lenin since his death. His disgrace was completed when Stalingrad was renamed Volgograd. Stalin was reburied in the Kremlin wall with lesser mortals in 1961, and among the Central Committee members who approved this action was a rising star from the Ukraine called Mikhail Gorbachev. He was to finish the process of de-Stalinisation two decades later.

THE DEFEAT OF THE 'ANTI-PARTY GROUP'

Khrushchev's reservations about freedom of expression have to be seen in the context of the threat from the conservatives in the Politburo. They certainly blamed him for the Hungarian uprising in 1956, after leaks about the secret speech had reached the Soviet satellite states. He was also forced to make considerable concessions to the new Polish leader Gomulka to avoid a full-scale national uprising in Poland.

This hostility to Khrushchev resulted in the so-called 'Anti-Party' conspiracy of 1957, which involved Molotov and the embittered Malenkov. Their plan was to outvote him in the Praesidium (the renamed Politburo) where they had a majority. In this situation, the peasant cunning of Khrushchev once again proved to be more effective than the intellectualism of Malenkov and the experience of the veteran foreign minister, Molotov, 'Mr Nyet' (No) as he was known to Western diplomats by the fifties. Khrushchev's solution was simplicity itself. He used his ally Zhukov, the defence minister and legendary war hero, to fly in all the Central Committee delegates before the Praesidium could meet. The Central Committee, which was responsible for electing the Praesidium in the first place, then gave Khrushchev the majority he needed.

Malenkov and Molotov were ousted from the Praesidium and replaced by Khrushchev supporters, but they could count themselves lucky: Malenkov was sent to manage a power station in Siberia and Molotov became ambassador to Outer Mongolia. Khrushchev sacked Prime Minister Bulganin who was then made chairman of the State Bank. The latter, who had replaced Malenkov in the post of premier, and was a rather colourless figure, although the British tabloid press invented the slogan 'Mr B and Mr K' when the two men visited Britain in 1955. They were roundly booed wherever they went, but the attempt to make 'B and K' into a political tandem was misplaced. In the Soviet hierarchy the post of general secretary was far more important than the premiership. Nevertheless, Khrushchev took on this position as well, and the defeat of the 'Anti-Party' group was complete. He had achieved this, as a British study has pointed out, 'without bloodshed, but in Communist terms by constitutional means'.[4]

The Satellites

When Stalin died he left the Soviet Union in control of the whole of Eastern Europe except Yugoslavia. But the response of the new collective leadership to his death was immediately to try and mend fences with the Yugoslavs. Khrushchev visited Belgrade in 1955, but Marshal Tito would not be lured back into the Soviet system.

On the surface the satellite states gave an impression of independence, but they all had Soviet troops on their soil and could do nothing without Moscow's approval. This loss of real sovereignty was difficult enough to bear, but it was compounded by the failure of central planning. Even Czechoslovakia, which had been relatively prosperous in the inter-war years, stagnated in the 1950s and 1960s.

The first physical resistance to Soviet domination had come in East Berlin in the summer of 1953. It was primarily a protest against food prices, but Soviet tanks were sent in to crush the uprising in which forty-two people died. The strategic position of the GDR made it impossible for the Kremlin to contemplate any meaningful changes there. Two years later, the USSR bound her satellites even more tightly in the military agreement known as the Warsaw Pact. This was the Soviet response to NATO, and the setting up of COMECON (Council for Mutual Economic Assistance) in 1949 strengthened Soviet control of the satellite economies as well. There was a superficial resemblance between COMECON and the EEC, but whereas the latter encouraged the development of a free market in Western Europe, COMECON remained 'a collection of countries with centrally planned economies, and most of the industry in state hands'.[5] COMECON was designed primarily for the benefit of the USSR, which sometimes caused bizarre anomalies (jokes circulated within the membership, about vast surpluses of tinned Bulgarian tomatoes which other members were obliged to buy regardless of whether there was any demand for them).

POLAND AND HUNGARY 1956

Whispers about Krushchev's speech reached Eastern Europe.

In October a full-scale revolt against the repressive regime of Matya Rakosi broke out in Budapest with a symbolic attack on the headquarters of the hated AVH (secret police). A new leader was found in Imre Nagy, himself purged by Rakosi who, only that month, had got back his communist party card. The Red Army withdrew from Hungary, and, for a while, it seemed that the Kremlin might acquiesce with the process of reform. But when Nagy wanted to leave the Warsaw Pact, and allow non-communists into his government, this was too much for Khrushchev and his colleagues.

The Red Army smashed its way back into Budapest, while the West was absorbed by the Suez Crisis. Vainly did the Hungarian Freedom Fighters scan the skies over their capital for American help. Nagy himself was tricked out of his sanctuary in the West Germany embassy and executed. The Hungarian October was over, but it was not forgotten.

In Poland, dissatisfaction with Russian domination was sharpened by the sudden death of Party Secretary, Bierut. The Poles rejected Ochab, Moscow's candidate as his successor, and insisted on the appointment of Vladislaw Gomulka who had been purged in the early fifties and, in his own way, was a Polish nationalist of sorts. Khrushchev, although reluctant to accept Gomulka, saw that he might otherwise have a second bloodbath on his hands. Gomulka was installed as General Secretary of the Polish Communist Party, and the 'Polish October' therefore resulted in a tactical victory for the Poles.

Foreign Affairs to 1964

The collective leadership which replaced Stalin adopted a more open stance towards the outside world, which was shown as early as the 1954 Geneva Conference. Malenkov represented the USSR, and acted as its co-chairman with the then British foreign secretary, Anthony Eden. The astmosphere was friendly and from it emerged a settlement on Indo-China. Seasoned observers of the international scene thought that they detected a new 'Spirit of Geneva'.

Malenkov certainly wanted 'peaceful coexistence' with the West, but his days as general secretary were numbered and the events of 1956 did little to improve relations between the USSR and the West. In a possible attempt to divert the world's attention away from events in Hungary, Bulganin made a belligerent statement threatening Britain and France with Soviet rockets if they did not end their attack on Egypt, which was designed to reoccupy the Suez Canal (Nasser had nationalised it in July 1956). Bulganin was almost certainly bluffing, but the Suez operation saved the USSR from embarrassment by involving two western democracies in a war with a backward Third World country.

In 1959 Soviet–Western relations had improved enough to allow Khrushchev to visit the USA and create quite a hit, so that a superpower summit was set up for 1960 in Paris. Unfortunately the proposed summit coincided almost exactly with the shooting down of a U2 American spy plane by the Russians and the capture of its pilot, Gary Powers. There was nothing new about aerial espionage, but the unfortunate Powers made the mistake of getting caught and handing the USSR an invaluable propaganda victory. Khrushchev went to the summit to berate and humiliate President Eisenhower and then storm out of the building.

East–West relations worsened still further in 1961, when the East German authorities, with Soviet backing, built a wall between the eastern and western parts of Berlin. In reality there wasn't the slightest prospect of any western intervention, but Soviet and American tanks did face one another for a while across 'Checkpoint Charlie' (the most famous crossover point between East and West Berlin). This followed a meeting between Khrushchev and the new American President, John F. Kennedy, at Vienna, where Khrushchev formed the impression that Kennedy was a rather gauche young man who could easily be pushed around. His biographer, Mark Frankland, believes that the Soviet leader wanted to test the president and that 'Kennedy himself found it an unpleasant experience, and Khrushchev seems to have left Vienna convinced that he could get away with some daring moves'⁶ The age difference may have been a factor (Kennedy was only 44 when he became president, Khrushchev was (66) but the absence of an armed US response to the Berlin Wall crisis seems to have strengthened this faulty analysis. It was to have serious consequences for Khrushchev himself.

THE SINO–SOVIET SPLIT

When the Chinese People's Republic was set up in 1949, it was despite rather than because of Soviet policy. Nevertheless, a Sino–Soviet treaty of friendship was signed in 1950, and Soviet experts were sent to China to assist Mao Zedong's attempt to modernise his country.

Only after Stalin's death did tensions appear between the two biggest Communist states. At first they centred on Khrushchev's de-Stalinisation campaign, which Mao and his colleagues could not accept; Stalin was still accorded as much honour as Lenin in China. Further disagreement arose over the Malenkov–Khrushchev doctrine of peaceful coexistence with the West, which Mao regarded as 'revisionism' (i.e. rejecting true communism). Soviet policy was based on the military primacy of the nuclear bomb but Mao dismissed it in a famous phrase as 'a paper tiger'. In doing so he was stressing the revolutionary potential of the masses, rather than denying the lethal effects of the weapon. But its existence was not, in Chinese eyes, an excuse for coming to terms with the Western imperialists.

Finally there was a disagreement over economic planning, which was inflated by Khrushchev's blunt and insensitive style. The Chinese had begun in 1958 what Mao called 'the Great Leap Forward', or Second Five Year Plan. An important part of it was to be the establishment of peasant communes throughout China, despite the collapse of such schemes in the USSR after the civil war in the 1920s. When Khrushchev visited China in 1958 he told Chairman Mao about the Soviet experience and was ignored for his pains. Relations worsened in 1959 when he visited the USA and disgusted the Chinese in the process. Khrushchev was by now acutely aware (as Malenkov had been) of the horrors of nuclear war, while the Chinese were, in Soviet eyes, indulging in Cold War brinkmanship with the Americans over Taiwan (Formosa). This island off the Chinese coastline was a bolthole for Jiang Jieshi and his routed Nationalist army after the Communist victory of 1949, but Mao regarded it as part of China proper. Intensive shelling by the Chinese communists in 1958 provoked an invasion scare, and the American Sixth Fleet was sent to the seas around Taiwan as a warning to Peking. There was no invasion but the Russians were concerned about Chinese sabre-rattling in the Far East.

It was clear by the end of the fifties that Mao Zedong was really challenging Khrushchev's right to lead the communist world. Whereas Mao had his own coherent theory of Marxism–Leninism, Khrushchev was essentially a pragmatist who saw that the commune system, with its lack of material incentives, would not work, and said so in his usual forthright manner. Ultimately, Khrushchev was proved to be quite right in his criticisms, and the 'Great Leap' had to be abandoned in 1961.

By 1960 Sino–Soviet relations were at an all-time low. It was obvious that there was personal animosity between Mao and Khrushchev, who made a violent attack on the Chinese in a speech in Bucharest. Later that year Khrushchev began to withdraw Soviet technicians from China, even though this left the Chinese with half-completed projects. He even indulged in crude racism of the sort used at the turn of the century about 'the yellow peril', and tried to prevent China attaining a dominant position in the Third World (the Chinese foreign minister, Zhou Enlai, had played a significant role at the Bandung Conference of non-aligned states in 1955).

All these moves helped to make the Sino–Soviet split irrevocable, and the schism was to last for three decades. Underlying it was a basic nationalism stretching back to the times when Imperial China was a pawn of the colonial powers. The Russians might be communists but they were still 'foreign devils'. Both sides emerged badly from the split of 1960. There were now two rival empires in the communist world, even if only tiny Albania followed the Peking line. Her maverick dictator, Enverr Hoxha, was a Stalinist who refused to accept the new Moscow line and left COMECON and the Warsaw Pact in 1961.

THE CUBAN MISSILE CRISIS

In 1959 Communist insurgents led by a youthful Fidel Castro overthrew the squalid American-backed dictatorship of Batista on the island of Cuba. As Cuba is only ninety miles from the coast of Florida, the US administration viewed this development with some alarm. But in its early phase the Cuban revolution, with its genuine popular support, seemed to be moving towards some form of democracy. Only when Castro nationalised all US property on the island did the Americans become really concerned and the American Central Intelligence Agency formulated a rather desperate scheme to remove him from power, and which was inherited by Kennedy from the Eisenhower administration. Early in 1961 this wildly optimistic plan to land anti-Castro exiles on the Cuban coast was presented to Kennedy who, rather against his better judgement, endorsed it. The result was the Bay of Pigs fiasco which ended in the capture or massacre of the exiles by Castro's forces while Washington stood by helplessly.

The combination of the Bay of Pigs disaster, the Vienna Summit and the Berlin Wall crisis may well have tempted Khrushchev and his colleagues to take a gamble of their own and place Soviet missiles in Cuba, ostensibly to protect the island from US attack, but also as a deterrent to some of the wilder anti-Communist ideologues in the Pentagon. (Soviet motivations have to be a matter of guesswork until their archives are opened.) The missiles were duly installed, accompanied by their Soviet technicians, but their existence was discovered by US spy planes by the autumn of 1962.

For some weeks the Kremlin denied all knowledge of the missiles, until a memorable confrontation between the US Ambassador at the UN, Adlai Stevenson, and his Soviet opposite number resulted in the production of blown-up US intelligence photographs of the missile sites. Soviet denials were then replaced by a refusal to remove the weapons. President Kennedy was adamant: if the Russians did not remove the missiles from their silos, the USA would consider invading Cuba once more, an act which could easily precipitate a nuclear war. Aggressive language was used by both sides but Kennedy kept a cool head. He rejected the idea of invasion or bombing (urged by Pentagon advisers) in favour of a blockade to prevent spare parts for the missiles arriving. This option also had the great advantage of giving the Kremlin a breathing space to consider whether Cuba was worth a nuclear war.

The crucial point turned out to be 28 October 1962. On that day, while some twenty-five Soviet merchant ships were sailing towards Cuba, some carrying missile spare parts, Khrushchev received a conciliatory message from Kennedy inviting further negotiation. Two days earlier Kennedy had received two messages from the Soviet leader: one was private and conciliatory, the other public and belligerent. Wisely Kennedy, taking his brother Robert's advice, responded only to the milder version. In his final response Khrushchev now agreed to remove the missiles, but demanded the end of U2 spy flights over Cuba (one had strayed into Soviet airspace on 27 October). The Soviet ships were also turned back, to avoid possible confrontation with US warships. One important technical result of the crisis was the installation of a 'hotline' telephone system between Washington and Moscow, in the interest of preventing another superpower confrontation in the future. Months later, with minimal publicity, US Jupiter missiles were removed from Turkey and Italy. Although the Russians had demanded their removal during the crisis, Kennedy had refused to trade while Soviet missiles were in Cuba. But the Russians did have a case and Kennedy recognised the Soviet right to more security.

The Kremlin decision-making process at this time was shrouded in a fog of secrecy which the West could not penetrate. Was Khrushchev the puppet of the Soviet military, or was the Cuban adventure a personal initiative? Mark Frankland believes that the Cuban decision 'was Khrushchev's most dangerous miscalculation in the nearly ten years that he dominated the conduct of Soviet foreign policy',[9] thereby suggesting that the policy was largely his own. Yet there is subtle evidence that Khrushchev may have been under some pressure from hawks in the Soviet military establishment. Three months after the crisis Marshal M.V. Zakharov, the army chief-of-staff, was transferred to an obscure post in a military school.[7]

THE TEST BAN TREATY

The narrow escape from a nuclear holocaust in 1962 concentrated the minds of the superpower leaders on the problem of ensuring that there never was one. The desire for disarmament, probably strongest at that time in the British premier Harold Macmillan, was to lead within a year to a real recognition of the danger hanging over the whole of mankind.

The 1963 Test Ban Treaty outlawed nuclear bomb testing in the atmosphere (though not underground). The Americans and Russians were joined by Britain, but the other two nuclear powers, China and France, refused to sign. The Chinese had been able to begin a nuclear programme without Russian assistance which Khrushchev withheld.

Khrushchev's Fall

There is no doubt that Khrushchev's reputation was badly damaged by the Cuban crisis, but it did not force him from office. Nor did the Sino–Soviet split. Even his tendency to behave like a one-man band, which infuriated fellow members of the Praesidium, was tolerated while his economic policies were working. It was in that sector that Khrushchev gave a hostage to fate by boasting about how the USSR would rapidly catch up with, and overtake, the US standard of living. This prediction was, of course, nonsense, particularly as far as Soviet agriculture was concerned, and a series of bad harvests gave his critics their opportunity.

In October 1964 Khrushchev was on holiday in his villa on Georgia's Black Sea coast when the Praesidium summoned him back to Moscow. The assault on his record was led by the chief party ideologist Mikhail Suslov, and although Khrushchev defended himself vigorously he had clearly lost the confidence of most of his colleagues. He then tried his old 1957 tactic of summoning the Central Committee, but this time his opponents were one jump ahead of him. They had already summoned and prepared the Central Committee for his elimination, and the Party Secretary was outvoted and lost his seat on the Praesidium.

The people of the USSR were told that Khrushchev had retired 'on health grounds', and he rapidly disappeared from public view. His last years were lived out as an ordinary pensioner in Moscow, and no representative of the Soviet government attended his funeral in 1971. The final mark of official disapproval was shown when he was buried, not in the Kremlin wall with the other heroes of socialism, but in the Novodevichi cemetery.

For all his faults Khrushchev was (bar one) the most obviously human of the leaders the USSR has had since the 1917 Revolution. The verdict of his biographer is apt because 'he left his country a better place than he found it, both in the eyes of the majority of his own people, and of the world'.[8]

The Brezhnev Years

Khrushchev was replaced as general secretary of the Soviet Communist Party by Leonid Brezhnev, while the post of prime minister went to Alexei Kosygin. This duo conformed to the image of leadership wanted by the grey party bureaucracy. Where Khrushchev had been brash and extrovert, Brezhnev and Kosygin were boring and safe. There were to be no more extravaganzas in Hollywood.

AGRICULTURE

Since the failure of his agricultural reforms had been largely responsible for Khrushchev's fall, Brezhnev set himself the task of making the state farming sector more efficient. He restored the ministry of agriculture, which Khrushchev had abolished, and gave the peasants the security of a minimum wage, and a 50 per cent increase in payments for their produce if they exceeded the quota laid down. A crash programme for the production of fertilisers was introduced, and by the 1970s considerable progress had been made.

The production figures confirm this development. Grain production, for example, which had a yearly average of 121 million tonnes between 1956 and 1960, had risen to an average of 162 million tonnes between 1966 and 1969. Real peasant incomes rose in the sixties, and the state encouraged the development of private peasant plots by subsidising them. Yet despite these innovations a bad harvest in 1975 forced the USSR to purchase large amounts of US grain. The food distribution system was often woefully inadequate, so that a citizen of Moscow or Leningrad would have to pay well above official price levels to obtain staple foods like fruit from private peasant markets. Endless queuing was a depressing feature of urban Soviet life.

INDUSTRY

The Brezhnev–Kosygin regime continued what has become known as 'goulash communism', an industrial policy devoted to the production of consumer goods, which also gave due recognition to the need for technological help from the West. A typical example was the agreement with Fiat, which was invited to build a car plant at Togliatti-on-Volga (named after Palmiro Togliatti, the leader of the Italian Communist Party for most of the post-war period). Although the plant was supposed to produce 600,000 cars a year, possession of a car remained a hopelessly Utopian dream for the average Soviet citizen. In 1966 car ownership stood at 5 per 1000 population compared with 398 per 1000 in the USA).

Housing posed another problem. With individual house ownership virtually unknown in the USSR, many Soviet citizens were forced to live in tiny flats in huge unattractive blocks. Although a big housing programme in 1968 provided some 11 million new flats, most of them only had two rooms. There is, it should be remembered, another side to this particular coin. Housing and fuel costs were (and are) heavily subsidised in the USSR, and part of the problem with the Soviet economy was that some better-off citizens were left with a surplus of roubles, but nothing to spend them on.

THE MINORITIES

Stalin had treated the national minorities of the USSR with extreme ruthlessness. But in the easier climate of the Khrushchev years, hopes had been raised that the rights of national minorities might be recognised. Brezhnev and Kosygin did not encourage such aspirations and adopted a policy of repression towards the minorities. Particular brutality was reserved for the Crimean Tartars whom Stalin had uprooted from their homeland. Between 1956 and 1974, 200 Tartars were imprisoned for agitating about the loss of their traditional lands, and those who returned to the Crimea without permission were expelled.

Baltic nationalism was also severely repressed, which provoked riots in Lithuanian in 1972 when a student burnt himself to death in protest at the Russian occupation. In Lithuania, the strong link between the Catholic Church and nationalist aspirations was demonstrated. Priests were also arrested for indulging in 'anti-Soviet propaganda'.

Further suffering was also inflicted on the Jewish minority by discriminating against those who wished to emigrate to Israel. A stock excuse for refusing a visa was that the individual concerned had access to state secrets, however long ago. Here at least western protests were effective. There was a large and vocal Jewish minority in the USA with a good deal of political influence, and the 1970s were the decade of détente and American pressure brought about the release of 100,000 Soviet Jews, although many were still refused permission to leave. The most celebrated case concerned the dissident Anatoly Shcharansky.

THE DISSIDENTS

The division between local nationalism and the right to freedom of expression and worship was often blurred. Hence Baptists could be imprisoned for trying to circulate bibles, and the Ukrainian mathematician Leonid Plyushch could be given two years in a psychiatric hospital for signing open letters to the UN on the subject of human rights. The disgraceful practice of sending quite sane people to mental hospitals was so prevalent during the Brezhnev period that Soviet psychiatrists became the pariahs of international medicine. The 'treatments' were horrific and often involved excessive use of the drug sulpamazine and the binding of victims in wet cloths. Although the Soviet authorities denied that such abuses were taking place, their behaviour did have a sinister

Alexander Solzenhitsyn

kind of logic behind it. This was because in the USSR, according to the official version, a perfect socialist society had been created, so that those who criticised it must therefore be deranged (schizophrenia was a favourite diagnosis) and removed from society. The existence of social problems like crime, alcoholism and drug-taking was also denied.

The response of dissidents to this persecution was to circulate samizdats (underground newspapers) both inside and outside the USSR. This took great courage because the penalty for those who were caught was draconian. In 1973, for example, Vladimir Borisov was given compulsory psychiatric treatment for supporting Solzhenitsyn, and kept in hospital for refusing to disavow him. Solzhenitsyn had become well known in the West and an international campaign had been started to secure his release. In 1974, after being stripped of his Soviet citizenship, he was forced to leave the USSR. Others like Borisov were not so fortunate.

Another celebrated case concerned Andrei Sakharov, a scientist of international repute, who is generally credited with being the 'father of the Soviet hydrogen bomb'. Sakharov's criticisms of Soviet society were deeply embarrassing to the Brezhnev government but they would not allow him to leave the USSR. Instead, he suffered 'internal exile' to the town of Gorky and, together with his wife, Elena Bonner, another noted dissident, was obliged to await better times.

EDUCATION

Immense efforts were made in the immediate post-war period to rebuild the educational system. At the famous 20th Party Congress in 1956 Krushchev spelt out the priorities. 'To arrive at communism,' he said, 'that most fair and perfect society . . . we must start right now educating the man of the future.' He then committed the party to provide every Soviet citizen with ten years education. This was a herculean task. Only 58 per cent of the population of the USSR had Russian as their mother tongue, and this was one of the reasons why special language schools were set up for promising young linguists. Similar provision was made for mathematics, science and theatre (surprisingly, no special provision was made for music). The ordinary schools in the Soviet system were to be comprehensive and coeducational.

Under the Soviet system each boy or girl was trained to be a loyal, hard-working and politically reliable citizen. It demanded a close relationship between schools and the Party youth organisations. At the age of seven Soviet children could join the Octobrists, before moving on to the Pioneer organisation. At fourteen it was possible, if a child were well-behaved and had good grades, to become a member of the Komsomol (communist youth movement). Normally Komsomol members remained in that organisation until the age of twenty-eight, when they would have expected to become members of the Communist Party.

Equal attention was given in the 1950s to the restoration of the university system. By 1966 four million young people were being taught in universities and institutes of higher learning. In most of its aspects the Soviet education system was highly centralised, but there were exceptions. The provision of nursery and kindergartens, for example, was the responsibility of local authorities.

CZECHOSLOVAKIA

The pattern of popular discontent in the satellite states continued. Its most dramatic manifestation was in Czechoslovakia during the six-month period of the 'Prague Spring'. The Czechs had grown more and more restless under the Stalinist regime of Antonín Novotný and eventually this malaise affected Party members as well. At the end of 1967 therefore, Novotný lost his post as Party Secretary. His replacement was the Slovak, Alexander Dubcek, a Soviet-trained communist who saw the desperate need for reform in his country. Dubcek's motto was 'communism with a human face', which meant allowing freedom of expression and the right to travel abroad. He became immensely popular in the brief period from January to August 1968 that the 'Prague Spring' continued. But he was careful to emphasise that Czechoslovakia would remain a member of the Warsaw Pact and COMECON. Despite such assurances, the Kremlin was alarmed at the course of events, particularly because of Czechoslovakia's pivotal position in the Soviet bloc. The hardline East German leader, Walter Ulbricht, was also extremely hostile to Dubcek's reformism and advised the Soviet government to intervene.

Meanwhile, the people of Czechoslovakia threw off their Stalinist shackles, and enjoyed their all too brief flirtation with freedom. A flavour of the period is given by this typically wry Czech joke:

> Dubcek has established a Ministry of the Marine.
> *Soviet Ambassador*: What's the point of having a Ministry of the Marine in a totally landlocked country?
> *Dubcek*: Well, you have a Ministry of Justice and the Bulgarians have a Ministry of Culture!

Although they enjoyed poking fun at their giant neighbour, the Czechs were not in fact anti-Soviet and were careful to learn from Nagy's experience in 1956. But there were ominous signs in the Soviet press which began to talk about 'anti-social elements' in Czechoslovakia. In Poland, too, Gomulka (no longer the hero of the 'Polish October') was irritated by crowds chanting 'We want a Polish Dubcek'.

In retrospect, it may seem that Dubcek and his colleagues were tempting fate by entertaining the mavericks of the communist world, Tito and Ceausescu, that summer (Rumania had diplomatic relations with China and Israel), but the Czech leader was a convinced communist and there was no suggestion of non-communists being invited into the government.

Dubcek seems to have been unlucky that his 'communism with a human face' coincided with the imposition of more hardline policies in the USSR after the relatively liberal period under Khrushchev. Evidence suggests that the Politburo (which replaced the term Praesidium again in 1965) made the decision to intervene in the early summer of 1968. The Soviet leadership then played a mendacious double game, pretending to approve the Dubcek reforms, while secretly planning counter measures.

Then what the Czechs had deemed impossible happened, as they were betrayed for the third time in three decades. Over the night of 20–21 August 1968 Warsaw Pact formations poured over the Czechoslovak borders, and the people awoke to find their country occupied. Dubcek, Cernik, Smerkovsky and other members of the Politburo were arrested and taken to Moscow for interrogation. But President Svoboda (the word translates into English as 'freedom') courageously refused to dismiss them. In this he mirrored the contempt and rage felt by the

Czech people for their invaders; many of the Warsaw Pact troops obviously did not know where they were, and were bewildered by the hostility of the crowds.

Dubcek came back from Moscow a broken man, but remained in his post until the beginning of 1969 because the Russians feared his popular appeal. He was then replaced by Gustav Husák, who had been imprisoned by Novotny and now played the shoddy role of a Soviet puppet. Some half a million Czech party members were purged in the aftermath of the invasion, and Dubcek himself was forced to accept a humble clerical job in the forestry commission at Bratislava.

For Brezhnev in particular the Czech experiment was a heresy too dangerous to be indulged. Its sequel was the 'Brezhnev Doctrine', by which the USSR reserved the right to intervene in any communist state where the regime was endangered by bourgeois nationalism or counter-revolution. The barest pretence of national sovereignty was therefore stolen from the satellite states.

The course of events two decades later only increases the sense of tragedy involved in the destruction of Dubcek's experiment. When a prominent aide of President Gorbachev was asked what the difference was between his boss and Dubcek, he replied, 'Twenty years'.

MORE POLISH OCTOBERS

Gomulka's 'honeymoon' with the Polish people lasted barely a year and he soon proved to be both inflexible and dogmatic. He was brought down in 1970 after a huge price rise across the board just before Christmas in 1970 infuriated the people, and led to strikes and protest demonstrations. The crucial events took place in the shipbuilding centre of Szczecin in mid-December when workers were shot dead; more died in Gdansk. Gomulka could expect Soviet assistance because of his loyalty in 1956, but the defence minister Jaruzelski told him that he would not use army units against the workers. At this point Gomulka had a slight stroke which incapacitated him, and with the Kremlin's approval Edward Gierek became Party Secretary instead.

Gierek tried to buy support by encouraging a consumer boom, which Poland could not pay for, and in 1980 he repeated his predecessor's blunder. This time, in the context of massive food shortages, the government announced meat price rises. Once again the workers rose, now led by the Gdansk shipyard workers and an organisation called Solidarity. This evolved into a free trade union led by a former electrician in the giant Lenin shipyard, Lech Walesa.

Solidarity demanded, and got, the right to negotiate with the government, although many Poles were afraid of Soviet intervention. But Poland is not Czechoslovakia and the Soviet leadership seems to have realised that such an intervention could end in a blood-bath. They knew in any case that General Jaruzelski (he of the dark glasses), who had taken on the posts of general secretary and prime minister, was planning his own solution to the problem of Solidarity. He implemented his plan on 13 December 1981 when martial law was introduced and leading Solidarity activists were arrested. From Moscow's perspective an internal solution was far more desirable, and once again force was used to crush Polish aspirations.

FOREIGN POLICY

In the early post-Khrushchev period the leading role in Soviet foreign policy fell to Alexei Kosygin, who acted as a mediator in the Indo–Pakistan war of 1965 and met President Johnson in 1967 at Glassborough to ensure that the third Arab–Israeli war did not lead to a superpower conflict. Although Soviet influence in the Middle East increased after Suez, it did suffer some major setbacks: most notable was the expulsion of all Soviet advisers from Egypt by President Sadat in 1971. But Soviet weaponry played a key role in the Yom Kippur war of 1973, and the USSR continued to support UN Resolution 242 which demanded the evacuation of the territory conquered by Israel in the 1967 war.

In Europe, the initiative taken by West German Chancellor Willy Brandt (1969–74) now won Soviet approval. Separate treaties with the GDR, Poland and the USSR gave formal recognition to the East Germans and accepted the Oder–Neisse line as the new frontier between East Germany and Poland. Brandt's so-called 'Ostpolitik' (Eastern policy) also played an important part in reducing Soviet fears about attack from the West. The most important aspect of Soviet foreign policy, as always in the years since 1945, was the relationship with the

USA. Moscow was certainly wary about the new détente between the Americans and China which President Nixon set up in 1971–2, but Brezhnev was anxious to remain on good terms with Washington. He and Kosygin achieved a considerable success in 1972 when Strategic Arms Limitation Talks (SALT) led to a reduction in both superpowers' nuclear arsenals.

AFGHANISTAN

Much of the good work done in the 1970s (including the 1975 Helsinki Agreement with its emphasis on human rights) was destroyed by the Soviet Union's decision to invade Afghanistan in December 1979. Most of the blame for this decision must fall on Brezhnev, who was clearly taken aback by the strength of feeling in the West against the Soviet move. Although USA continued to sell grain to the USSR, rather than risk the wrath of the farming lobby, so that much of the force of US protests was weakened.

The USSR claimed she was intervening to help Babrak Karmal's beleaguered communist government, but with the memories of Czechoslovakia barely a decade old the West found this excuse difficult to swallow. It was much easier to sympathise with the heroic Muslim hill tribesmen, who hated their own government and the Russians with equal ferocity. Sympathy was soon translated into large arms shipments from America.

For the Red Army, with a high proportion of raw conscripts, Afghanistan was to prove a hard slog in an alien environment. Its morale can hardly have been improved by the extraordinary attitude of the Soviet government to its own soldiers, which continued after the Brezhnev period. No recognition was accorded to the dead and wounded, which seemed to reflect the government's embarrassment about the whole venture.

BREZHNEV'S DEATH

Brezhnev's last years were not happy ones. Kosygin retired on health grounds in 1980, the casualty list in Afghanistan grew longer by the month, and the détente with the USA for which he had laboured was virtually destroyed by the invasion. Ronald Reagan, who became US president in 1981, took to referring to the USSR as 'the evil empire' as the two superpowers seemed to enter a new version of the Cold War. Sino–US friendship also bothered Brezhnev at a time when Chinese anti-Soviet propaganda was at its most strident (although it did not result in the frontier clashes of 1969). By now Brezhnev himself was a very sick man, and looked it in his public appearances, while the whiff of corruption surrounded his family. He died in November 1982, with little fanfare and even less public remorse.

CHAPTER SIXTEEN

The USSR in the Eighties

The Brezhnev Succession

When Brezhnev died in 1982 the succession reverted to the men of his generation who had lived through the Stalinist horror of the thirties and fought in the Second World War. But the new General Secretary, Yuri Andropov, was not the run-of-the-mill, septuagenarian, characterless clone, otherwise represented on the Politburo. He had been in charge of the KGB, but was both cultured and incorruptible, which were unusual characteristics in Brezhnev's entourage. Just as important, perhaps, was Andropov's ability to spot the rising men in the Party bureaucracy who were not corrupted by the old regime's penchant for bribery and nepotism.

Unlike Brezhnev, Andropov both recognised the serious weaknesses of Soviet society and was prepared to do something about them. Together with his protégé, Mikhail Gorbachev, whom Andropov had made Secretary to the Central Committee, the new General Secretary had tried out a degree of liberalisation by allowing factories in the electronics industry to offer cash incentives to workers. The problem, the workers bluntly told him, was that extra roubles were useless unless there was something to spend them on. Ordering a car, for example, required exemplary patience and a wait of many months.

Andropov had been effective at dealing with dissidents and institutionalised corruption when he was KGB chief, but reforming the creaking monster which was the Soviet economy was another matter. In the event, he had just eight months to assess his task before a chronic kidney disease turned him into an invalid for the last six months of his life.

Andropov wanted Gorbachev, a dynamic reformer like himself, to succeed him but the Old Guard would not have it. Instead, the Politburo insisted on appointing 72-year-old Konstantin Chernenko, although Andropov did extract a promise from his colleagues that Gorbachev would get his chance next. So it was that, in the words of one recent analyst of Soviet affairs, 'in February 1984, the third in a sad line of elderly invalids was elevated to the general secretaryship of the Communist Party'.[1] Chernenko, in fact, was suffering from chronic emphysema, a serious lung disorder which made his demise only a matter of time. As the same writer has pointed out, in any other country this elderly cabal (Foreign Minister Gromyko was 74 and Defence Minister Ustinov 75) would have been pensioned off, but the slogan of the Politburo seemed to be 'thou shalt not retire'.

Chernenko's term of office lasted for just one year, and in March 1985 Mikhail Gorbachev was elected Party Secretary – arguably the most significant decision made in the USSR since Stalin's death.

Gorbachev's Background

Mikhail Gorbachev was born in 1931 in the village of Privolnoya near Stavropol in the Caucasus region, lying between the Black and Caspian Seas. His grandfather was both a founder and the chairman of the local collective but little is known of his father, although his mother Maria still lives in the region. During 'the Great Patriotic War', Privolnoya was occupied by the Germans, and Mikhail was probably evacuated into Soviet Asia (the details about this period are somewhat sketchy).

Considerable play is often made by the Western media with the fact that Gorbachev is the first Soviet leader not actually to have experienced the national trauma of the thirties and forties. This is an oversimplification because, as Gorbachev himself has pointed out, while he didn't fight in the war he was surrounded by its devastating effects on his own region. He travelled regularly from Stavropol to Moscow in the late forties and 'saw with my own eyes the ruined Stalingrad, Rostov, Kharkhov, Orel, Kursk and Voronezh ... Everything lay in ruins: hundreds and thousands of cities, towns and villages, factories and mills.'[2] An intelligent and patriotic young man like Gorbachev was bound to have been profoundly affected by such an experience.

He began work at the age of fifteen as assistant to a combine-harvester operator. Recognised at once to be a hard worker, he was awarded the Order of the Red Banner of Labour before moving on to the University of Moscow in 1950; and had made 'a remarkable leap from a north Caucasus village school to Moscow's law faculty'.[3] His choice of subject was perhaps unusual, because in the USSR law was not a springboard to a political career. But in Moscow he confirmed his reputation for being a hard worker, and it was at the university that he met his wife Raisa. His appointment as the Komsomol representative for his year also gave an indication that he hoped for a Party career. In 1952, Gorbachev became a full Communist Party member, and was set on the slow movement up the Party hierarchy which was to put him into the Kremlin.

Even in those Stalinist days Gorbachev gave subtle indications that his view of the Soviet future might differ from that of the careerists and apparatchiks around him. One of his closest university friends was the Czech Zdenek Mlynar who became a member of the Czech Politburo and was expelled from the Czech Communist Party after the overthrow of the Dubcek government in August 1968. After graduation in 1955 Gorbachev returned to Stavropol, where he became successively secretary of the city Komsomol and of the territory Komsomol. In 1966 he became secretary of the Stavropol city committee of the Communist Party of the Soviet Union (CPSU).

Mikhail Gorbachev

At this point Gorbachev had the stoke of luck which every aspiring political leader needs. In 1967 the newly appointed head of the KGB, Yuri Andropov, came on holiday to Krasnye Kamni (red rocks), one of several pleasant spa towns in the Caucasus foothills around Stavropol. Protocol demanded that he meet the area's first secretary, and that man was Mikhail Gorbachev. The two hit it off at once and became firm friends. Gorbachev was a graduate from Moscow University whereas Andropov had acquired his education in night classes, but the KGB chief was far and away the most intelligent man on the Brezhnev Politburo. Gorbachev shared the older man's distaste for the corruption which surrounded the Brezhnev regime, and he became a frequent visitor at the Andropov flat in Moscow after his election to the Supreme Soviet in 1970.

In 1971 Gorbachev moved up another rung on the Party ladder when he was elected onto the Central Committee. Then in 1978 he became Secretary of the CPSU Central Committee. Seven years later it was foreign minister Gromyko who proposed Gorbachev for the post of General Secretary of the CPSU. If this move was intended to save Gromyko's position it didn't work, because Gorbachev first gave him the titular position of President of the USSR and then took the post for himself after sacking him. It was the end of the biggest surviving act in the history of the USSR.

The inertia of the Soviet system meant that, despite his talents, it had taken Mikhail Gorbachev nearly thirty years to reach the top. After the 'Gromyko-inspired' promotion, he had to wait another year to become an alternate member of the Politburo in 1979, and a further year after that to become a full member of the Soviet executive.

Glasnost and Perestroika

Mikhail Gorbachev came to power in 1985 with a clear-cut programme. His greatest task was to revitalise the moribund Soviet economy and his chosen slogan was 'perestroika' (restructuring). Marginally less importance was attached to 'glasnost' (openness) in the press and broadcasting media, but it proved a less difficult nut to crack than perestroika, with its years of muddle and overmanning to overcome. After half a lifetime in the Party apparatus he was well aware of the difficulties perestroika would cause in the USSR.

> Everyone from General Secretary to worker has to alter his thinking. And this is understandable, for many of us were formed as individuals and lived in conditions when the old order existed.[4]

In the brave new Soviet world after 1985 Brezhnev was very much part of 'the old order', and his period in office was designated 'the years of stagnation'.

Perestroika was made to work at a very basic level. The authorities tackled the long-standing problem of alcoholism and absenteeism in the Soviet workforce head on. Drink shops were closed down by the score, and Gorbachev earned the (not entirely flattering) nickname of 'Mr Lemonade'. Police squads also roamed around cities like Moscow and Leningrad, arresting malingerers who were work-shy.

Although this new puritanism was resented by the workforce, it paled into insignificance in comparison with the major task of making the Soviet economy competitive and up to date. Incentive bonuses and employers who sacked people were striking innovations for workers who, were feather-bedded in many respects, and used to fixed price levels (going back to the thirties) and jobs for life.

The USSR had a large nuclear industry but it was badly discredited in 1986 when an accident at the Chernobyl nuclear power station polluted the surrounding area. The Chernobyl accident showed not only that Soviet nuclear power safety standards were too low, but that old habits

Tallinn, the capital of Estonia

died hard as far as 'glasnost' was concerned. Efforts were made both to keep knowledge of the accident secret and to play down its seriousness. This angered [foreign governments like] the Swedish and British government whose livestock and forests were affected by fallout from Chernobyl.

The eighties demonstrated beyond argument that the USSR was also falling behind the West as far as computer technology was concerned. Soviet models were archaic, and American hostility made it difficult for any Western firm to export the latest computers to the USSR even if they wished to do so. What Soviet industry did demonstrate was a remarkable capacity to get by with what westerners would regard as ancient hardware. The most striking example was to be found in the field of space exploration, where apparently obsolete space probes were able to reach Venus, and Soviet cosmonauts were able to beat all the records for staying in space. Just as in World War II the famous T34 tanks were crudely designed but immensely effective, so Soviet space hardware proved to be both durable and effective.

If the Chernobyl disaster represented a setback for glasnost, great efforts were made elsewhere to dust off the cultural cobwebs in Soviet society. An important aspect of this was to continue the process started by Khrushchev in 1956 and admit the truth about the Stalinist Terror. The film *Repentance* did this admirably, and Soviet Television also showed some bitingly accurate documentary footage about the Stalinist period. The sleazy corruption of the Brezhnev period of 'stagnation' was also well portrayed in films like *Plumbum, or A Dangerous Game*, which was released in 1986. In literature, too, glasnost made its impact, with the publication in the USSR of banned texts like Pasternak's *Doctor Zhivago*.

There were lapses into Stalinist ways, of course. In 1989, for example, *Pravda*, which had been showing a welcome capacity for living up to its name, reverted to type by trying to smear Boris Yeltsin, a former party boss in Moscow and ex-Politburo member who had proved to be too radical even for Mikhail Gorbachev. *Pravda* claimed that Yeltsin was a drunkard with a seamy private life, but it was subsequently forced to print an apology.

The more he sallied out to meet the crowds, the more the General Secretary became aware of the link between glasnost and perestroika. It was nice to be able to write critical letters to *Pravda* without being punished, but nicer still to find shops which sold fruit and meat in adequate amounts. So when Ukrainian miners went on strike in 1989, they were not just exercising a worker's basic right, but showing their impatience with the progress made by pererstroika.

THE POLITICAL STRUGGLE

The battles for perestroika and glasnost were only part of the wider struggle Gorbachev was involved in with his more conservative colleagues on the Politburo. But whereas Khrushchev had been testy and volatile with his colleagues, Gorbachev was subtle and conciliatory. If the hardliners were appalled by Yeltsin's bravado, he was sacked to show that Gorbachev could keep the progressives in line. If conservatives dragged their feet, like Gromyko and Romanov, they too were removed. Most subtle of all perhaps was Gorbachev's tolerance of a hardliner like Yegor Ligachev despite his anti-glasnost speeches and generally obstructive attitude. It has been suggested, not implausibly, that the retention of Ligachev is a deliberate ploy which allows Gorbachev to have a reactionary scapegoat who attracts popular hatred. But this is a high-risk strategy if things go badly wrong, because Ligachev would be a natural leader for the conservative factions in the CPSU. Most of Gorbachev's real allies are outside the Kremlin's walls, a fact which the General Secretary acknowledged when he allowed proper elections to a Soviet-style parliament in 1989. While far from being democratic in the fullest Western sense, these elections did allow a well-known dissident like Andrei Sakharov to win a seat, after Gorbachev had freed him and his wife from internal exile. It did Gorbachev no harm to have his ideas endorsed by a scientist and human rights campaigner of international reputation. His deft footwork and political realism had placed Mikhail Gorbachev head and shoulders above his Politburo colleagues, but he has been careful to assert that the political primacy of the CPSU must be maintained.

Gorbachev and the Satellites

The wind of change blowing through the Kremlin has inevitably brought demands for reform inside the Soviet bloc. But the dizzying pace of change in the satellite countries has amazed even the most well-informed analysts of East European affairs. This time also, the hopes of the Poles, Hungarians and Czechoslovaks were far more soundly based.

Poland was the catalyst for change, despite the fact that the military repression of 1981–2 had broken up Solidarity and repressed the group of intellectuals who supported it. Lech Walesa was imprisoned for a while, but he had a valuable ally in the Catholic Church, and Polish spirits would not be crushed. Even the most hard-faced Polish general, and General Jaruzelski was more flexible than most, felt uneasy about repressing his own people.

The attitude of the USSR was absolutely crucial in the return to democracy in Poland and her neighbours. Once it became clear that Soviet troops would remain in their barracks and not intervene in the process of change, the grey-faced Moscow men of the late sixties and seventies were doomed. In 1988 Kadar, the turncoat of 1956, was brought down in Hungary, and in 1989 the GDR's Erich Honecker was sacked together with his wife Margot who had been minister of education since 1963! This followed a visit by Gorbachev to the GDR, when he gave Honecker a blunt warning about the need for reform which went unheeded. Vast demonstrations in Leipzig and Dresden then kept the new general secretary, Egon Krenz, under pressure (ironically he had been in charge of the infamous Stasi or secret police). When he was forced to resign, the subsequent elections in 1990 brought a Christian Democrat/Social Democrat coalition to power. Down had come the Berlin Wall, a desperate, fruitless gesture by a regime whose vital young life-blood was fleeing westwards over the Hungarian and Czech frontiers.

The Hungarians had already torn down their segment of the Iron Curtain, and they amended their country's title of 'People's Republic' to just 'the Hungarian Republic'. More important, for those Magyars who remembered 1956, was the dignified ceremony in Budapest which ended with Imre Nagy's body being given an honourable grave. Free elections were also promised, and the official lie about the 1956 'counter-revolution' disavowed forever. The elections took place in 1990, in which the centre-right won and the Communists were routed.

Poland was the most advanced of all when Solidarity secured the appointment of the devout Catholic and non-communist Tadeusz Mazowiecki as the new prime minister. Jaruzelski remained as president but his party was humiliated at the polls. There was no euphoria in Solidarity as yet because the communists still controlled the armed forces and the police.

In Czechoslovakia the communists tried to play musical chairs. Gustav Husák was relegated to the post of state president, but his successor Miklos Jakes was little better and no one was fooled by this transparent effort to cling to power. Huge demonstrations in Prague culminated in excessive police brutality which infuriated the protesters. Without Soviet aid the Czech leadership was helpless and they were swept away in a few hectic weeks in November 1989. The most moving sight of all was the reappearance of Alexander Dubcek, now sixty-eight, speaking once more to a vast crowd in Wenceslas Square. His resurrection came just before Gorbachev's condemnation of the 1968 invastion. Equally extraordinary was the appointment of the dissident poet Vaclav Havel as President of the Republic.

The most amazing feature of all, in this exciting but turbulent year, was the relaxed low-profile reaction to all this in Moscow. When asked to comment on all the changes in Eastern Europe, Gorbachev's foreign policy adviser Gennady Gerasimov quipped, 'It's the Frank Sinatra doctrine – they are doing it their way.' As the Bulgarian leadership had also been driven from office, only the absurd personality cult of the Rumanian President, Nicolae Ceausescu, remained intact. In a six-hour address to his sheeplike Party Congress, Ceausescu received no less than sixty-seven 'spontaneous' ovations.

At that stage, bets would have been laid that Ceausescu and his stooges would survive into the nineties. The events of the last two weeks of December 1989 in Rumania which brought the dictator down, were therefore extraordinary even by the standards of that extraordinary year.

During all these events the USSR was apparently a passive onlooker. Yet even its 'non-role' was significant. No suggestion of Soviet intervention was ever made, and yet this was probably the only thing which could have saved Ceausescu's neck. The irony was that the squalid

Rumanian dictatorship had waxed fat for years in the West on Ceausescu's ill-deserved reputation as a defender of Rumanian rights, who would not allow the Red Army on his country's soil.

Totalitarianism is totalitarianism wherever it rears its ugly head, as the people of Tibet would acknowledge.

The Nationalities

Gorbachev's strategy of devolving economic power from the centre to the regions was always going to be a risky one. This was because, if he wanted help to introduce perestroika, he had to make concessions in the sphere of glasnost, which pushed that principle to its furthest limits.

Baltic nationalism had to be tolerated to the extent of allowing national flags to reappear in Lithuania, Latvia and Estonia, together with the foundation of nationalist parties which demanded secession from the USSR. The same nationalist currents also swept through Georgia and the Ukraine, and rekindled an ancient feud between Christian Armenia and Muslim Azerbaijan. This concerned the largely Christian enclave of Nagorno-Karabakh which was administered by Azerbaijan, another troublesome legacy of the Stalinist period. In this instance the situation was complicated by a terrible earthquake in Armenia in November 1988, which killed thousands of people. This disaster took place in the midst of Azerbaijani masscres of the Armenian minority in their republic, which forced Moscow to send in regular troops. But they could not prevent disruption of rail traffic into Nagorno-Karabakh by the Azerbaijanis, or a spate of sectarian murders. For ten months in 1988–9 Moscow had to impose direct rule on Nagorno-Karabakh, but it could not resolve the basic issue of who was to administer the enclave. With one eye on the large and potentially restive Muslim minority Gorbachev was forced to tread very carefully.

This caution may in the long run have proved to be counterproductive, as the situation in the Soviet southern republics got more and more out of hand. With an eye to the potential disaster in the making if 70 million Soviet Muslims revolted against Moscow, Gorbachev had limited the scale of military intervention in Nagorno-Karabakh and Azerbaijan, and was thus accused of tolerating anti-Armenian pogroms.

The Azeris then accused him of failing to talk to their representatives directly, as, for example, he did in Lithuania early in 1990.

A crisis point was reached in the last weeks of January 1990 as Armenia and Azerbaijan were virtually in a state of war. On 22 January large army units supported by KGB and internal security units broke into Baku and killed a large number of Azeris (the official figure was around sixty). The next day a million Azerbaijanis were on the streets of Baku in protest against this Soviet 'occupation'. The Azerbaijan parliament gave Moscow forty-eight hours to get out of the republic, or face a referendum on secession from the USSR. The Soviet declaration of a state of emergency in Azerbaijan was further declared null and void.

The only positive aspect of the crisis from the Soviet viewpoint was the cautious strategy adopted by the mullahs in Teheran, who were anxious to retain Soviet friendship. Although Moscow opened the Azeri–Iranian frontier as a conciliatory gesture, the Russians soon became alarmed by the vision of hundreds of people flocking into Iran with its radical Pan-Muslim doctrines. The frontier was closed again, and the Iranians contented themselves with verbal warnings to Gorbachev about ill-treating his Muslims. This was just as well in a situation where Soviet warships had to be used to sink Azeri boats, which were trying to blockade Baku harbour and prevent Red Army families being evacuated.

Gorbachev's emergency measures won the support of the conservatives in Moscow, who tried to pretend that the southern emergency was a consequence of 'perestroika'. It was not, of course. Hatred between Azeris and Armenians was centuries old, and had both religious and ethnic roots. These were then accentuated by Stalin's absurd territorial settlement in the area. But the racial complexity of the Soviet republics, mirrored in neighbouring Yugoslavia, was bound to erupt in intercommunal clashes unless Gorbachev resorted to Stalinist methods. His handling of the Azerbaijan crisis, rather than showing pro-Armenian bias as the Azeris claimed, demonstrated the Soviet leader's reluctance to fall back on the military option. No force after all was used in the Baltic Republics, even when in 1989 Estonia passed a law giving itself the right to secede from the USSR. Lithuania went a step further early in 1990 and seceded from the Soviet Union altogether, a move which the

Soviet parliament declared to be illegal. Gorbachev then demanded a referendum in Lithuania, and a five-year transition period before independence. By April 1990 an impasse had been reached.

As a Caucasian Gorbachev is still probably more sensitive to national rights issues than some of his Greater Russian colleagues, and his homeland is a hotchpotch of different nationalities. Writing in 1988, Gorbachev noted how

> the Karachai–Cherkess autonomous region – part of the Stavropol territory – is populated by Karachais, Cherkess, Russians, Abazins, Nagais, Ossetians, Greeks and representatives of other nationalities, and that they all live in harmony with one another.[5]

But this harmony was a fragile flower which could easily be destroyed by inept decision-making in Moscow, and local nationalism was easily encouraged in the permissive atmosphere of glasnost.

The most striking example of this was in the republic of Georgia, which enjoyed a comfortable life-style under communism but had a proud and independent history of its own. There were nationalist demonstrations in the Georgian capital, Tbilisi, particularly against the corrupt party boss Patiashvils, and the authorities lost their heads. On 9 April 1989, 'Bloody Sunday' as the Georgians now call it, Soviet troops made a barbaric attack on a crowd of peaceful demonstrators in which twenty people were killed (fourteen of whom were girls and women). A particularly shocking aspect of the affair was the crudity of the methods used by the soldiers to attack the demonstrators. Some were gassed, and the remainder were beaten with truncheons or hacked with trenching shovels. The whole episode suggested that a deliberate, cold-blooded attempt was being made to terrorise the people.

Mikhail Gorbachev had only just returned from one of his many foreign trips when the Tbilisi massacre occurred, and the evidence suggests that the decision to use such brutal tactics may have come from his deputy Ligachev. Although an inquiry was set up to examine the events of that April day, disturbing aspects of the affair remained. One was the refusal of the Red Army to provide Tbilisi doctors with technical information about the highly toxic gas used against the demonstrators. Such behaviour could only remind infuriated Georgians of the institutionalised secrecy of the bad old days.

The reformers in the Kremlin also had to keep a wary eye on the Ukrainian republic, with its important industries and equally distinct culture and history. The Chernobyl disaster had not helped, and a wave of strikes by Ukrainian miners showed their growing impatience with the pace of perestroika. Warnings from Gorbachev about the economic damage caused by such strikes did not cut much ice with these men who were usually regarded as the aristocracy of the Soviet labour force.

THE CHURCHES

There was an important link between Ukrainian nationalism and the status of the Uniate Church, which was affiliated to the Catholic Church. Four million Ukrainian Catholics live in the formerly Polish Western Ukraine and its capital Lvov, but Stalin banned their Church in 1946 and handed their churches over to the Orthodox Church. The old resentment between the Orthodox and 'Latin heretics' remained, and Ukrainian Catholics often regard the Orthodox Church as merely the religious agency of the KGB.

Here, as elsewhere, Gorbachev has brought an open mind to the problem, and a tolerance appropriate to the last decade of the twentieth century. In 1985 the Catholic cathedral in Lvov was handed back on his orders, to be followed by the closing down of the Museum of State Atheism in which Pope John Paul II had been described as 'a warmonger' (an odd description in the context of Stalin's famous dismissal of papal influence: 'How many divisions has the Pope got?' he once asked a Vatican diplomat). In the political whirlwind which blew through Eastern Europe in 1989, a visit by General Secretary Gorbachev to Rome may seem unremarkable. But a visit by Pope John Paul II to the USSR in 1990 would certainly appease the affronted Catholics of the Ukraine and Lithuania. It is worth remembering that freedom of worship was written into the Soviet constitution, but that Soviet leaders have indulged in collective amnesia about this clause. The spiritual strength of Soviet Christianity alone has allowed it to survive seventy years of persecution and harassment.

SOVIET WOMEN

If the criterion for assessing how civilised a society is depends on its treatment of women, the USSR has a mixed record. Since 1985 its first lady has been Raisa Gorbacheva, a snappy dresser with a doctorate in sociology and an intellectual vigour and curiosity which caused Mrs Nancy Reagan to complain about being upstaged. Yet if Mikhail Gorbachev represents 'New Soviet Man', it is by no means clear that Raisa represents the norm for her own sex.

In some ways the Soviet achievement has been impressive. Soviet women have gone into space, won Olympic gold medals, and become doctors, engineers and teachers. There are, in fact, more women doctors in the USSR than men, a situation which is not reflected in the West. It is also true that Raisa Gorbacheva has buried forever the Western tabloid stereotype of the typical Soviet woman as an Amazonian discus thrower. But Mrs Gorbacheva is very much alone in her high profile in the modern world. No woman had held an important post for twenty-five years until Alexandra Biryukova was promoted to the position of Secretary to the Central Committee of the CPSU Secretariat in 1986.

Gorbachev himself seems to have a blind spot in this area. In his book *Perestroika*, the General Secretary stresses the importance of the female contribution in a communist society, but does not address the issue of the absence of women from the corridors of power. He allows just two pages to 'Women and the Family' and his conclusions are on the conservative side, acknowledging women's contribution in various sectors of the economy, but referring to the increase in social problems which are 'a paradoxical result of our sincere and politically justified desire to make women equal with men in everything'. He is equally worried by the fact that labour shortages force women to take on heavy physical work which may damage their health, but ends with the rather lame statement that 'women's role in our society will steadily grow'.[6]

Western observers would agree that the lot of the Soviet woman is a far harder one than her western counterpart. More Soviet women go out to work than those in the West, and child-care provision is limited. So are contraceptives, and abortion is very common in the USSR, often in the bleakest of surroundings. Soviet women have stated that giving birth to a baby in a Soviet maternity hospital is an even worse experience than having an abortion. This also means that infant mortality rates are strikingly higher than in the West.

Having children in the USSR is a decidedly mixed blessing because so many Soviet citizens have to live in tiny flats where privacy is at a premium, and the most basic foodstuffs are unavailable. Until recently, too, Soviet society paid the merest lip service to modern fashion, and women's clothes were badly designed and badly made. It is not surprising therefore that Raisa Gorbacheva's patronage of Paris fashion houses did not always go down too well at home. Although she presented a far more attractive role model than the almost invisible spouses of Brezhnev, Andropov and Chernenko, good clothes and a pleasant life-style can easily be equated with corruption in a country where most women had little chance of ever wearing the latest Western clothes. On the other hand, Soviet women need to make the quantum leap from having the stern-faced Valentina Tereshkova (the USSR's first woman cosmonaut) as a role model, to the sophisticated Raisa Gorbacheva.

Foreign Relations

When Mikhail Gorbachev was elected general secretary of the CPSU in 1985, his foreign policy inheritance was a difficult one. The Red Army was bogged down in a fruitless guerilla war in Afghanistan and relations with the USA were at an all time low.

Gorbachev was quick to recognise an unpalatable fact which his immediate predecessors had shied away from. The USSR could *not* spend some 18 per cent of its GNP on defence, while meeting its citizen's demands for a better standard of life. In the teeth of American suspicion, and opposition in the military establishment, he therefore suggested that significant cuts should be made in the conventional and nuclear arsenals of the superpowers. A sort of pattern emerged in the late eighties whereby Gorbachev would make significant offers of nuclear-force reduction and the US administration would be taken by surprise. The most striking example of this sort of diplomacy was in the Icelandic capital, Reykjavik, when Gorbachev offered to destroy all nuclear weapons and the Americans refused to abandon their Star Wars antimissile system. But in 1988 Gorbachev did persuade President Reagan to agree to a 5 per cent cut in missile systems, and small cuts in conventional forces.

Another important breakthrough came in the summer of 1989 when Gorbachev visited the Chinese leader Deng Xiaoping in Peking and brought about a normalisation of relations. This allowed the Russians to reduce their military establishment on the Sino–Soviet border.

A further Gorbachev theme in foreign policy was 'our common European home', and before the extraordinary changes in Eastern Europe came to the fore in 1989 he had visited France, Britain and the Federal German Republic. The chants of 'Gorby, Gorby' wherever the Soviet leader went in the West (he visited New York in 1988) suggested that he was more popular there than at home, where the food queues were as long as ever.

Domestic opinion was then partly appeased, when Gorbachev negotiated the withdrawal of Soviet forces from Afghanistan in February 1989, so ending a war which had cost 50,000 Soviet lives. The campaign for glasnost also ensured that wounded Afghan veterans did not suffer in the silence of the Brezhnev era. Meanwhile the battle for perestroika has also brought about a scaling down of military aid to Nicaragua, Cuba and Angola. Superpower pretensions had to be curbed in the interests of the sickly Soviet economy.

Whither Russia?

In every sense, Gorbachev is in a difficult position because the uprising of the nationalities has in turn aroused Greater Russian nationalism. In the Baltic Republics, for example, Russian incomers have protested against linguistic reforms which discriminate against them.

There are also Soviet citizens who object to the 'blackening' (*ochernitelstvo*) of Soviet history in Gorbachev's glasnost, and others who do not accept that twenty million of their fellow citizens died in Stalin's camps. Such views are represented in a new Soviet film called *Is Stalin with Us?*, in which a middle-aged woman teacher makes an amazing statement that, in the Stalin period, 'they arrested people openly, exiled them openly and executed them openly'. This may be an extreme reaction, but there are many of the older generation who look back longingly to the order and discipline of the Stalin period. This basic Russian nationalism still survives, as Sakharov found out in the new Soviet parliament when he tried to criticise the Red Army's role in Afghanistan (he died in 1989).

Gorbachev needs Western aid and encouragement but Westerners need to remember, firstly that the Russians are a proud people, and secondly that the Russia of Stalin and Beria was also the Russia of Tolstoy, Chekhov, Borodin and Tchaikovsky.

The coming of Democracy

The USSR continued to hurtle down the path to pluralism and democracy in the late winter of 1989–90. On 5 February a huge crowd of 200,000 demonstrators in Moscow demanded an end to the dominant position of the CPSU, using slogans like 'Dinosaurs into retirement'.

The very same week Gorbachev made a dramatic switch in his position by agreeing that Article 6 of the Brezhnev constitution should be revised, so that the CPSU did not 'claim full governmental authority'. He also demanded the creation of an executive presidency 'with all necessary power to implement perestroika'. This demand, which the Soviet parliament approved in a draft law in March, worried the reformist wing of the CPSU which detected in the executive presidency, an attempt to revive the authoritarianism of the Stalin period.

Nevertheless in the first week of March 1990 the first round of elections to the Soviet parliament went ahead, and the reformers polled well in the cities of the Russian Federation, Byelorussia, and the Ukraine (Yeltsin got 80 per cent of the vote in his own town of Sverdlovsk in the Urals) in the country areas.

Another feature of the elections was the success of the Ukrainian separatist party (Rukh). It did especially well in the Western Ukraine, where the legalisation of the Uniate Catholic Church was a central issue. In Lithuania, despite Gorbachev's criticism of their expressed intention to secede from the USSR, the nationalist bloc (Sajudis) maintained its dominance by winning 90 out of the 141 seats in the Vilnius parliament (Lithuania followed this up by declaring itself independent).

The overall impression left on analysts by the election results was that in the three Slav Republics (Ukraine, Byelorussia, the RSFSR), the Communist Party, though down, was by no means out.

Further Disturbances in the Asian Republics

Despite the gradual Soviet drift to democracy, underlined by Gorbachev's announcement of direct election of the Soviet president by 1994, there was still clear evidence of chronic internal discontent in the non-Russian republics.

In February 1990 there were serious riots in Tadzhikistan following rumours that Armenian refugees were to get housing priority in the republic's capital Dushanbe. Thirty-seven people died, and at one stage Moscow Radio admitted that the situation was 'out of control', before troops crushed the riots. Protests in the neighbouring republic of Kirghizia took a more peaceful course, until the serious rioting in June 1990.

Subsequently in March there was another outburst of ethnic violence in the Central Asian republic of Uzbekistan. In this instance, the arrival of ethnic Turks in the town of Parkent, near Tashkent, sparked off riots in which an undisclosed number of people were killed. The disturbances took place at the same time as the local elections, but there seems to have been no link between the two.

The Shifting Foreign Policy Perspective

In foreign relations too, 1990 brought important changes of emphasis for the USSR. President Gorbachev, initially opposed to German reunification, then gave it his blessing, although his conservative opponent Ligachev tried to use the horrors of the Great Patriotic War as a stick with which to beat the reformers.

Foolish attempts by the Federal German chancellor Helmet Kohl to question the status of the Oder–Neisse line (the Polish-German frontier) did nothing other than to underline the unanimity of the former wartime allies on this issue. In early March, Kohl, motivated it seemed largely by electoral factors, had to back down in embarrassing fashion.

Elsewhere the USSR maintained its drive to improve Soviet–Western relations and finally see off the Cold War which had been resurrected in the Reagan–Brezhnev period. Soviet troops began to withdraw from Czechoslovakia, and Gorbachev promised President Havel that they would all be gone by 1991. Similar arrangements were made with Hungary.

The USSR also indicated a willingness to reduce its forces in the former GDR to 30,000 by 1991, providing the West did the same in what is now the FGR. But Gorbachev and his foreign minister Shevardnadze have been firm in their refusal to agree to the integration of a united Germany into NATO.

The Future

President Gorbachev's daring foreign policy initiatives (for which he deserves every credit) are nonetheless overshadowed by the crucial developments at home. For despite the introduction of privately run co-operatives, it remains true that 98 per cent of the Soviet economy remains under the control of the unwieldy central state planning apparatus. Ominous rumblings among the ethnic Russians centre on the chronic shortages in the shops, and the undoubted failure of perestroika to improve matters. Gorbachev cannot be unaware that some Soviet citizens have compared him to Stalin in unfavourable terms, and that cities like Leningrad have given birth to unpleasant manifestations of crypto-fascism. Conversely, the Soviet leader must be given immense credit for the fresh wind of glasnost which has blown into many dark corners of Soviet society (an example being the long-overdue admission in 1990 that Stalin's secret police had murdered thousands of Polish officers in the Katyn Forest). In the words of the great Soviet cellist Rostropovich, he has destroyed a system which was based on 'an ocean of lies'.

Mikhail Gorbachev himself has said, 'To understand Russia you must understand our past,' but the future of the Soviet Union as a political entity must also depend on that legendary patience and stoicism of the Russian people, which saw off both Napoleon and Adolf Hitler. One day, hopefully in the not too distant future, Pushkin's lament about 'how sad our Russia is', which seemed to have such constant relevance, will be but a distant memory.

CHAPTER SEVENTEEN

The End of the Soviet Union

In 1990 the structure of the USSR, although sorely pressed, was still intact. Certainly Mikhail Gorbachev and his colleagues did not envisage the total collapse of the Union. Indeed at the end of 1990 Gorbachev's position seemed to be strengthened when the USSR Congress of Deputies granted him wide executive presidential powers.

This however proved to be an illusion as far as Gorbachev was concerned, for throughout the Union Soviet power was in retreat. In January 1991 brutal military intervention by interior ministry troops in Lithuania and Latvia resulted in civilian deaths. Gorbachev claimed to be unaware of the decision to send troops into the two Baltic states. This move merely strengthened the desire for independence in both Latvia and Lithuania. Two months later in March 1991 Gorbachev held an all-union referendum on the issue of the preservation of the USSR, and although there was a 76.4 per cent 'yes' vote the referendum was boycotted by Armenia, the Baltic States, Georgia and Moldova (Moldovia).

On the economic front matters were no better, for in the Russian heartland of the Union, a two-month-old miners' strike in Siberia was settled only when the Russian prime minister Boris Yeltsin (Gorbachev's old Politburo colleague and rival) transferred the ownership of the mines from the USSR to the Russian Federation. It was clear that the miners, the aristocrats of the Russian working class, trusted Yeltsin rather than Gorbachev. Yeltsin then challenged the authority of the Communist Party of the Soviet Union (CPSU) itself, by banning all political activity at the workplace in July. As the workplace was normally one of the bastions of party power and privilege, the inference was clear. The month before, Yeltsin had strengthened his own political position by defeating five other candidates in the battle for the Russian presidency. Did Gorbachev realise that real power and influence was slipping out of his fingers?

It seems not, and his rival Yeltsin accused Gorbachev of never really being willing to give up the power and privilege associated with the general secretaryship of the CPSU. In his memoir *Against the Grain*, Yeltsin wrote: 'He likes to live well, in comfort and luxury. His meetings with workers in public are nothing but a masquerade.' While a degree of personal animus must be allowed for here (Gorbachev did sack Yeltsin in 1987) it seems clear that in the course of 1990–91 Gorbachev was moving steadily away from the cause of reform to the side of the conservatives on the Politburo. Whether this was another of Gorbachev's clever tactical manoeuvres must remain a matter for speculation, but the real nature of Gorbachev's beliefs by August 1991 remain a matter of intense controversy.

The 1991 Coup

Between 19–21 August 1991 Gorbachev was the apparent victim of an attempted *coup d'état* in Moscow led by important party figures like the Defence Minister Marshal Yazov, Boris Pugov and Gennady Yaneyev. Gorbachev claimed that he was held captive by the conspirators at his Black Sea holiday home, while the conspirators claimed later that the general secretary had known in advance about the intended coup and approved of it. The motive behind the coup was clear. To reverse the policies of perestroika and glasnost, and to prevent the national minorities like the Balts and the Georgians breaking away from the USSR.

But it failed. Partly as a result of the ineptitude on the part of the conspirators, and partly as the result of the courage and initiative of Boris Yeltsin. Bizarrely the coup leaders failed to capture the 'White House' in Moscow where the Russian parliament held its sessions, or even to sever its communications. Yeltsin was able to denounce the coup from the top of a tank (friendly troops had rallied to the Russian president) and he was joined in the parliament building by other leading liberals like the former foreign minister Eduard

Shevardnadze. The previous December Shevardnadze had resigned his post after warning dramatically that 'dictatorship is coming'.

But dictatorship did not come partly because the conspirators lacked the nerve to attack the Russian parliament building, and partly because they failed to win the support in the army necessary to secure their power base. Soon they were under arrest and Gorbachev returned from the Black Sea, claiming that he and his family had heroically resisted the plotters, who had visited his *dacha* at Pitsunda and tried to bully him into submission.

Whatever the truth of the matter, Gorbachev totally misjudged the mood of the capital on his return. He failed to render immediate congratulations to Yeltsin, and two days later was humiliated in front of the Russian parliament when his rival produced documents showing that the whole Politburo was in on the plot. For Gorbachev there was to be no way back after that fateful forty-eight hours in August.

Gorbachev's prospects were certainly not improved by the apparent unwillingness of the western democracies and Japan to loan him the funds needed to restructure the ailing Soviet economy. His critics argued that Gorbachev, for so long the darling of western crowds and media, lacked sufficient commitment to the concepts of privatisation and the free market economy.

The Fall of Gorbachev

The supposed president of the crumbling USSR was by now seriously discredited by the events surrounding the August coup, although he made desperate attempts to prevent his authority being further eroded by Yeltsin.

His lack of a popular mandate was another serious weakness during the last months of 1991 when he battled for his political life. This period was one of relentless erosion of Soviet power and victory for nationalist secessionist movements. Even though Gorbachev had issued a presidential decree dissolving the CPSU, and resigned his post as general secretary, he was inevitably linked in the minds of people throughout the USSR with the Communist Party.

He was forced to accept the official withdrawal of all three Baltic Republics from the Union, and in November only seven of the

Soviet republics agreed to resume talks about the formation of a so-called 'Union of Sovereign States'. A further snub to Gorbachev in that month was the appointment of Eduard Shevardnadze as Russian foreign minister, after he refused Gorbachev's request to take back his old job as Soviet foreign minister.

He was now effectively without authority in a Union which was dissolving itself, for since 1990 (when Byelarus, Moldova, Kirgitzstan, Tajikistan, Ukraine, Turkmenistan and Uzbekistan had declared themselves sovereign) membership of the Union had effectively become voluntary. Yeltsin, with the support of the other independent republics, insisted at the end of 1991 on both Gorbachev's resignation as Union president, and the dissolution of the Union itself. After seventy-four years of life the USSR had ceased to exist.

GORBACHEV'S AGREEMENT

After the heady days of the mid-eighties, Gorbachev's dismissal from the scene was a sad anti-climax. But his glamorous foreign policy successes could not cover one damning reality. Never in the years after 1985 was Mikhail Gorbachev really able to tackle the former USSR's economic problems, and his failure to do so doomed perestroika to failure. It could also be argued that the freedom of discussion allowed under glasnost also doomed the USSR to failure, because it encouraged the feelings of nationalism and separatism which were ultimately to destroy the Union. But this was surely to Gorbachev's credit, and in recognising his ultimate failure, due credit must be given to his achievements too. His sternest critic, Boris Yeltsin, has left us with this assessment:

> What he has achieved will, of course, go down in the history of mankind. He could have gone on existing just as Brezhnev and Chernenko existed before him. Yet Gorbachev chose to go quite another way. He started by climbing a mountain whose summit is not even visible.

YELTSIN'S BACKGROUND

Boris Nickolayevich Yeltsin was born in February 1931 in the village of Butko in the Talitsky district of Sverdlovsk province. He came of peasant stock and in his early years the family shared their small house with a cow, but his father developed a second career as a construction worker. Boris, one of six children, was to follow his father in his own career.

He was a natural leader and an extrovert, but with ability in technical subjects. A childhood accident with a grenade cost him two fingers on his left hand, but this did not prevent him becoming a volleyball player of some reputation and almost manic dedication. Young Boris studied civil engineering at Sverdlovsk Polytechnic, hitched the length and breadth of the Soviet Union (according to him by hitching rides on the roofs of passenger trains) and graduated in 1955. He joined the Communist Party while working as an engineer in the Urals. For fourteen years Yeltsin worked in the construction industry until he was invited to head the section of the provincial committee of the Party responsible for construction.

Then, after a personal interview with Leonid Brezhnev, Yeltsin was appointed first secretary of the Sverdlovsk provincial committee of the party. It was during this period that Yeltsin first came into contact with Mikhail Gorbachev, who was first secretary at Stavropol. The relationship was a cordial one, and Yeltsin greeted Gorbachev's appointment as secretary to the central committee for agriculture in 1978 'with enthusiasm'. But he was soon disillusioned by his performance.

In 1985, Yeltsin made the crucial move to Moscow when he was offered the post of head of the central committee section responsible for construction. He seems to have accepted this post somewhat reluctantly, but further promotion came in December 1985 when Gorbachev gave him the important post of head of the Moscow city committee of the Communist Party. He owed his appointment to Gorbachev's desire as the new general secretary of the CPSU to clean up the corrupt city administration.

Difficulties soon arose as Yeltsin threw himself wholeheartedly into his work. He already had the popular touch with the people, and alienated conservatives in the Kremlin by making gestures like personally riding in the Metro (unheard of for party bosses who normally travelled everywhere in Zil limousines). Moscow newspapers and TV were encouraged to be lively and open-minded, rather than pompous and smug as in the Brezhnev era. There were mass sackings in the Moscow party itself. All this made Yeltsin personally very popular in the city.

According to Yeltsin's personal account, Gorbachev too became uneasy about his reforms in Moscow and resented his criticisms at Politburo meetings (normally the general secretary's decisions were agreed with minimal discussion). Yeltsin was then sacked as Moscow city boss and lost his position on the Politburo. He was offered a more lowly position on the state construction committee. But ultimately Yeltsin was a political animal and in June 1988, he was put forward as one of thirteen delegates to the nineteenth party conference, representing Karelia. Throughout this period he was a pariah whose name was never mentioned in the Soviet press, lest it be to smear him by suggesting that he was a drunk. In December 1988 Yeltsin made the decision to stand in the election for people's deputies in Moscow, and retaining his popularity with the Muscovites, he was elected in March 1989 with 89.6 per cent of the vote. But deputies for the new Supreme Soviet were chosen from among the people's deputies, and it was still possible for Gorbachev and the Politburo to block Yeltsin's election to it. (Andrei Sakharov was kept out of the Supreme Soviet by these means.)

In fact, Yeltsin's election to the Supreme Soviet was blocked, even though more than half the people's deputies voted for him. He was saved only by the decision of Alexei Kazannik, a deputy from Siberia who had already been elected to the Supreme Soviet, to stand down in his favour. By now Yeltsin had moved to a position where he was demanding the deletion of Article 6 of the Soviet constitution, which gave the CPSU a monopoly of power in the USSR. He had soon ceased to be a member of the party at all, and became prime minister of a separate, sovereign Russian Federation.

The Founding of the Commonwealth of Independent States, CIS

We left Russia's story during the last weeks of the life of the USSR. But its replacement was already in preparation, for in the second week of December 1991 Russia, Ukraine (which had voted for complete independence the previous week) and Byelarus, recognising that the USSR was now defunct, agreed to form a new federation.

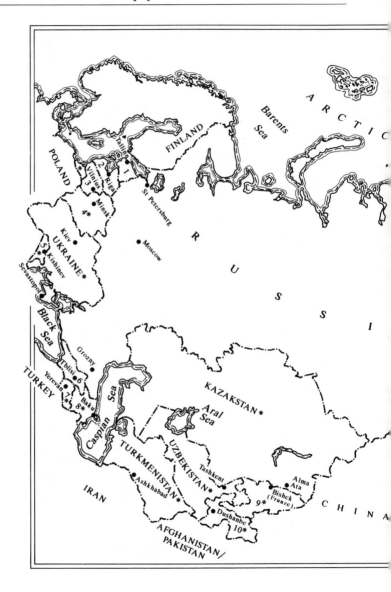

1 ESTONIA
2 LATVIA
3 LITHUANIA
4 BYELARUS *
5 MOLDOVA *
6 GEORGIA
7 ARMENIA *
8 AZERBAIJAN *
9 KIRGITZSTAN *
10 TAJIKSTAN *

Members of CIS *

A *

OCEAN

Sea of Okhotsk

MONGOLIA

CHINA

JAPAN

0   800 km
0   500 miles

Modern Russia and
the Commonwealth of Independent States

This was to be called the Commonwealth of Independent States. In the following April of 1992 Armenia, Kazakstan, Kirgitzstan, Tajkistan and Uzbekistan joined the founder members in agreeing to create an inter-parliamentary assembly for the CIS. But the new federation was to be in no way comparable to the old, heavily centralised USSR. Each member state was fully sovereign, and some former Soviet republics like Georgia opted not to join the CIS at all.

Russia's Problems

By 1991, Russia consisted only of the Russian Social Democrat Federation, the largest of the old Soviet republics. In June 1992, as outlined above, Boris Yeltsin was elected executive president of the new Russian republic. He faced tremendous difficulties.

Yeltsin and his reformist deputy prime minister Gaider were pledged to introduce privatisation and a market economy. But this aroused such fierce opposition that in April 1992 Yeltsin felt obliged to sack Gaidar to placate conservative opponents in the Russian parliament led by Khasbulatov. Meanwhile inflation soared upwards, and groups like health workers and teachers responded by putting in 300 per cent pay claims. By August 1992, Russian national income had actually fallen by 14 per cent.

On the political front, Yeltsin seemed a little more secure. A farcical attempt by political conservatives to revive the old defunct Congress of the USSR's people's deputies ended when a rump of deputies, unable to meet anywhere in Moscow, were forced to meet by candlelight outside it! This was in March 1992, the same month that the Russian Federation Treaty was signed by eighteen of the twenty autonomous republics. Ominously, as it turned out, one that did not was Chechen Ingushetia.

Increasingly also, Yeltsin's authority as president came under challenge from the Russian Federation Parliament led by Khasbulatov. By the autumn, Yeltsin's ministers in the Russian government were warning about the dangers of a right-wing coup, and he was at loggerheads with his own vice president. Meantime, another unwanted feud began with the newly-independent Ukraine about who was to control the former Black Sea fleet. This situation had, in fact, been created by Khrushchev's bizarre decision to give the Crimea to the former Soviet republic of the Ukraine, and the main Black Sea naval base was at Sevastopol.

When 1993 began, the portents for the Russian Federation were not auspicious. Yeltsin and Khasbulatov continued to argue, with the latter accusing his president of presiding over a 'bankrupt economic programme'. The privatisation programme seemed to be progressing at a snail's pace and inflation soared. This in a country where for decades prices for fuel and basic foodstuffs had remained virtually static.

Relations with the surrounding republics also remained uneasy, with accusations that the Russian government was encouraging the ethnic Russian minority in Moldova to resist union with Rumania. The Balts also accused the Yeltsin government of deliberately delaying the withdrawal of Russian troops from the former Soviet bases there.

In this situation, Boris Yeltsin decided to call a national referendum which would, in effect, be a vote of confidence in him. The referendum was held in April, and gave Yeltsin 56 per cent of the vote, but even this did not resolve the constitutional crisis. His opponents, somewhat spuriously, pointed out that many Russian citizens had not voted at all, ignoring the fact that Yeltsin now had a bigger popular mandate than most western leaders. He had in any case been strengthened by the G7 group of top industrial nations' decision to vote Russia more funding for her modernisation. And the new US president Clinton hoped that a strengthening of Yeltsin's domestic mandate would allow him to play a more positive role in the tragic Yugoslav crisis which had been worsening since 1991. Up to this point Yeltsin had been forced to move cautiously, aware of Russia's historical ties with Slavic Serbia. But he had at least been able to continue Gorbachev's work in running down the nuclear arsenal of the former USSR.

The Failed 1993 Coup

Despite his referendum victory, Yeltsin faced serious internal dissent, and the so-called 'White House' in Moscow was the focal point for this. This was the meeting place for the Russian parliament, a leftover from the Gorbachev period which, under the leadership of the speaker Ruslan Khasbulatov, consistently obstructed Yeltsin's free market reforms. Yeltsin was so enraged by Khasbulatov's behaviour and that of his vice-president Alexander Rutskoi, that he sacked the vice-president and dissolved the parliament (both men had formerly been supporters of his).

For a few days in September 1993 there was a complete impasse. Yeltsin cut off the telephones and the electricity supply to the White House and surrounded the building with interior ministry troops. The parliament responded by declaring Yeltsin's dissolution illegal and making Rutskoi acting president of the Russian Republic. The parliamentary deputies continued to meet in candlelight.

Then came the bizarre climax, in circumstances which are still shrouded in mystery. Inept policing allowed a demonstration by anti-Yeltsin agitators to get out of hand, break the siege of the White House and attack Moscow's main TV station (opponents of Yeltsin had long complained about his control of the TV system). Interior ministry troops and police were unable to cope with the situation and Yeltsin's presidency seemed in danger. Only the belated deployment of army units crushed what seemed to be a genuine attempt at a coup, to follow the fiasco of August 1991. Tanks shelled the White House into surrender, although a few diehard fanatics went on resisting the security forces desperately.

Alexander Rutskoi and Khasbulatov were arrested and imprisoned, and Yeltsin confirmed that new parliamentary elections would be held in December. Draconian security measures, including the censorship of papers and a curfew in Moscow, were taken. But aspects of this second coup within two years left many Russians uneasy. How would Yeltsin use the virtually dictatorial powers now available to him? Could the army, which had only sided with Yeltsin at the last minute be relied upon to support him (some ex-army officers had taken part in the defence of the White House). Would the civilian population put up indefinitely with soaring crime rates and runaway inflation in the context of harsh free market reforms? The evidence of September 1993 was that although Russians were not enthusiastic supporters of Yeltsin and his market reforms, they were not attracted by the alternatives. It was never clear what the ragbag coalition of nationalists, former communists and disillusioned war veterans led by Rutskoi and Khasbulatov had to offer the Russian people.

Boris Yeltsin received strong foreign support, notably from the USA in the September crisis, as the only democratically elected leader in Russia. Not least because of the instability in Russia's sister republics. The ethnic and religious war between Armenia and Azerbaijan dragged on, but it was the former Soviet foreign minister Eduard Shevardnadze who faced the most serious problems in Georgia. A separatist revolt in the northern part of the republic found him both short of support and indecisive in his handling of events. Complaints from him that Russia had instigated the crisis lacked conviction.

THE CHECHEN WAR

A much more serious internal problem confronted the Russian authorities in 1994, with the attempted defection of the Chechens (a tough warlike race who had long resented Russian rule) from the Federation. By the end of that year, the Chechen capital Grozny was under heavy Russian air attack and ground forces reached the outskirts of the city in mid-December forcing 300,000 inhabitants to flee.

Efforts by Yeltsin to achieve reconciliation in 1995 failed, and the problem became more intractable culminating in the deaths of 150 people in Buddenovsk when Chechen extremists held over 1,000 people hostage before retreating into their breakaway republic. A bloody war which cost 30,000 Russian casualties was only halted by a tentative ceasefire in 1996 (which depended too much on the role of Yeltsin's then-security boss Alexander Lebed). There was little real trust between the two antagonists. War was to erupt again in 1999.

Meanwhile the economy continued to present real problems. In March 1995 Prime Minister Chernomyrdin (a rather colourless ex-communist bureaucrat) introduced a second wave of privatisations, which gained the approval of the International Monetary Fund to the extent of sanctioning a loan of $6.8 billion. But this did little to change a situation where inflation eroded the living standards of many Russians on fixed incomes (it was not unusual to see old women on the streets of St Petersburg trying to raise a few roubles by selling off their cutlery). The authoritarian security of the old USSR was, in fact, replaced by the perils of unregulated capitalism, crimes and drugs (in 1995 the well-known TV journalist Vladislav Listyev was gunned down by the Russian Mafia). This chronic underlying economic insecurity was underlined by the Duma (Parliament) decision to endorse a 1995 budget which left Russia in deficit to the tune of 73,000 billion roubles (approximately $25 billion). And in August 1995 Russian banks refused to lend each other money following rumours that some were on the point of collapse.

Such economic problems were bound to have political repercussions. Thus in December 1995 the reformed Communist Party under Gennady Zguyanov, promising to reject 'old style' socialism, became the largest single party in the 450 seat Duma with 157 seats. This was despite Yeltsin's warning that voting communist would mean the end of democratic Russia.

This setback undoubtedly shook Yeltsin, and made him even more determined to win the June 1996 presidential election. Rather absurd cavortings on TV were designed to reassure people about his health (there had been constant rumours about heart trouble and drinking), and the communists were rigorously excluded from the broadcasting media which were in any case blatantly pro-Yeltsin. In the event Yeltsin failed to win the first round of the presidential election, requiring 51 per cent of the vote but did so comfortably enough in the second ballot. But it was obvious that in rural areas, and the so-called 'Red Belt' of the South, there was much disillusionment with the Yeltsin government. In addition, the strong showing (14 per cent) in the first ballot of the renegade general Alexander Lebed forced Yeltsin to take him on (albeit briefly — he was sacked in October) as security chief. Fears about Yeltsin's health were amply justified by a post-election heart attack followed by a stay in hospital for pneumonia, which reduced him to little more than a watching brief over state affairs.

The Financial Crisis

The severe financial crisis facing Russia worsened in 1997–8. Yeltsin's health remained a serious concern, and he seemed to have little answer to the growing inflationary problems, and the parallel collapse in the value of the rouble. Faced with economic difficulties on such a massive scale, Yeltsin's response was just to shuffle the pack of political leaders. The colourless Chernomyrdin was replaced by the young, and absurdly inexperienced Kiriyenko, who in turn was replaced by the former foreign affairs expert Primakov. Miners and factory workers remained unpaid for months on end, yet Yeltsin attempted still to play the role of a significant international leader. Thus, in the autumn of 1998, Yeltsin objected to NATO threats to launch air strikes against Serbia because of atrocities in Kosovo. The future for Russia remained uncertain not least because potential successors to Yeltsin, like Lebed, were nationalist hawks. Even the discredited Chernomyrdin had presidential aspirations, and rumours spread that Yeltsin would not see out his presidential term to the year 2000.

Yeltsin, however, continued to demonstrate an almost inspired capacity for survival, and a keen nose for potential rivals. By 1999, Primakov had become too popular as prime minister, and was abruptly sacked.

The Kosovo Crisis

As discussed above, Yeltsin's handling of the Chechen war had been inept. But in 1998–99 he found himself involved in an external crisis which brought him into conflict with the West (tensions already existed because of the adherence of Hungary, Poland and the Czech Republic to NATO). This concerned the Yugoslav republic of Kosovo with its overwhelmingly Muslim population, which had long been repressed by the Serb military since the withdrawal of its autonomous status by Yugoslav President Slobodan Milosevic in 1989.

NATO had persistently warned Milosevic about the shelling of Albanian Muslim villages by his security forces, supposedly in response to terrorism by the Albanian KLA, but in reality a thinly disguised form of 'ethnic cleansing'. In October 1998, Milosevic was threatened with bombing unless he agreed to cease the persecution of the Albanians. Under this threat, Milosevic agreed to meet western and Russian representatives at Rambouillet to discuss the Kosovo problem. Russia, with its cultural and religious links with the Orthodox Serbs, had long been sympathetic to the Yugoslav position while deploring human rights breaches by Milosevic's forces in Kosovo.

The Rambouillet talks achieved nothing. Milosevic flatly refused to allow NATO forces into Kosovo, or to withdraw his own forces even though it was made clear that NATO opposed independence for Kosovo as demanded by the KLA resistance front. He knew though that Russia (and indeed China) opposed the bombing of Serb forces in Kosovo. When bombing of Serb forces in Kosovo, together with attacks on strategic targets in Serbia itself began in March 1999, Yeltsin came under pressure from extreme right-wing nationalists. Some Russians offered their services as mercenaries on the Serb side, and the NATO bombing campaign was deeply unpopular in Russia. Yet Russia alone of the great powers had influence in Belgrade, and this fact was heavily played upon in bi-lateral diplomacy between Russia and the United States, the leader of the NATO alliance. On the other hand, Yeltsin had to be seen to take a stand against western policy. Russia was, after all, the mother Slav country, and the centre of Orthodox culture. It had been an ally of Serbia in both World Wars, and these factors fused together with growing resentment about Russian financial dependence on the West, and the roaring inflation which affected many Russians' lives. When the bombing stopped in June 1999, it was agreed that Russia would take part in the NATO occupation of Kosovo, as the Serbs trusted them while being fiercely hostile to the Americans, British, French and Germans (especially the latter). Yeltsin then stole a march on the western powers by sending paratroopers to seize the airport at Pristina, well ahead of the NATO incursion into Kosovo. Disputes continued about the exact size of the Russian force and, most importantly, about the command structure. The Russian government refused to take direct military orders from NATO commanders. Nevertheless, by July 1999, some 5,000 Russian troops were on their way to Kosovo, replicating the role played by Russia in Bosnia after the civil war there.

The Kosovo crisis reminded the world that Russia was still a great power whose views had to be taken into account in global politics. It could not disguise, nonetheless, the chronic lawlessness and insecurity inside the country. Many Russian workers had not been paid for months, if not years, and subsisted on vegetables grown in domestic plots. Gangsterism was rife. Even ice-hockey players and their coaches were not safe from assassination by Mafia killers, and the head of the Russian Ice Hockey Federation, Valentin Sych, was killed just after he had attacked the level of corruption and intimidation in the sport. Law enforcement forces were grossly inadequate for their tasks. Under-funded and under-armed, they faced an almost hopeless job in dealing with sophisticated gangsters, some of them former KGB and security force operatives.

The Chechen Conflict

The dangers of becoming involved in a bloody conflict like Afghanistan have also resurfaced in 1999. As indicated above Russia had become involved in a fruitless struggle in the Muslim Republic of Chechnya in 1994, which resulted in a hard won ceasefire in 1996. But in the summer of 1999 Moscow and other Russian cities were rocked by a series of devastating explosions, in which hundreds of civilians were killed. The Russian government assumed, rightly or wrongly, that Chechen guerrillas or 'bandits' as the authorities called them were responsible.

The Russian military, backed by President Yeltsin and the new Prime Minister Vladimir Putin (there were suggestions that both were using the Chechen war to enhance their popularity), launched a new invasion of Chechnya. Heavy bombing of Chechen towns and villages was carried out, and by the end of the year the Chechen capital Grozny was almost surrounded. Western condemnation of Russian tactics, which resulted in many civilians' deaths, was rebuffed by Yeltsin in abrasive style. The military were confident of victory, but these were unpleasant parallels with another war with a Muslim people, the Afghans, in which the old Soviet army had been worsted. The Russian justification was that Chechen 'terrorists' had to be dealt with, and that this was an internal Russian matter. Outsiders believed that the Russians were engaged in a war of revenge, which performed the useful function of distracting public attention from internal problems.

The 1999 Russian Elections

The impact of the Chechen war on Russian politics was dramatic. In December 1999 the so called 'glorious six', a coalition of parties led by Vladimir Putin's 'Unity' or 'Bear' party won the Parliamentary elections. Six months before the renewal of the war no one had heard of Putin, or the Unity Party. But the sudden surge in popularity of Putin and his party plainly made him a front runner for the 2000 presidential elections in Russia. The Duma had been dominated by the Communists under Gennady Zguyanov, who had frequently tried to impeach Boris Yeltsin. Putin was now the apparent heir to the outgoing president.

Yet Putin's elections strategy was perilous in its short terminism. The media had, as a western journalist pointed out, been the victim of 'ruthless manipulation by the war party'. This allowed Putin to get away with ignoring other major issues like the economy and the crime rate. Russia has been the casualty of earlier short patriotic wars in its history, and Putin and the Unity party could only offer a vacuum where there should have been a domestic policy.

A Surprise Resignation

Throughout his political career Boris Yeltsin was surrounded by controversy. It was to be expected therefore, that he would depart in spectacular fashion, and he duly did so on New Year's Eve 1999. Yeltin's presidential powers were handed over to Putin who returned the favour by issuing a decree protecting Yeltsin and his family (long suspected of corruption), from prosecution for any misdeeds committed while the former president was in office.

The perils of Putin's nationalist, authoritarian approach were soon demonstrated. Although cutting a moderate figure at international conferences he was guilty of attempts to muzzle the media. And in August 2000 a tragic disaster involving the loss of 118 men in the nuclear submarine 'Kursk' marked a reversion to old, bad habits. Putin himself showed marked insensitivity in failing to visit the naval base at Murmansk, and the Russian navy was consistently evasive about details of the disaster, and churlish about accepting foreign help. Putin was roundly condemned by opposition politicians, the media and the relatives of the dead men. Neither was he able to prevent another mysterious bomb explosion in Moscow, a particular blow to a man who had stood on an anti-corruption law and order platform in 1999 (although to his credit Putin did not immediately blame the Chechens). Yet it could be argued that despite its manifest shortcomings and corruptions, the attacks on Putin were a healthy sign in Russian society.

Pushkin's lament 'O God, how sad our Russia is' resonates down the centuries. The Russian people, courageous and long-suffering as ever, deserve better. Mikhail Gorbachev has written that 'Democracy is the only way to Russia's revival, to a life of dignity for its great people'. Yet more than a decade since perestroika and glasnost were implemented, the transition to democracy and a market economy is fraught with dangers.

Notes on Sources

CHAPTER ONE
1. Quoted in B.H. Liddell Hart, *History of the Second World War* (London, 1970).
2. Robin Milner-Gulland, with Nikolai Dejevsky, *Atlas of Russia and the USSR* (Oxford, 1989), p. 30.
3. Lionel Kochan and Richard Abraham, *The Making of Modern Russia* (Harmondsworth, 1983), p. 12.
4. Tibor Szamuely, *The Russian Tradition* (London, 1988), p. 10.
5. Kochan and Abraham, pp. 12, 14.
6. Henri Pirenne, *A History of Europe* (London, 1939), p. 465.

CHAPTER TWO
1. James Chambers, *The Devil's Horsemen* (London, 1979).
2. *Ibid.* p. 58.
3. *Ibid.* p. 60.
4. Szamuely, *Russian Tradition*.
5. Quoted in *The Cambridge Economic History of Europe*, Vol. I (Cambridge, 1941), p. 427.

CHAPTER THREE
1. Szamuely, p. 24.
2. Milner-Gulland and Dejevsky, p. 55.
3. *Ibid.* p. 56.
4. N.M. Karamzin, *Memoirs on Ancient and Modern Russia*, ed. R. Pipes (Cambridge, Mass., 1959), p. 109.
5. G. Vernadsky, *A History of Russia* (New York, 1944).
6. Karl Marx, *Revelations of the Diplomacy of the Eighteenth Century* (1857).

CHAPTER FOUR

1 Kochan and Abraham, p. 44.
2 Szamuely, p. 44.
3 *The Correspondence between Prince A.M. Kurbsky and Tsar Ivan IV of Russia 1564–1579*, ed. & trans. J.L.I. Fennell (Cambridge, 1955), p. 27. Now thought by many to be a forgery.
4 Garrett Mattingly, *The Defeat of the Spanish Armada* (London, 1959), p. 166.
5 Runciman, in *The Christian World*, ed. Geoffrey Barraclough (London, 1981) p. 120.
6 See Szamuely, p. 43. Although born in Hungary Szamuely defected to the West in 1964. There is more than a hint of traditional Magyar anti-Russian feeling in his writing.

CHAPTER FIVE

1 Runciman p. 115
2 Kochan and Abraham, p. 62.
3 *Ibid.*
4 B.H. Sumner, *Survey of Russian History* (London, 1961) p. 182.

CHAPTER SIX

1 Kochan and Abraham, p. 73.
2 Robert K. Massie, *Peter the Great* (London, 1981), p. 15. This Pulitzer prize-winning biography gives a brilliant description of Old Muscovy, cf. pp. 3–18.
3 Szamuely, pp. 66–7.
4 Massie, p. 62.
5 *Ibid.* p. 61.
6 Kochan and Abraham, p. 90
7 B.H. Sumner, p. 235.

CHAPTER SEVEN

1 Massie, p. 52.
2 Kochan and Abraham, p. 103.
3 Szamuely, p. 122.
4 Massie, p. 136.
5 Kochan and Abraham, p. 105.
6 Runciman, *loc. cit.* p. 121.
7 The account of the battle owes much to Chapter 37 of Massie's book. This gives a detailed but very readable description of it.
8 Massie, p. 670.
9 T. Riha (ed.), *Readings in Russian Civilization* (Chicago, 1964), p. 85.
10 V.O. Klyuchevsky, *Kurs russkoy istorii*, Vol. IV, pp. 47–8.
11 Alexander Herzen, *Byloye i dumy* (Moscow, 1947), p. 46.

CHAPTER EIGHT
1   John T. Alexander, *Catherine the Great, Life and Legend* (Oxford, 1989), p. 17.
2   Kochan and Abraham, p. 142.
3   For a detailed account of the circumstances surrounding Ivan's murder, see Alexander, pp. 89–94.
4   Henri Troyat, *Catherine the Great* (London, 1978), p. 22.
5   *Ibid.* p. 112.
6   For speculation about Peter's death, see Alexander, pp. 10–16.
7   *Ibid.* p. 16.
8   Sumner, p. 245.

CHAPTER NINE
1   Surprisingly, Kochan and Abraham give a figure of fifty.
2   Alexander, p. 226.
3   Runciman, *loc. cit.* p. 121.
4   Troyat, p. 211.
5   Szamuely, p. 156.
6   N.P. Pavlova-Silvanskaya, Uchrezhdenie No. 16 (21 April 1785), Art. 20 (Moscow, 1964).
7   E.M. Almedigen gives more details about Catherine's last hours in *So Dark a Stream* (London, 1959), ch. 13.
8   Neal Ascherson, *The Struggles for Poland* (London, 1987), p. 22.

CHAPTER TEN
1   Curtis Cate, *The War of the Two Emperors* (New York, 1985), p. 15.
2   *Ibid.* p. 15.
3   Alastair Horne, *Napoleon. Master of Europe 1805–1807* (London, 1979), p. 131.
4   Cate, p. 23.
5   Felix Markham, *Napoleon* (London, 1963), p. 175.
6   Corelli Barnett, *Bonaparte* (London, 1978), p. 164.
7   *Ibid.* p. 169.
8   See Markham, p. 181; Cate, p. 273.
9   Cate is particularly critical of his handling of the battle of Malo-Yaroslavets, pp. 335–7.
10   Graham Stephenson, *Russia 1812–45* (London, 1969).
11   Jacques Droz, *Europe between Revolutions 1815–48* (London, 1967), pp. 182–3.
12   *Ibid.* pp. 183–4.
13   Sumner, p. 316.
14   Hugh Seton-Watson, 'The Expansion of Russia', in Asa Briggs (ed.), *The Nineteenth Century* (London, 1985), p. 223.
15   *Ibid.*
16   C. De Grunwald, *Tsar Nicholas I* (London, 1954), p. 34.
17   Ascherson, p. 26.

18   Albert Seaton, *The Crimean War. A Russian Chronicle* (London, 1977), p. 35.
19   *Ibid.* p. 50

CHAPTER ELEVEN
1   Kochan and Abraham, p. 180.
2   Hugh Seton-Watson, *The Russian Empire 1801–1917* (Oxford, 1967), p. 130.
3   Ascherson, p. 29.
4   J.N. Westwood, *Endurance and Endeavour. Russia 1812–1980* (Oxford, 2nd ed. 1981).
5   Quoted from F. Venturi, *Roots of Revolution* (New York, 1960), p. 184.
6   E.H. Carr, Introduction to *What is to be Done?* by N.G. Chernyshevsky (New York, 1960), p. 17.
7   Marc Slonim, Afterword to Fyodor Dostoyevsky's *The Possessed* (New York, 1962), p. 697.
8   *Ibid.* p. 696.
9   W.E. Mosse, *Alexander II and the Modernisation of Russia* (London, 1958).
10   Stephenson, *op. cit.*
11   *Ibid.*
12   Kochan and Abraham.
13   Seton-Watson, 'The Expansion of Russia', p. 218.

CHAPTER TWELVE
1   Richard Charques, *The Twilight of Imperial Russia* (Oxford, 1958).
2   Alex de Jonge, *The Life and Times of Grigorii Rasputin* (London, 1982), p. 156.
3   Geoffrey Regan, *Someone Had Blundered . . . A Historical Survey of Military Incompetence* (London, 1987), p. 37.
4   Andrew Wheatcroft, *The World Atlas of Revolutions* (London, 1983), p. 78.
5   *Ibid.* p. 85.
6   Norman Stone, *The Eastern Front 1914–17* (London, 1975), p. 36.
7   Kochan and Abraham, p. 281.
8   Stone, ch. 7.
9   de Jonge, p. 346.
10   Joel Carmichael, *A Short History of the Russian Revolution* (London, 1967), p. 59.

CHAPTER THIRTEEN
1   E.H. Carr, *The Bolshevik Revolution*, Vol. I (London, 1966), p. 103.
2   Kochan and Abraham, p. 323.
3   John Silverlight, *The Victor's Dilemma. Allied Intervention in the Russian Civil War* (London, 1970), p. 367.
4   Carr Vol. II, p. 271.
5   David Shub, *Lenin* (New York, 1948), p. 420.

CHAPTER FOURTEEN
1   B. Bazhanov, *Stalin – Der Rote Diktator* (Berlin, 1931), p. 79.

2   John Scott, *Behind the Urals* (Indiana, 1973).
3   Christopher Andrew, *Secret Service* (London, 1985), p. 365.
4   Alexander Solzhenitsyn, *The First Circle* (London, 1968), p. 134.
5   Aino Kuusinen, Before and After Stalin (London, 1974) p. 134.
6   *Iblid*. p. 134.
7   Christopher Thorne, *The Approach of War 1938–9* (London, 1967), p. 18.
8   A recent definitive study of Soviet foreign policy suggests that Soviet preparations for intervention were genuine. Jonathan Haslam, *The Soviet Union and the Struggle for Collective Security in Europe 1933–9* (London, 1984), pp. 192–4.
9   Solzhenitsyn, *First Circle*, p. 134.
10   Albert Seaton, *Stalin as Warlord* (London, 1976), p. 271.
11   A.J.P. Taylor, *How Wars Begin* (London, 1979). p. 170.
12   In the magazine *Soviet Culture*.

CHAPTER FIFTEEN

1   Andrei Gromyko, in *Memories* (London, 1989), p. 322, quotes Molotov's version of Beria's arrest but says nothing about his subsequent fate.
2   Martin Walker, *The Waking Giant. The Soviet Union under Gorbachev* (London, 1986), p. 5.
3   Mark Frankland, *Khrushchev* (London, 1966), p. 107.
4   Charlotte Waterlow and Archibald Evans, *Europe 1945–70* (London, 1973), p. 128.
5   Ben R. Jones, *The Making of Contemporary Europe* (London, 1980), p. 142.
6   Frankland, p. 192.
7   Arthur Schlesinger Jnr makes this point in his biography of President Kennedy, *A Thousand Days. John F. Kennedy in the White House* (New York and London, 1965), p. 712.
8   Frankland, p. 209.

CHAPTER SIXTEEN

1   Walker, *op. cit.* p. 24.
2   Mikhail Gorbachev, *Perestroika. New Thinking for Our Country and the World* (London, 1988), p. 41.
3   Walker, p. 4.
4   Gorbachev, p. 65.
5   *Ibid.* p. 120.
6   *Ibid.* p. 118.

Grand Princes and Tsars of Kiev and Muscovy

Rurik *862–879*

Kievan Russia

Oleg *879–912*
Igor *912–945*
Olga (Igor's widow) regent
945–964
Svyatoslav *964–972*
Yaropolk I *973–978/80*
Vladimir I *978/80–1015*
Svyatopolk I *1015–1019*
Yaroslav the Wise *1019–1054*
Succession struggle between
Yaroslav's sons *1054–1093*
Svyatopolk II *1093–1113*
Vladimir Monomakh *1113–1125*

Muscovy

Alexander Nevsky *1252–1263*
Yuri III *1303–1325*
Ivan I (Moneybags) *1328–1340*
Ivan II *1353–1359*
Dimitri Donskoy *1359–1389*
Vasily I *1389–1425*
Vasily II *1425–1462*
Ivan III (The Great) *1462–1505*
Vasily III *1505–1533*

Ivan IV (The Terrible)
1533–1584
Fyodor I *1584–1598*
Boris Godunov *1598–1605*
Fyodor II *1605*
False Dimitry I *1605–1606*
False Dimitry II *1607–1610*

The Romanovs

Mikhail (Michael)
1613–1645
Alexis *1645–1676*
Fyodor III *1676–1682*
Ivan V *1682–1689*
Peter the Great *1682–1725*
Catherine I *1725–1727*
Peter II *1727–1730*
Anna *1730–1740*
Ivan VI *1740–1741*
Elizabeth *1741–1762*
Peter III *1762*
Catherine II *1762–1796*
Paul *1796–1801*
Alexander I *1801–1825*
Nicholas I *1825–1855*
Alexander II *1855–1881*
Alexander III *1881–1894*
Nicholas II *1894–1917*

Prime Ministers, People's Chairman, General Secretaries and Presidents

Provisional Government Prime Ministers

Prince Lvov *February–May 1917*

Alexander Kerensky *May–October 1917*

People's Chairman of the Council of Commissars

V.I. Lenin *1917–1924*

General Secretaries of the CPSU

J.V. Stalin *1924–1953*

G.M. Malenkov *1953–1955*

N.S. Khrushchev *1955–1964*

L.I. Brezhnev *1964–1982*

Yu.V. Andropov *1982–1984*

K.U. Chernenko *1984–1985*

M.S. Gorbachev *1985–1991*

Presidents of Republics

Armenia	Levon Ter-Petrosyan *1991–1998*
	Robert Kocharya *1990–*
Azerbaijan	Abulfaz Elchibey *1991–1994*
	Geidar Aliyev *1994–*
Byelarus	Stanilas Shushkevitch *1991–1994*
	Alyakshandar Lukashenka *1994–*
Estonia	Lennart Meri *1991–*
Georgia	Zviad Gamsakhurdia *1991–1992*
	Eduard Shevardnadze Head of State *1992–1995*
	President *1995–*
Kazakhstan	Nursultan Nazarbayev *1991–*
Kirgitzstan	Askar Akayev *1991–*
Latvia	Anatolis Gorbunovs *1991–1994*
	Guntis Ulmanis *1994–*
Lithuania	Vytautis Landsbergis *1991–1992*
	Algirdas Brazauskas *1992–1998*
	Valdas Adamkus *1998–*
Moldova	Mircea Muravschi *1991–1994*
	Mircea Snegur *1994–1997*
	Petru Lucinschi *1997–*
Russia	Boris Yeltsin *1991–1999*
	Vladimir Putin *2000–*
Tajikistan	Rakhman Nabiyev *1991–1994*
	Imomali Rakhmonov *1994–*
Turkmenistan	Saparmurad Niyazov *1991–*
Ukraine	Leonid Kravchuk *1991–1994*
	Leonid Kuchma *1994–*
Uzbekistan	Islam Karimov *1991–*

★ = not members of the Commonwealth of Independent States.

Chronology of Major Events

A.D.

1367	Construction of Moscow Kremlin begins
1380	Dimitri Donskoy defeats Mongols at Kulikovo
1392	Muscovy obtains Nizhny-Novgorod (Gorky)
1453	Ottoman Turks capture Constantinople
1475–9	Construction of Dormition Cathedral in Moscow
1477	Ivan III (1462–1505) captures Novgorod
1480	Ivan III ends payment of tribute to the Mongols
1510	Vasily III (1505–33) annexes Pskov
1547	Beginning of Ivan the Terrible's (1533–84) personal rule; adopts title 'tsar'
1552	The 100 Chapters; Ivan IV conquers Kazan
1553	Richard Chancellor's voyage to White Sea
1562	Failure of Muscovite campaign against Livonia
1563–7	Period of the *oprichnina* terror
1569	Poland and Lithuania united by Union of Lublin
1571	Crimean Tartars raid Moscow
1584	Death of Ivan the Terrible
1584–6	Regency of Nikita Romanov
1586–98	Regency of Boris Godunov
1588	Moscow attains status of Patriarchate
1591	Death of Prince Dimitry (son of Ivan IV by 2nd marriage)
1603	Appearance of the first 'false Dimitry'
1605	Death of Tsar Boris
1606	Uprising against false Dimitry
1607	Defeat and execution of first false Dimitry (Grigory Otrepyev); failure of Ivan Bolotnikov's uprising; appearance of second 'false Dimitry'
1609	Smolensk falls to Poles
1610	Vladislav of Poland proclaimed tsar
1612	Poles driven out of Moscow
1613	Michael Romanov becomes tsar after nomination by Zemsky Sobor
1617	Peace of Stolbovo
1618–48	The Thirty Years War
1619	Return of Filaret Romanov from exile in Poland; municipal reform programme
1632	Death of Gustavus Adolphus
1633	Death of Filaret Romanov
1649	The Russian Code of Laws (Ulozhenie)
1652	Tsar Alexis does penance for the murder of Archbishop Philip
1654	First book printed in Moscow
1655	Muscovy lays siege to Riga

1658–67	Russo–Polish War
1660	Deposition of Patriarch Nikon
1666	Nikon exiled
1669	Death of Tsaritsa Maria Miloslavskaya
1676	Death of Tsar Alexis
1682	Abolition of the *mestnichestva* (systems of aristocratic preference); death of Fyodor III; Sophia becomes regent
1689	Overthrow of Sophia; joint rule of Peter and Ivan V
1696	Death of Ivan V; Peter annexes Azov
1697	Peter begins grand tour of western Europe
1698–9	Destruction of the *Streltsy*
1700	Start of the Great Northern War; battle of Narva
1709	Russian victory over the Swedes at Poltava
1711	Peter's army surrounded by Turks on the River Pruth
1712	Peter the Great moves capital to St Petersburg
1718	Death of Charles XII of Sweden
1721	Treaty of Nystadt ends Great Northern War
1722	Table of Ranks instituted
1723	Russians annex Baku
1724	Catherine crowned tsaritsa
1725	Death of Peter the Great
1727	Death of Catherine I; fall of Menshikov
1730	Death of Peter II from smallpox
1733–5	War of the Polish Succession
1735–9	Russo-Turkish War
1739	Treaty of Belgrade
1740–1	Anna Leopoldovna regent for Ivan VI
1741	Deposition of Ivan VI, after coup by Guards regiments puts the Tsaritsa Elizabeth on the throne
1745	Marriage of Charles Peter of Holstein to Sophie of Anhalt-Zerbst
1748	End of the War of the Austrian Succession
1756–63	Seven Years War
1757	Apraksin defeats Prussians at Gross-Jägersdorf
1759	Russian victory at Kunersdorf
1761	Death of Tsaritsa Elizabeth; Russians withdraw from Prussia
1762	Deposition and murder of Peter III; Catherine becomes tsaritsa
1763	Catherine II restores Collegium of Economy
1764	One million private serfs transferred to state control; Stanislaw Poniatowski elected king of Poland
1767	Catherine issues her 'Instruction'
1768	Confederation of Bar formed

1769	Russians occupy Moldavia and Wallachia
1772	First Partition of Poland
1773–4	Pugachev's uprising; battle of Tsaritsyn
1774	Treaty of Kuchuk-Kainardji
1783	Russian annexation of the Crimea
1791	Ochakov crisis; Polish constitution proclaimed
1792	Second Partition of Poland
1794	Polish uprising crushed by Suvorov
1795	Third Partition of Poland
1796	Death of Catherine II; accession of Paul (1796–1801)
1801	Assassination of Tsar Paul; Alexander I (1801–25) succeeds
1805	Battle of Austerlitz
1807	Battles of Eylau and Friedland; Treaty of Tilsit
1810	Alexander rejects marriage alliance with Bonaparte
1812	Russo–Turkish peace treaty; French invasion of Russia; battle of Borodino; burning of Moscow; passage of the Beresina and destruction of the French army; Speransky dismissed
1813	Treaty of Kalisch with Prussia; battle of Leipzig; battles of Lutzen and Bautzen
1814–15	Congress of Vienna; Alexander I secures creation of Congress Poland and puts forward concept of 'The Holy Alliance'
1818	Congress of Aix la Chapelle
1820	Congress of Troppau
1822	Monroe Doctrine proclaimed by USA to counter Alexander's desire for intervention in Latin America; Grand Duke Constantine gives up succession rights
1825	Death of Alexander and accession of Nicholas I (1825–55); Decembrist revolt crushed
1829	Treaty of Adrianople
1830–1	Polish uprising crushed; followed by the 'Great Emigration'
1833	Treaty of Unkiar Skelessi; Pushkin publishes *The Bronze Horseman*
1834	Gogol publishes *Taras Bulba*
1841	Straits Convention
1844	Visit by Nicholas I to Britain
1849	Russian intervention crushes Hungarian uprising
1850	Meeting at Olmütz
1853	Nicholas occupies Moldavia and Wallachia
1854	Franco–British declaration of war against Nicholas; battles of Alma, Inkerman and Balaclava
1855	Battle of Sevastopol; death of Nicholas and accession of

	Alexander II (1855–81), who releases surviving Decembrists
1856	Treaty of Paris
1861	Edict of Emancipation
1862	Turgenev's *Fathers and Sons* published
1863	Revolt in Russian Poland crushed
1863–9	Tolstoy's *War and Peace*
1864	*Zemstvo* reform
1866	Karakozov's attempt on Alexander's life
1869	First Russian edition of *Das Kapital* available
1870	Russia revokes the Black Sea clauses of the Treaty of Paris
1873–7	Tolstoy's *Anna Karenina*
1874	The narodniks 'go to the people'
1877	Treaty of San Stephano
1878	Congress of Berlin
1881	Alexander II assassinated by the 'People's Will'; accession of Alexander III (1881–94)
1887	Reinsurance Treaty with Germany
1888	Russia fails to obtain Reichsbank loan
1894	Franco–Russian Dual Alliance; death of Alexander III; accession of Nicholas II (1894–1917)
1898	Peasant redemption payments end
1900	Siberia loses status of penal colony
1903	Serious pogroms in Kishinev and Gomal
1904	Outbreak of Russo–Japanese war
1905	Port Arthur falls; battles of Mukden and Tsushima; Treaty of Portsmouth; Revolution of 1905; Bloody Sunday in St. Petersburg
1906	Fundamental Law of the Empire; First Duma meets
1907	Entente with Britain
1908	Bosnia–Herzegovina crisis
1911	Assassination of Prime Minister Stolypin
1913	300th anniversary of Romanov dynasty
1914	Outbreak of World War I; Russian defeats at Tannenberg and the Masurian Lakes
1915	Battle of Gorlice Tarnow
1916	Brusilov offensive against Austro-Hungarians; murder of Rasputin
1917	Abdication of Nicholas II (March); Provisional Government set up; return of Lenin; failure of Kornilov counter-coup; Bolsheviks seize power (November); Constituent Assembly abolished; Cheka set up
1918	Treaty of Brest-Litovsk; beginning of Allied intervention; murder of Romanovs

1920	Russo–Polish war; battle of Warsaw
1921	Treaty of Riga; Lenin introduces NEP; Kronstadt mutiny crushed
1922	Treaty of Rapallo with Germans
1924	Death of Lenin
1925	Trotsky removed from Politburo
1928	First Five Year Plan introduced
1929	Trotsky exiled from USSR
1930	Stalin's article 'Dizziness with Success'
1933	Second Five Year Plan
1934	Murder of Kirov; USSR joins League of Nations
1935	Franco–Soviet Treaty
1936	Purge of former Left Bolsheviks; death of Maxim Gorky
1937	Army purge; execution of Marshal Tukhachevsky
1938	Purge of Right Bolsheviks; USSR excluded from Munich Conference
1939	Fighting with Japanese on Mongolian frontier; Nazi–Soviet pact
1939–40	Winter war with Finland
1940	Soviet annexation of Baltic Republics and Bessarabia; assassination of Trotsky
1941	USSR attacked by Nazi Germany
1941–4	Siege of Leningrad
1942	German advance into Caucasus
1943	German surrender at Stalingrad; battle of Kursk
1944	Red Army drives into Poland
1945	Battle of Berlin; Yalta and Potsdam meetings; war in Europe ends; USSR enters war against Japan
1946	Persian settlement
1947	Truman Doctrine
1948	Berlin blockade; Tito defects from alliance with USSR; Communist takeover in Czechoslovakia
1949	Purges of East European Communist parties; USSR explodes first atomic bomb
1950	Outbreak of Korean War
1953	Death of Stalin; workers' uprising in East Berlin; disappearance of Beria
1954	Geneva summit
1955	Austrian State Treaty; Warsaw Pact created
1956	Khrushchev denounces Stalin in secret speech; Hungarian uprising crushed; Suez crisis
1957	Khrushchev defeats 'anti-party' group; Sputnik launched
1960	Gary Powers shot down over USSR; Paris summit cancelled

1961	Yuri Gagarin becomes first man in space; Berlin Wall built; Bay of Pigs
1962	Cuban missile crisis; Solzhenitsyn's *One Day in the Life of Ivan Denisovich* published
1963	USSR signs nuclear test ban treaty; publication of Yevtushenko's *Precocious Autobiography*
1964	Fall of Khrushchev; Brezhnev becomes General Secretary of CPSU
1965	Prime Minister Kosygin mediates at Tashkent
1967	Six Day War in Middle East; Johnson–Kosygin meeting at Glassborough
1968	Red Army crushes 'Prague Spring'; Brezhnev Doctrine promulgated
1969	Fighting on Sino–Soviet border
1970	Gomulka overthrown in Poland; Solzhenitsyn wins Nobel Prize for Literature
1971	USSR launches world's first manned space station
1972	SALT I agreed; Sino–US agreement
1973	Yom Kippur War
1974	Solzenhitsyn leaves USSR for exile
1975	Helsinki Conference
1976	Brezhnev takes post as Soviet President
1977	SALT II discussions with USA
1978	KGB crushes attempts to form independent unions
1979	Soviet invasion of Afghanistan
1980	Death of Kosygin; Western boycott of Moscow Olympics; fall of Gierek in Poland
1981	Martial law in Poland after Soviet pressure
1982	Death of Brezhnev; succeeded by Andropov
1983	USSR shoots down Korean airliner in error
1984	Death of Andropov; succeeded by Chernenko; USSR boycotts Los Angeles Olympics
1985	Death of Chernenko; succeeded by Gorbachev, who introduces glasnost and perestroika
1986	Reyjavik summit
1987	Chernobyl disaster; INF Treaty signed
1988	Serious earthquake in Armenia; Gorbachev in New York
1989	Soviet evacuation of Afghanistan; Gorbachev in China; Tbilisi massacre; fall of Honecker, Ceausescu, etc.
1990	Soviet troops assault Baku; Lithuanian declaration of independence; elections to Soviet parliament; Soviet economic blockade of Lithuania; USSR Congress of Deputies grants Gorbachev executive presidential powers

1991	Military intervention in Lithuania and Latvia; all union referendum on future of USSR boycotted in six republics; Yeltsin elected executive president of Russia; failure of Moscow coup attempt; dissolution of CPSU; resignation of Gorbachev and dissolution of USSR; CIS formed; Comecon disbanded; dissolution of Warsaw Pact
1992	Signing of Russian Federation Treaty by 18 autonomous republics; growing tensions between Yeltsin and Russian parliament; inter-parliamentary assembly for CIS set up; dispute with Ukraine over Black Sea fleet; first US–Russian summit; Russian ratification of Strategic Arms Reduction Treaty
1993	Dispute with Baltic states over former Soviet garrisons; Yeltsin wins Russian federation referendum; Yeltsin dissolves parliament after failed coup by Khasbulatov and Rutskoi; Parliamentary elections called for December
1994	Defection of Chechens; Outbreak of Chechen War
1996	Yeltsin wins June Presidential Election
1999	Russia opposes NATO bombing of Kosovo; Russian troops enter Kosovo as part of peacekeeping force; Russia reopens war with Chechyna; Armenian prime minister assassinated in parliament; Vladimir Putin wins the Parliamentary Election in Russia
2000	Boris Yeltsin resigns; Vladimir Putin is elected President; 118 men are lost in the nuclear submarine *Kursk* disaster

Further Reading

ALEXANDER, J. *Catherine the Great* (Oxford, 1989)

CHAMBERS, J. *The Mongols* (London, 1979)

DEUTSCHER, I. *Stalin* (Oxford, 1949)

FRANKLAND, M. *Khrushchev* (London, 1966)

GROMYKO, A. *Memories* (London, 1989)

KOCHAN, L. & ABRAHAM, R. *The Making of Modern Russia* (Harmondsworth, 1983)

LYNCH, M. *Stalin and Khrushchev. The USSR 1924–64* (London, 1990)

MASSIE, R.K. *Peter the Great* (London, 1981)

MILNER-GULLAND, R. & DEJEVSKY, N. *Atlas of Russia and the Soviet Union* (Oxford, 1989)

MOSSE, W.E. *Alexander II and the Modernization of Russia* (London, 1958)

OBOLENSKY, C. *The Russian Empire. A Portrait in Photographs* (London, 1980)

PALMER, A. *Alexander I* (London, 1974)

SEATON, A. *The Crimean War* (London, 1977)
        Stalin as Warlord (London, 1976)

SETON-WATSON, H. *The Russian Empire 1801–1917* (Oxford, 1967)

SILVERLIGHT, J. *The Victor's Dilemma. Allied Intervention in the Russian Civil War* (London, 1970)

SOLZHENITSYN, A. *August 1914* (London, 1972)

STONE, N. *The Eastern Front 1914–17* (London, 1975)

TUCHMANN, B. *The Guns of August* (London, 1962)

WALKER, M. *The Waking Giant. The Soviet Union under Gorbachev* (London, 1986)

WESTWOOD, J.N. *Endurance and Endeavour: Russian History 1812–1980* (Oxford, 2nd ed. 1981)

YELTSIN, B. *Against the Grain* (London, 1990)

Historical Gazetteer

Numbers in bold refer to the main text

Alma-Ata The capital of the Republic of Kazakhstan, with a population of over a million (its name translates in English as 'Father of Apples'). It was established as the local capital by the Russians in the nineteenth century under the name of Verny, and has since acquired a cosmopolitan character. Currently only a third of the population are ethnic Kazakhs. Once famous for its nomadic horsemen (Kazakh translates as 'rider'), Kazakhstan, which became a constituent republic of the USSR in 1936, now has a cosmodrome (at Baykonyr) and a nuclear testing centre (Semipalatinsk). Became an independent republic when the USSR broke up in 1991.

Archangelsk (Archangel) The city port of Archangel was established as a direct consequence of Richard Chancellor's pioneering voyage of 1553. Situated at the mouth of the northern branch of the River Dvina, it became the key link in the trade between England and Muscovy. Allied troops landed there during the civil war period after 1917, and the port played an important role during World War 2 when Anglo-American munitions were landed there. Archangel has now become an important outlet for the exports of the Kola peninsula and one of the three great ports of the north-western region (with Murmansk and Leningrad). **52, 58, 74, 193, 224**

Ashkhabad The capital of the Republic of Turkmenistan. The Turkmens (who are Sunni Moslems) are a Turkic people, living in an ancient area which was occupied successively by Huns, Arabs, Sassanids and Parthians, and finally by Mongol Oghuz. The southern section was under Persian rule in the 15th–17th centuries, then reunited with the northern by the Russians in 1881. It became a constituent republic of USSR in 1924. Ashkhabad is situated in the Kara-Kum Desert (the largest in USSR). It is only 25 miles from the Iranian border, a fact of more significance since the 1979 Iranian Revolution. A noteworthy Fine Art Museum contains examples of Turkmeni and European artists and examples of local carpets. Museum of Local History and Ethnography, and Botanical Garden behind local Agriculture College.

Baku Baku, the capital of the

Republic of Azerbaijan, has a population of 1.7 million. Its castle includes the Mohammed Mosque dating from 1093 and the oldest building in the city. The 20th-century Kirov Monument, the city's highest point, gives a fine panoramic view of the entire city. The oil deposits around Baku were of tremendous importance in the tsarist period, and even today oil is the single most important contributor to the Azerbaijani economy. Despite its absorption into the Russian empire in the 1920s, the city has retained its distinctive Azeri culture. Islamic influence (both Sunni and Shiite) is still strong and the attraction of nearby Iran is growing. During the civil war an independent anti-Bolshevik republic was set up for a time, but it was crushed by the Red Army and much of the city destroyed in the process. The city makes up for this historical disaster through its fine situation, built on a hillside around a bay of the Apsheron Peninsula. A mild climate is occasionally transformed by a fierce wind, akin to the French Mistral, called the 'Nord of Baku'. Since 1991 capital of the new independent Azerbaijan. **79, 162, 267**

Batumi   The resort town of Batumi on the Black Sea is just 12 miles from the Turkish frontier and its very mild winters make it a popular holiday venue. Buildings of historic interest are few in number, although the Adzhar State Museum in Dzhinsharadze Street has interesting items about Batumi before 1917. There is a Drama Theatre in Rustaveli Street and a special Summer Theatre in Pimorsky Park.

Bishkek   Formerly known as Frunze, the capital of the Republic of Kirghizistan lies in the valley of the Chu river. Bishkek has little of historical interest itself although it is only 50 miles from the 11th-century Burana tower. Pervogo Maya Street has the Fine Arts Museum and the Kirghiz Drama, as well as a museum built to honour the early Soviet general Mikhail Frunze who was born in the city which recently bore his name.

Kirghizia, which became a separate republic in 1936, is the furthest republic from Moscow and shares a long frontier with China. The population is 90% Muslim. Capital now of independent Kirghizistan. The second capital Osh is known as 'a second Mecca'.

Bukhara   The city of Bukhara fell to Genghis Khan in 1220, and during the course of the occupation the largely wooden city was burnt to the ground (this seems to have been an accident, as the Mongols hadn't stormed the city). The 'White Horde', so named to distinguish them from the Golden Horde which was based in European Russia, made Bukhara their headquarters and it retains its medieval character to this day. Bukhara also became an important trading centre across the routes to Europe and Central Asia.

Cherkassy   Cherkassy is in the Ukraine on the River Dnieper and an important regional and cultural centre. Museum of Local History traces the city's development since 16th century. The development of the Kremenchug Reservoir has also promoted Cherkassy's role as a river port.

Dushanbe   Dushanbe (formerly Stalinabad), the capital of Tadzhikistan, is a modern city which only really began to expand after the coming of the railways in 1929. It is noted for its steam power plants. Most of the points of interest are concentrated in or around the Lenin Prospekt. They include the Museum of History and Regional History, which also contains interesting examples of Tadzhik art. The Firdansi Library houses an important collection of Eastern manuscripts and is almost opposite the Science Museum. The two municipal markets with their flavour of ordinary Tadzhik life are also recommended (many still wear the *tubeteyka* or embroidered skullcap). The Ayni Park is named after the founder of modern Tadzhik literature.

Tadzhikistan, like Uzbekistan, was first ruled by the Bukhara emirate and then by the Russians. It is 90% mountainous and noted for its poverty. The Tadzhiks speak an Iranian-type language, and they fought strongly against Soviet expansionism 1921–5. Traditional carpet-making still survives (a relic of old links with Persia) but most are now mass-produced. Serious nationalist riots broke out in Dushanbe in the winter months of 1990. Became independent republic in 1991. **274**

Echmiadzin   Founded in AD 117, it was formerly the capital of Armenia (its old name was Vargarsapat). As the current seat of the Catholicos (or Patriarch) the city is often known as 'Holy Echmiadzin' and is regarded as Armenia's religious capital. The cathedral dates from the beginning of the fourth century AD and serves as a model for many Armenian churches abroad. The nearby Gayane Convent, built in the 7th century, is also worth a visit. Echmiadzin is 20 km west of Yerevan.

Frunze   See **Bishkek.**

Kalinin   Formerly known as Tver, a rival to Moscow until the time of Ivan the Terrible, the city has two cathedrals: the Pobrovsky, built in 1689, and the Uspensky (1777). The latter has a large bell which was cast in 1841 to commemorate the defeat of Napoleon's invading army in 1812. There is also a 19th-century university. **26, 27, 31**

Kerch   One of the oldest settlements in the USSR, dating from the 6th century BC when it was founded by the Greeks as Panticapaeum. Important archaeological remains from the Scythian period have been found. It dominated what was then known as 'the Cimmerian Bosphorus', giving access to the Sea of Azov. It was successively a Byzantine, Genoese and Ottoman colony, until the Treaty of Kuchuk-Kainardji (1774) gave it to Tsarist Russia. This is traced in the city's Historical and Archaeological Museum. **116**

Kiev   The capital of the Ukraine and the place where Christianity was first established. Its most striking building is the Cathedral of St Sophia which was dedicated by the Grand Prince Yaroslav the Wise in 1037. Yaroslav was buried in the cathedral when he died in 1054. St Andrew's Church was built on the orders of the Empress Elizabeth. Among several buildings in Red Square are Peter the Great's headquarters at the time of the Great

Northern War, and the ruins of the Bratsky Monastery. Kiev's university dates from 1834. The city became the capital of independent Ukraine in 1991. **2, 11, 20–1, 198, 222**

Kishinev The capital of the Soviet Republic of Moldavia and site of a notorious anti-Jewish pogrom in 1903. **168–9**

Kursk Completely destroyed in 1240 during the Mongol invasion. The greatest tank battle of World War 2 was fought around the town in 1943. Relics from the battle area are on show at the Park of the Battle of Kursk. Kursk also has the Cathedral of St Sergey. **223–4**

Minsk Minsk is the capital of Byelorussia and a big industrial and cultural centre. The earliest settlement dates from AD 900, and until the eve of the Mongol invasion the city was in the principality of Polotsk. In the 15th century it was absorbed into Lithuania before becoming part of Poland in the 17th century. Only in the 19th century did Minsk become part of Russia, and the first Congress of the RSDP was held there in 1898. Minsk suffered severely in the Great Patriotic War, and has an obelisk in Pobeda Square to the war dead. A separate war museum can be found in Svoboda (Freedom) Square. The old-style wooden houses in Victory Square are also a tourist attraction. Minsk has several theatres, a circus, and provision for opera and ballet in its Bolshoi Theatre. Capital of independent Byelorussia since 1991.

Moscow Moscow is the capital not only of the USSR but also of the Russian Soviet Federal Socialist Republic. The RSFSR makes up three-quarters of the entire land mass of the USSR, including the whole of Siberia and smaller areas such as Finno–Karelia.

Moscow has a population of almost 9 million (1987 figure). The dominant architectural feature is the Kremlin (which is never done real justice in western TV coverage) which contains no less than four cathedrals inside its walls: the Archangel, the Annunciation, the Assumption, and the Twelve Apostles (where the Orthodox patriarch lives today). The Cathedral of the Archangel, which was built by the Milanese Alevisio Novi, contains the tombs of all the tsars before Peter the Great (apart from Boris Godunov who is buried at Zagorsk).

Near the Tower of Ivan the Great stands the great Tsar's Bell (Tsar Kolokol) which weighs some 200 tons, but has cracked open on the two occasions, in the reigns of Boris Godunov and Tsaritsa Anna, when efforts were made to use it. Close by is the Tsar Cannon (Tsar Pushka), a sixteenth-century relic which weighs 40 tons, but has never been fired in anger. Also inside the Kremlin walls is the Faceted (Granovitaya) Palace which was built for Tsar Ivan III. The more modern Great Kremlin Palace was built on the order of Tsar Nicholas I between 1839 and 1849. Outside the Kremlin walls, in the adjacent Red Square, is the Lenin Mausoleum (from which Stalin was removed in 1961) where the corpse of the former leader is preserved. At the far end of the Square is St Basil's Cathedral, built for Ivan the Terrible between 1554 and 1560 and now a museum. The biggest monument to the Stalin period is the Metro system, with its ultra-cheap travel and spotless, grafittiless stations. No visit to Moscow would be complete without a visit to the Bolshoi Theatre, the home of classical ballet (whose dancers showed their support for the 1905 Revolution by refusing to perform). The original Bolshoi was destroyed by fire and rebuilt in the 1850s. New capital of the new Russian republic. **23, 26, 29, 50, 91, 125**

Novgorod Arguably the most historic of Russian cities. It escaped the ravages of the Mongols in the 13th century, and was a centre of resistance to the Teutonic Knights before the battle of Lake Peipus. Sacked by Ivan the Terrible. The most striking landmarks are its Kremlin, which has been carefully preserved, and the 11th-century Cathedral of St Sophia. A bell-shaped military monument was erected in 1862 in the Kremlin's square to commemorate 1000 years of Russian history. There are surviving examples of the 12th-century Novgorod school of church building. **2, 6, 11, 20, 31, 35–6, 50, 64**

Narva Site of an important victory by the Red Army in 1918. Occupied by the Swedes during the Great Northern War. Gave its name to the battle in which Charlex XII beat the Russians in 1700. The Ivangorod castle was built by Ivan III in the 16th century. **75–8, 80**

Ochakov The town was the object of a dispute between Catherine II (who eventually annexed it) and Britain. Close by are the remains of the old Greek settlement of Olvia, over 2000 years old. **116**

Odessa Best remembered perhaps for the memorable Odessa steps sequence in the famous Eisenstein film *Battleship Potemkin*. The poet Pushkin lived in the city in 1823–4 and a statue of him was erected in 1888. The Opera House, a legacy from the 1880s, is reputedly one of the finest in Europe. A series of catacombs runs for hundreds of miles under Odessa and the surrounding area.

Petrodvorets (Peterhof) is 18 miles from St Petersburg and the site of Peter the Great's summer palace. Built by the Frenchman Le Blond, this large two-storeyed structure if handsomely decorated, and opens out into a large French-style garden. Petrodvorets is much smaller than the Winter Palace or Versailles (on which Peter modelled it). The glory of Petrodvorets (or Peterhof as it would have been known to the imperial family) is its fountains and water displays. Exquisitely arranged by Le Blond the 64 fountains have as their centrepiece a Golden Samson prising open the jaws of a lion which spouts water (the modern version is a replica as the original was destroyed by the Germans in World War 2). The water display around the palace flows into the sea through a canal which is large enough to allow small sailing ships to sail up to the façade, and the canal itself is flanked by yet more fountains. Surprisingly the water supply for Petrodvorets comes not from the nearby Gulf of Finland, but from higher ground some 13 miles away. The water is then pumped down to the palace through wooden pipes which have survived almost intact from 1721. The Lower Garden contains three summer pavilions, the Hermitage, Marly, and Monplaisir, the last named being Peter's personal favourite. (Marly was named after Louis XIV's private retreat.) Monplaisir was built between 1714 and 1723 and follows the Petrine style as to decorations, furniture, and household artifacts. Its study reflects the great tsar's interest in all things nautical, and the tulips in the back garden will remind the knowledgeable tourist of Peter's important visit to Amsterdam. Monplaisir was virtually the only part of Petrodvorets to escape destruction in World War 2, and the palace, its pavilions and grounds are a tribute to meticulous Soviet restoration.

Poltava Site of Peter the Great's famous victory over the Swedes in 1709. The Holy Cross Monastery dates from the 17th century. **77–8, 86**

Pskov First referred to in the 10th century, and for a long period ruled over by Novgorod. An independent republic from the 13th–15th centuries, when it withstood many attacks by the neighbouring Lithuanians and the Teutonic Knights. Conquered by the Muscovites in the 15th century. Completely destroyed in World War 2 and subsequently rebuilt. **24, 35, 37**

Pushkin (Tsarskoye Selo) is 15 miles south-west of Leningrad. Originally Tsarskoye Selo, the 'Tsar's village' was built in the middle of a swamp by the Tsaritsa Catherine, Peter the Great's second wife. Later embellished by Catherine the Great it reflects the Baroque style of 18th century Enlightenment. There are two palaces, Catherine's Palace (Yekaterinsky Dvorets), sometimes known as the Old Palace, and Alexander's Palace, both being fully restored after war damage. The Catherine Palace, built by Rastrelli, has a blue and white façade and some 200 rooms, several like the Amber Room and the Blue Room being named after their colours.

As its name suggests, the Alexander Palace, with 100 rooms and a yellow and white façade, was built by Quarenghi and the Scotsman Charles Cameron for Catherine the Great's grandson, the future Alexander I. It was the home of Nicholas II and the Tsaritsa Alexandra for over 20 years (only Nicholas and his grandfather Nicholas I liked it) although bizarrely Alexandra couldn't abide the existing imperial furniture and ordered her own by mail order from the London firm of Maples! In her day the palace façade was overlaid by sweet-smelling lilac which was (curiously) cut away by the Bolsheviks in 1920. An interesting feature of Tsarskoye Selo is the railway station, built specially for the imperial family because the secret police thought it too dangerous to use the village station. It dates from 1837 and terminates the oldest railway line in Russia. The road from the railway line to the two palaces has the houses of the former nobility on either side. The palaces are set in 800 acres of parkland which contain artificial lakes, follies, a pagoda, a Turkish bath, and bridle paths. A prominent feature is the so-called 'Great Pond', an artificial lake between the palaces which is next to the Chesma Column commemorating a victory over the Turks in 1770. Visitors should also see the Lyceum, originally built as a school for Catherine the Great's grandsons, which later became a school for the sons of the nobility. Alexander Pushkin enrolled there as a student in 1811. **96, 176–7**

Riga The capital of Latvia and an important port and shipbuilding and fish-processing centre. The largest and most cosmopolitan of Baltic cities it suffered badly in both world wars and most of its medieval buildings were destroyed. Riga has an old castle which houses three museums. There is also a 13th-century church of St Peter, the town's patron saint. Peter the Great lived in a house off Lenin Street when he visited in 1711 and helped to plant the Vestura Garden off Eksporta. New capital of independent Latvia. **198**

Rostov-on-Don Founded in the 18th century. Its Museum of Local History has among its exhibits the sword of the Prussian King Frederick the Great which was captured when the Russians were involved in the Seven Years War. **58**

St Petersburg Formerly Leningrad and the home of the imperial family after Peter the Great moved there with his family in 1710. In 1712 it was proclaimed capital of Russia. The Peter and Paul fortress contains the Church of SS Peter and Paul where Peter the Great and his successors are buried. The fortress also contains the tsarist Mint and Arsenal. Peter also built the Monastery of St Alexander Nevsky and moved the former Grand

Prince's remains there from Vladimir. The classic splendour of St Petersburg is a legacy from the reigns of the Tsaritsas Elizabeth and Catherine II. Empress Anne had commissioned the Italian Rastrelli to rebuild the Winter Palace in 1732, and the merchant adventurer Stroganovs got him to build a palace for them in 1752. In 1744 Rastrelli was responsible for the building of the Convent and Cathedral of Resurrection at Smolny for Elizabeth. Next to it is the Smolny Institute which was built by Quarenghi. Catherine II founded it as a school for the daughters of the aristocracy, and it became first Lenin's headquarters in 1917, and then headquarters of the Leningrad Communist Party. Sergei Kirov was murdered there in 1934. The old Winter Palace was demolished in 1754, and the Tsaritsa Elizabeth ordered Rastrelli to build a new one. It was only completed in 1762 and had 1500 rooms and 8 staircases. A serious fire in 1837 damaged much of the palace, but it was rebuilt in the original style by the architect Stasov. The Little Hermitage was built for Catherine II, partly to house her great picture collection. But this had grown so much by 1774 that she had a second place, known as the Old Hermitage, built to house the remainder. Even then part of the collection ended up in the Winter Palace.

The Winter Palace was the last refuge of the Provisional Government in 1917. Close by the Winter Palace is the Alexandrinsky theatre (now called the Pushkin theatre) which dates from 1832, and immediately behind it is Palace Square where the demonstrators were massacred on 'Bloody Sunday' in 1905.

The Hermitage contains a vast collection of paintings and historical artifacts. There are sections on Russian history, prehistoric times (including Scythian relics), Byzantium, and the republics of Central Asia. Art lovers will be particularly attracted by the sixth section of the museum, which contains many examples of Renaissance art from Leonardo and Raphael to Titian. The art collection also includes dozens of Rembrandts and Rubens, and there is a French Impressionists room where the visitor will find paintings by Cézanne, Monet, Degas and Renoir. The collection of modern art includes many Picassos. The English interest is represented by Gainsborough and Reynolds, and there is a bust of Charles James Fox waspishly commissioned by Catherine the Great to annoy his great political rival Pitt the Younger. The great 'Frog' Dinner Service ordered by the tsaritsa from the pottery baron Josiah Wedgwood can also be found in the Hermitage (it was originally intended for the Chesma Palace whose coat of arms includes a green frog motif). Decembrists Square commemorates the abortive uprising of December 1825 which attempted to remove Nicholas I, and in it is the famous statue of Peter the Great by the Frenchman Falconet. It is commonly known as the 'Bronze Horseman' after Pushkin's poem in which he refers to the tsar as the 'lord of doom', and was erected on the orders of Catherine the Great. At the southern end of Decembrists Square is Saint Isaac's Cathedral, the biggest church in modern St Petersburg named after Peter the Great's favourite saint. Started by Alexander I, it took forty years to build at immense expense. It was turned into a museum of atheism by the Bolsheviks. **68, 77, 79–81, 176–8, 186–91, 223**

Samarkand Samarkand was an ancient city even before the onslaught of the Mongols. At the beginning of the 13th century its population was already in excess of half a million and it was an important centre for silk and cotton. The city fell to the forces of Genghis Khan in 1220 after a siege which lasted just five days. In the later Middle Ages it became an important cultural and scientific centre under Ulegh-Beg. Unlike Tashkent, Samarkand (together with its sister Uzbek cities of Bukhara and Khiva) is a well-preserved medieval city. Its inhabitants can still be seen wearing the traditional clothes of Turkic peasants. Samarkand has a museum of Uzbek Art, and not far outside the city is Ulegh-Beg's Observatory. **145**

Sevastopol Most noted for its resistance to the Anglo–French siege during the Crimean War. Its fall made the Russian defeat inevitable. There is a statue to Totleben who was the Russian hero in the war. The Cathedral of Peter and Paul (built 1843) is opposite the statue of Maxim Gorky (it is now a Palace of Culture). **140**

Smolensk One of the oldest Slav settlements in Russia, dating from the 9th centurey AD. In the 12th century, Smolensk was the capital of an independent principality and then became part of the Grand Duchy of Lithuania in the 13th and 14th centuries. Captured by the Poles in 1609 and Napoleon in 1812. Occupied by the Nazis from 1941 to 1943 and devastated, so that only 300 buildings were left intact. **2, 6, 11, 126, 50, 64, 66**

Suzdal The old capital of the principality, and the first to be conquered by the Mongols in 1237. First mentioned in historical records in the year 1024, it was the capital of Rostov–Suzdal in the 12th century. Later sacked by the Poles and the Crimean Tartars. **17**

Tallinn Capital of Estonia and an important Baltic port, only a short ferry ride from Helsinki and Finland. Beautifully preserved Hanseatic buildings underline the fact that Tallinn, and the rest of Estonia, is essentially western and has the most interesting medieval houses in the Baltic Republics. The St Alexander Nevsky cathedral only dates from the end of the 19th century but the building 'Look-into-the-Kitchen' dates from 1470 and old cannon-balls remain from the siege of 1577. The most interesting relic in Tallinn is the Toomkirk (Cathedral) on Castle Hill which has a Baroque roof and dates from the 13th century. The so-called Great Castle was destroyed by a fire in 1684, but with its sister Small Castle it survived the occupation by the Danes and the Teutonic Knights. Pikk Street contains 'Stout Margaret', another 16th-century remnant (it has a large naval museum inside it).

The October 16th Park commemorates the anti-tsarist uprising of 1905. In 1940 Tallinn was occupied by Soviet troops under the terms of the Nazi–Soviet pact. This occupaion has always been bitterly resented, although Gorbachev's experiments with 'perestroika' have found a natural testing ground in Tallinn. The Estonians, unlike the Great Russians, are natural entrepreneurs. Tallinn means 'Dames Town' and is usually known as Reval outside Estonia. Most Estonians are Lutheran, a residue of historic links with Germany. Once again it is the capital of independent Estonia.

Tashkent Tashkent is the capital of Uzbekistan, one of the Central Asian Republics of the USSR. It was sited on a major trade route across the Chirchik river, becoming part of the Russian empire in 1865. Today it is the fourth largest city in the USSR (2.1 million). It is also the most important Islamic centre in the USSR, where mullahs go for their training and many Islamic tracts are published. In 1966 the city was devastated by a severe earthquake. Remnants of the old city remain in its bazaars, but in most respects Tashkent is now thoroughly modern. In 1986 the population was over 2 million. Capital of independent Uzbekistan since 1991. **261**

Tbilisi (Tiflis) Capital of Georgia, Tbilisi lies on the banks of the River Kura and has a population of more than a million. It has a temperate climate good for fruit-growing. Its inhabitants have a reputation for longevity which may owe something to the medicinal properties of the famed hydrogen sulphide springs.

Georgia's relationship with Russia goes back to Kievan times. It came under Russian protection in the 1780s and full absorption took place under

Tsar Paul (1796–1801). It was an independent republic under the Mensheviks, 1918–21; then incorporated into Transcaucasian SFSR. Full republic 1936.

Tbilisi's finest street is the Rustaveli Boulevard which has many buildings of interest. They include the Georgian National Museum (founded in 1929) and the Kasvety Cathedral opened in 1910. At the end of the Komsomol Promenade is the Museum of Local History. It is in the centre of Lenin Square with the Georgian Art Museum. The museum has a good collection of icons and other works by Georgian artists. Formerly a seminary, it had Stalin as a student (until he was expelled for political activity). The Old Town in Tbilisi contains several buildings of considerable antiquity. The castle, for example, dates from the 4th century AD. The Anchiskhati Church dates from the same period, although little of the original is left. On the left bank of the Kura, on top of a small hill, is one of the Georgian capital's landmarks, the Metekhi Chapel. A 13th-century foundation, it has also doubled as a prison and a theatre. Many of the old buildings in the Old Town have examples of the intricate Georgian style of wood carving. Resumed role as capital of independent Georgia in 1991. **268**

Vilnius   The capital of Lithuania, a constituent republic of the USSR which declared itself independent in 1990. In the 13th century Lithuania was a great power in its own right and it was later united to Poland by the Union of Lublin (1569). The city is situated on the banks of the River Neris with its most historic quarters on the left bank. The Catholic Cathedral of St Stanislaus is a major feature which contains a chapel dedicated to Lithuania's only saint, St Casimir. The cathedral was reconsecrated in 1989 after years first as a garage and then as an art gallery following the Soviet occupation of 1940. Castle Hill has a restored 14th-century tower which has a museum with an exhibition of Vilnius' history. A bigger historical museum can be found at the bottom of the hill. The city has an interesting old quarter starting with the former palaces of the bishops of Vilnius in Kutuzov Square (it now houses the Artists' Union). The university dates from 1570 and is the oldest in the USSR. Close by are the churches of St Anna and St Bernard. The former is a beautiful example of 16th-century Gothic. The Ausros Vartai (The Gate of Dawn) is all that is left of a wall that was once 1½ miles long. It contains a religious shrine centred on the painting of Our Lady of Vilnius (17th century). Kaunas was the inter-war capital. Capital once again of independent Lithuania. **273**

Vladimir   Founded by Vladimir Monomakh, Grand Prince of Kiev, in 1108. It was sacked in the Mongol invasion of 1238 and came under Muscovite rule in the 15th century. Its cathedral is noteworthy. **20**

Yaroslavl   Founded by the Kievan Grand Prince Yaroslav. It was here that his wife and children were slaughtered by the Mongols in 1240.

Yalta   Holiday resort in the Crimea,

chosen by Roosevelt, Churchill and Stalin for their wartime meeting in February 1945. The home of the great playright Anton Chekhov from 1893 to 1903; his house has now become the Chekhov Museum. **226**

Yerevan (Erevan) Capital of Armenia. The terrible earthquake in December 1988 which devastated Armenia's capital was characteristic of the constant misfortunes inflicted on this tragic race. It also demonstrated the sloppy nature of Soviet building methods in an earthquake zone. This particular earthquake went hand in hand with a vicious ethnic feud with the Azeris. Just off Lenin Boulevard is a museum devoted to Armenia's tragic 2000-year past. Close by is the Museum of Modern Art, the only one of its type in the USSR. At the far end of the boulevard is the famous archive known as the Matenadaran which contains much important documentation about Armenia's history. One of its saddest episodes concerns the virtual genocide perpetrated by the Ottoman Turks against the Armenians in 1915 (although successive Turkish governments have denied responsibility). As Christians, the Armenians were suspect and their sufferings are commemorated by the large monument which overlooks Tsitsernaberd Park. Many Armenians died of hunger in the streets of Yerevan in the famine that followed.

Yerevan itself was a relatively obscure provincial town until after the Bolshevik Revolution. Even now it is capital of a Soviet republic which is only one-tenth of the size of historic Greater Armenia. But Soviet Armenia has acted as a refuge for the whole Armenian race because of the (relatively) good treatment they have received at the hands of the Soviet authorities. The Soviet Republic of Armenia is the only place in the world where Armenian, together with Russian, is used as the language of administration. Yerevan also contains fragments of the earlier Urartu civilisation. Capital of independent Armenia since 1991.

Zagorsk is 44 miles from Moscow in the RSFSR. It is most famous for the fortified monastery of Trinity St Sergius (founded in 1340), and contains much of historic interest. The monastery itself was destroyed in the Mongol raid of 1408, and was then rebuilt in stone. This enabled it to withstand the sustained Polish siege of 1608 to 1610. The Church of the Trinity contained paintings by Andrey Rublyev (later taken off to Moscow and replaced by copies) and is worth a visit, as is the Cathedral of the Assumption (founded 1554) where Boris Godunov is buried. Next to the Cathedral of the Assumption is the Dormition Cathedral with an elegant belfry by Rastrelli. There are two smaller, but picturesque churches within the monastery boundaries. Both St Paraskeva-Pyatnitsa and the Presentation of the Virgin date from the 16th century. **49**

Index

Interlink Bestselling Travel Publications

The Traveller's History Series

The Traveller's History series is designed for travellers who want more historical background on the country they are visiting than can be found in a tour guide. Each volume offers a complete and authoritative history of the country from the earliest times up to the present day. A Gazetteer cross-referenced to the main text pinpoints the historical importance of sights and towns. Illustrated with maps and line drawings, this literate and lively series makes ideal before-you-go reading, and is just as handy tucked into suitcase or backpack.

A Traveller's History of Australia	$14.95 pb
A Traveller's History of the Caribbean	$14.95 pb
A Traveller's History of China	$14.95 pb
A Traveller's History of England	$14.95 pb
A Traveller's History of France	$14.95 pb
A Traveller's History of Greece	$14.95 pb
A Traveller's History of India	$14.95 pb
A Traveller's History of Ireland	$14.95 pb
A Traveller's History of Italy	$14.95 pb
A Traveller's History of Japan	$14.95 pb
A Traveller's History of London	$14.95 pb
A Traveller's History of North Africa	$15.95 pb
A Traveller's History of Paris	$14.95 pb
A Traveller's History of Russia	$14.95 pb
A Traveller's History of Scotland	$14.95 pb
A Traveller's History of Spain	$14.95 pb
A Traveller's History of Turkey	$14.95 pb
A Traveller's History of the U.S.A.	$14.95 pb

The Traveller's Wine Guides

Illustrated with specially commissioned photographs (wine usually seems to be made in attractive surroundings) as well as maps, the books in this series describe the wine-producing regions of each country, recommend itineraries, list wineries, describe the local cuisines, suggest wine bars and restaurants, and provide a mass of practical information—much of which is not readily available elsewhere.

A Traveller's Wine Guide to France	$19.95 pb
A Traveller's Wine Guide to Germany	$17.95 pb
A Traveller's Wine Guide to Italy	$17.95 pb
A Traveller's Wine Guide to Spain	$17.95 pb

The Independent Walker Series

This unique series is designed for visitors who enjoy walking and getting off the beaten track. In addition to their value as general guides, each volume is peerless as a walker's guide, allowing travellers to see all of the great sites, enjoy the incomparable beauty of the countryside, and maintain a high level of physical fitness while travelling through the popular tourist destinations. Each guide includes:

• Practical information on thirty-five extraordinary short walks (all planned as day hikes and are between 2 and 9 miles), including: how to get there, where to stay, trail distance, walking time, difficulty rating, explicit trail directions and a vivid general description of the trail and local sights.

• Numerous itineraries: The Grand Tour which embraces all thirty-five walks; regional itineraries; and thematic itineraries.

• One planning map for the itineraries and thirty-five detailed trail maps.

• Trail notes broken down into an easy-to-follow checklist format.

• A "Walks-at-a-Glance" section which provides capsule summaries of all the walks.

• Black and white photographs.

• Before-you-go helpful hints.

The Independent Walker's Guide to France	$14.95 pb
The Independent Walker's Guide to Great Britain	$14.95 pb
The Independent Walker's Guide to Italy	$14.95 pb
The Independent Walker's Guide to Ireland	$14.95 pb

Wild Guides

An unrivalled series of illustrated guidebooks to the wild places far from home and work: the long walks, mountain hideaways, woods, moors, sea coasts and remote islands where travellers can still find a refuge from the modern world.

"The Wild Guides will be enjoyed by everyone who hopes to find unspoiled places."
—The Times (London)

Wild Britain	$19.95 pb
Wild France	$19.95 pb
Wild Ireland	$19.95 pb
Wild Italy	$19.95 pb
Wild Spain	$19.95 pb

Cities of the Imagination

A new and innovative series offering in-depth cultural, historical and literary guides to the great cities of the world. More than ordinary guidebooks, they introduce the visitor or armchair traveller to each city's unique present-day identity and its links with the past.

Buenos Aires: A Cultural and Literary Companion	$15.00 pb
Edinburgh: A Cultural and Literary Companion	$15.00 pb
Madrid: A Cultural and Literary Companion	$15.00 pb
Mexico City: A Cultural and Literary Companion	$15.00 pb
Oxford: A Cultural and Literary Companion	$15.00 pb
Rome: A Cultural and Literary Companion	$15.00 pb
Venice: A Cultural and Literary Companion	$15.00 pb

The Spectrum Guides

Each title in the series includes over 200 full-color photographs and provides a comprehensive and detailed description of the country together with all the essential data that tourists, business visitors or students are likely to require.

Spectrum Guide to Ethiopia	$22.95 pb
Spectrum Guide to India	$22.95 pb
Spectrum Guide to Jordan	$22.95 pb
Spectrum Guide to Maldives	$22.95 pb
Spectrum Guide to Mauritius	$19.95 pb

Spectrum Guide to Nepal	$22.95 pb
Spectrum Guide to Pakistan	$22.95 pb
Spectrum Guide to Tanzania	$22.95 pb
Spectrum Guide to Uganda	$19.95 pb
Spectrum Guide to the United Arab Emirates	$21.95 pb

The In Focus Guides

This new series of country guides is designed for travellers and students who want to understand the wider picture and build up an overall knowledge of a country. Each In Focus guide is a lively and thought-provoking introduction to the country's people, politics and culture.

Belize In Focus	$12.95 pb
Brazil in Focus	$12.95 pb
Chile in Focus	$12.95 pb
Costa Rica in Focus	$12.95 pb
Cuba in Focus	$12.95 pb
The Dominican Republic in Focus	$12.95 pb
Eastern Caribbean in Focus	$12.95 pb
Ecuador in Focus	$12.95 pb
Guatemala in Focus	$12.95 pb
Haiti in Focus	$12.95 pb
Jamaica in Focus	$12.95 pb
Nicaragua in Focus	$12.95 pb
Peru in Focus	$12.95 pb

We encourage you to support your local independent bookseller

To request our complete 48-page full-color catalog, please call us toll free at **1-800-238-LINK,** visit our website at **www.interlinkbooks.com,** or write to **Interlink Publishing** 46 Crosby Street, Northampton, MA 01060 e-mail: sales@interlinkbooks.com